THE ART OF STRATEGIC THERAPY

The Art of Strategic Therapy

Jay Haley and Madeleine Richeport-Haley

Routledge
Taylor & Francis Group
New York London

Published in 2003 by
Routledge
Taylor & Francis Group
270 Madison Avenue
New York, NY 10016

Published in Great Britain by
Routledge
Taylor & Francis Group
27 Church Road
Hove, East Sussex BN3 2FA

© 2003 by Taylor & Francis Group, LLC
Routledge is an imprint of Taylor & Francis Group

Printed in the United States of America on acid-free paper
10 9 8 7 6 5 4
International Standard Book Number-13: 978-0-415-94592-9 (Hardcover)
Library of Congress Card Number 2003009289

Chapter 2: Ethnicity Issues in Strategic Therapy, Copyright © 1998. Adapted from Ethnicity in Family Therapy: a Comparison of Brief Strategic Therapy and Culture-Focused Therapy by Madeleine Richeport-Haley. Reproduced by permission of Taylor & Francis, LLC.

Appendix A: Case report: How to Unbalance a Couple, © 1996 by The Guilford Press. From Haley, J., Live Supervision Example: Being Unfair, Learning and Teaching Therapy, pp. 140-151. Reprinted with permission.

Library of Congress Cataloging-in-Publication Data

Haley, Jay.
      The art of strategic therapy / by Jay Haley and Madeleine Richeport-Haley.
      p. ; cm.
  Includes bibliographical references and index.
  ISBN 0-415-94592-5 (hardcover : alk. paper)
  1. Strategic therapy.
  [DNLM: 1. Psychotherapy, Group—methods. WM 430H168a 2003] I. Richeport-Haley, Madeleine. II. Title.
  RC489.S76H35 2003
  616.89'15—dc21
                                                  2003009289

Visit the Taylor & Francis Web site at
http://www.taylorandfrancis.com

and the Routledge Web site at
http://www.routledge.com

To
Helen McCullough

Contents

Foreword, by Michael P. Nichols, Ph.D.   ix
Preface   xv

1   Strategic Therapy   1

2   Ethnicity Issues in Strategic Therapy   17

3   Strategic Therapy with Couples   31

4   Family Therapy at a Distance: 53
    A Case of Depression

5   Changing a Violent Family   79

6   Compulsory Therapy: A Violent Case   97

7   Paradox and Play with Children: 111
    The Boy Who Can't Stop Fighting

8   Mother–Daughter Incest   125

9   Cultural Confusions: 135
    How Many Clients Are in One Body?

10 A Positive Approach With a Psychotic Couple   157

Epilogue   175
Appendix A *Case Report: How to Unbalance a Couple*   179
Appendix B *Supplemental Video Programs*   191
Index   197

Foreword

W hen one of the founding geniuses of family therapy comes out with a new book, attention must be paid. There was a time when anything with Jay Haley's name on it would find an instant audience. In the golden age of family therapy, books like *Problem-Solving Therapy* and *Leaving Home* were crowning examples of what made strategic therapy the most compelling approach of the time. But that was before postmodernism, before the collaborative model, and before narrative and solution-focused therapies became so popular. Today, some people would say that strategic therapy is dead.

The strategic therapy that flourished in the 1980s was centered in three unique and creative groups: MRI's brief therapy center (Weakland, Watzlawick, and Fisch); Mara Selvini Palozzoli and her colleagues in Milan; and, of course, Jay Haley and his colleagues at the Family Therapy Institute of Washington, D.C. The master, Milton Erickson, was a school unto himself. What made strategic therapy so popular was that it offered a simple framework for understanding how families get stuck and a clever set of techniques to help them get unstuck.

According to the cybernetic metaphor, families become trapped in dysfunctional patterns when they cling to solutions that don't work. The trick is to get them to try something different. If the essence of neurotic behavior is stubbornly continuing to behave in self-defeating ways, the essence of strategic therapy is getting people to try something different. To accomplish this, strategic therapists introduced a number of ingenious techniques, many of them paradoxical, designed to break up homeostatic ("problem-maintaining") solutions and get families moving and on their way.

Like many people not lucky enough to receive training from an accomplished master like Jay Haley, I learned about strategic therapy from books and from sitting in with a group of graduate student therapists and their supervisor. What I remember about those sessions was that an earnest and intelligent group of people used to interview families with a wide range of complex dynamics. And yet, invariably, the group's "strategic solution" was to prescribe to the families that they continue doing exactly what they were doing. This "paradoxical injunction" (or reverse psychology as your grandmother would have called it) was designed to make clients rebel against this foolish directive and stop engaging in their problem-maintaining solutions. Unfortunately, this tactic left many people cold, myself included.

So, as you see, strategic therapy is manipulative, gimmicky, and superficial. No wonder the field moved on. Incidentally, if you want to see some of the most heartfelt criticisms of strategic therapy's whiz-bang techniquism, read the works of the leading narrative therapists. Many of them, it turns out, are refugees from their own manipulative brand of strategic therapy.

As you might guess, I've since discovered that there is more than meets the eye to strategic therapy. How did I learn this? By coming into contact with practicing clinicians who were actually trained by Jay Haley. These therapists were far more sophisticated in their understanding of families than any critic might imagine, and their artful use of directives was so subtle and so apt, that I've stolen (*borrowed*) many of their strategies for my own practice.

Sure, you can learn about strategic therapy by reading a chapter in some textbook. By the same token you can learn to do structural family therapy from Minuchin's *Families and Family Therapy*—where you will learn that all there is to it is to join with families, set up enactments, and then do whatever Minuchin does to restructure them. The problem is that the very elegance of the structural and strategic models, which made them so easy to summarize and teach, led to the illusion that they were easy to learn and simple to practice. As one who has been trying to get it right for 30 years, let me assure you: family therapy is not simple.

As anyone fortunate enough to have sat behind the one-way mirror with Jay Haley can attest, there is a wealth of understanding that goes along with the simple outlines of his brand of strategic therapy. As Haley himself says, "What makes therapy so difficult . . . is that life is so complex that you have to design therapy for each case."

What makes *The Art of Strategic Therapy* so special is that it invites readers to join Haley behind the one-way mirror to sit in on his fascinating observations of real families in treatment. All the familiar principles of strategic therapy are here, of course. Beginners will learn that action (not understanding) is the key to change, that to function well families must have a workable hierarchy, that most family problems involve triangles, and that directives must be tailored to the specifics of each family and their problems. Readers will also find guidelines for strategic intervention laid out in a clear, 10-step process. But the real meat of this book is found in Haley's subtle analysis of the individual cases described here in such rich detail. Where, for example, in a set of general guidelines would you find a supervisor saying, "If things aren't going well, maybe you should bring in more family members"? Or, something so simple and yet so helpful as, "Give them a call in a week or so to make sure things are okay"?

In case after case, Haley's low-keyed suggestions are focused like a laser beam on the presenting problems families bring to therapy and the structural patterns underlying them. Readers will be reminded that a "systemic" therapist focuses on two things: the often obvious interpersonal interplay between someone with symptoms and someone else, and the often less obvious third persons who invariably shadow every troubled relationship. But, as I've said, it is in the specific suggestions for each case that Haley demonstrates his art. In one case, for example, he casually observes how a therapist's neutrality serves to support the unhealthy status quo in a couple. How's this for whatever the opposite of neutrality is: "You are in danger of losing your wife. I think what you are doing is absolutely wrong, that you are doing things to turn her off by not talking to her, by not being aggressive, by not courting her."

It is refreshing to see that Haley's insightful comments are directed not only to clients but also to the therapists trying to help them. In one case, for example, he makes wonderful suggestions about how therapists can take strategic advantage of their personal attributes. (I only regret that none of his examples included aged college professors who can't seem to remember anything. Perhaps I can extrapolate.) In another case, Haley explains the parallel process by which a therapist's response to the supervisor mirrors the clients' response to the therapist.

Invariably, Haley's gentle questions get to the heart of things. To one therapist who was describing at length a patient's history and his depression, Haley said, "Why don't you say what are the problems you are trying to solve with him?" And, just as he advises therapists to do with families, Haley never forgets to ask therapists who seem to be stuck, "What have you tried with them?" The point is, of course, that things won't change unless you try something different.

Although many of the clinical insights and examples in this book could have been written any time in the last 20 years, there is much here that could not have been. Twenty years ago few family therapists treated the kinds of court-mandated cases that Haley so brilliantly shows how to work with. Moreover, it is important to recognize that Haley did not write this book alone. It's one thing to say that a strategic therapist must tailor interventions to fit the unique characteristics of every case, but what is far more instructive are the numerous examples from other cultures in this book involving demonic possession, shamanism, faith healing, and spirit mediums from cultures as diverse as South and Central America, Japan, Bali, India, and Southern California.

Thanks to Madeleine Richeport-Haley's anthropological perspective,

readers are shown how the principles of strategic therapy apply in a variety
of strange and fascinating situations. But these colorful examples serve as
more than exotic curiosities. Rather, by showing how therapists and healers
can employ inventive strategies in a variety of unusual situations, Haley and
Richeport-Haley help us as readers unfreeze our own familiar habits of per-
ception. In order to be helpful to a Balinese woman suffering from "spirit
possession," you can't just sit back and reflect her feelings. Nor can you rely
on some formulaic paradoxical prescription. You have to be flexible, you
have to be inventive, and you have to tailor your approach to that person's
unique worldview. And that, as this book makes clear, is exactly the same
kind of mindset a therapist must bring to bear in every case, no matter how
apparently foreign or familiar.

Part of what makes *The Art of Strategic Therapy* so useful is that the
authors show rather than tell us how to do strategic therapy. Take, for example, the use of paradox. I don't know about you, but I never really liked
the idea of telling families to do something you didn't really think would be
helpful just to get them to react. It seemed too much like trickery. But after
reading this book, I think I finally get it. In one case, Haley recommends
that the good sibling take a turn pretending to be the bad one and that the
bad one pretend to be the good one. What my description won't make clear,
but what reading the case will, is this paradoxical injunction (prescribing
the symptom) accomplishes two very powerful things. First, it introduces a
playful, experimental atmosphere into the consulting room—an atmosphere
that the therapist and the family *share*. No one is being tricked by this use of
paradox. Instead, the clients are invited to join the therapist in experiment-
ing with becoming more flexible.

The second thing that Haley's use of paradox accomplishes may be the
most important element in any form of successful therapy. By maintaining
the kind, playful, and inventive attitude necessary to make paradoxical suggestions, a therapist avoids being inducted—that is, drawn into a family's
unproductive way of seeing things. The families who are our clients deserve
our unwavering respect; every one of them is doing the best that they can to
cope with life's difficulties. However, it's important to remember that what
brings people to therapy is that their actions and point of view aren't working for them. It is therefore a therapist's job to bring something different to
the table. Unfortunately, achieving some kind of new and more productive
perspective is often made difficult or impossible if a therapist succumbs to
the powerful pressure to accept the kind of assumptions most client families
come in with, such as that one person is the problem, that behavioral problems are physical, that good parents must always justify their rules to their
children, etcetera, etcetera.

In asking me to write this foreword, Jay and Madeleine suggested that I would be doing them a favor. As it turns out, the shoe is on the other foot, for in giving me a chance to read this splendid book, they did me the enormous favor of helping me to understand for the first time how truly inventive and effective strategic therapy can be. It's nothing like the formulaic and manipulative approach described in most textbooks. Rather, in Jay Haley's hands, strategic therapy is a rich concoction of structural understanding, clinical sensitivity, and, above all, a wonderful way to help families stuck in their ruts to try something different.

MICHAEL P. NICHOLS, PH.D.

Preface

*T*his book represents modern therapy. The cases come from places where the choice is jail or therapy, public clinics, abuse shelters, homeless shelters, addiction groups, juvenile halls, children in foster care, and people in day hospitals as well as full-time hospitals. Both the clientele and the trainees treating them are from a variety of ethnic groups including Latinos, African Americans, Middle Easterners, Pacific Islanders, Asians, and middle-class people from American suburbs. The cases were chosen on the basis of the interest in problems, effective techniques, ethnicity, and how the goals of therapy and supervision in strategic therapy in a one-way-mirror room were most clearly articulated.

Some ideas for this book were developed with poor people as therapists in training at the Philadelphia Child Guidance Clinic in the 1960s. The dilemma was how to train the middle-class to deal with the poor. We decided to train the poor. The professionals learned a lot from the poor including what it was like to be poor. Salvador Minuchin, Braulio Montalvo, and others were already experienced with that population. We learned to be practical about life and less esoteric than many therapists were. The one-way mirror and the guidance of a supervisor behind it protected the trainees and the families at the moment they needed it.

What makes therapy difficult for trainees is that life is so complex that you have to design therapy for each case and you have to be innovative. Up to the 1950s, if a therapist gave a directive he was considered wrong because he was supposed to reflect. Milton H. Erickson, M.D. was the exception. Some people used hypnosis that teaches how to give a directive. Then they learned they could give directives without hypnosis.

Erickson encouraged his students to study anthropology and anthropologists to study therapy. Richeport-Haley, one of a number of anthropologists (including Margaret Mead and Gregory Bateson) who studied with Erickson, benefited by his feedback for 10 years on her work in Latin America and the United States integrating medical and traditional healing systems. Understanding cultural background is important to planning therapy for individual cases. For 15 years, Richeport-Haley has been a participant-observer in Jay Haley's training while contributing an anthropological perspective on some cases.

We thought it would be worthwhile to film his process of supervision both in front of and behind the one-way mirror in training programs so that the step-by-step process of learning and teaching therapy could be made explicit. This book grew out of some of this well-documented material, which worked out some of the special problems of filming therapy and making film ethnographies of therapy cases. The finished films turned out to be powerful teaching tools (see Appendix B).

Milton H. Erickson, M.D., was the master strategist. Haley's directive approach is based on his 17-year association with Erickson, on which he published numerous works. The strategic approach was first presented in 1963. "Therapy can be called strategic if the clinician initiates what happens during the therapy and designs a particular approach for each problem. He or she must identify solvable problems, set goals, design interventions to achieve these goals, examine the responses he receives to correct his approach, and ultimately examine the outcome of his therapy to see if it has been effective." (*Uncommon Therapy: The Psychiatric Techniques of Milton H. Erickson, M.D.*, 1973).

Some people have a prejudice against strategic family therapy and some people don't understand it, having been trained as therapists in a different orientation. Some of the objections are it prevents spontaneity, it tells people what to do, it doesn't focus on feelings, it doesn't concentrate on the cause, it doesn't necessarily look for truth in a theory, and you have to design a therapy for each case instead of following a method. This book will alter and eliminate such objections as you learn how to do strategic therapy.

The therapy approach is influenced by the need for skillful therapists and supervisors. There have been so many people who have contributed to the ideas of this book. Braulio Montalvo, M.A., was an enthusiastic critic and guide. Scott Woolley, Ph.D., provided his administrative wisdom. Neil Schiff, Ph.D., could handle the most difficult of cases. Salvador Minuchin, M.D., likes to explore theories.[1] Michael Hoyt, Ph.D., offered his comments and reviews. The lasting influence was that of Milton H. Erickson, M.D., for the development of the strategic approach.[2] The Mental Research Institute carries on the systemic tradition. Our appreciation to the colleagues and students who adapted to the one-way mirror.

This book is for teachers, supervisors, and student and trainee therapists working in private and public settings. It is tailor-made to give you a practical model that formulates problems so they are solvable and the tools to deal with current issues. The emphasis is on a variety of ways to plan therapy, some of them unusual, and specific techniques to use. It gives the reader an insider's view of the process of dialogue between supervisor and trainee. Readers should come away with the idea that therapy can be enjoyable despite the severity of human problems.

NOTES

1. Michael Nichols, Ph.D. offered valuable suggestions.
2. The Erickson family gave support and encouragement.

1

Strategic Therapy

The ideas of strategic therapy are deceptively simple. Carrying out these ideas in action is not so simple. A simple idea of presenting strategic therapy is to notice that it is the opposite of the traditional therapies. One can outline a few of the opposing ideas between traditional and strategic ideas.

The Past

In the strategic approach, interviews are not focused upon abuse, trauma, and guilty pastimes. Unless there is a special circumstance, time is not spent on remembering in a strategic interview. Rather than beginning with a genogram or history, the therapist focuses on what task to follow. A traditional therapist often feels that it is improper to focus on the present, particularly when one is faced with the idea that what is caused now must have been caused by the past. It is difficult to minimize the past when established theories and even official diagnosis emphasizes the past as cause.

To illustrate, suppose a woman comes in who suffered sex abuse as a child. She now has difficulty with sex with her husband. Should one assume her sexual problem is caused by the childhood abuse or by the current problems with her husband? One might prefer the strategic current problem theory since that idea includes attention to the husband's problems as well her own.

Cause of Change

Other differences between a strategic and a traditional approach are more controversial. The cause of change is different. A common assumption in the traditional approach is that if people understand themselves they can change. Therefore, the interpretation is the tool of insight. The strategic approach does not assume that an understanding of oneself leads to change.

1

In fact, it can be a negative intervention in many situations since many clients change without insight, and many do not like interpretations.

For example, when the therapist interprets to parents that their daughter was attempting suicide to help the parents with their problems, this interpretation upsets the parents and so increases the frequency of the daughter's suicide attempts. The idea that insight is the basis of change could be the result of being educated in universities where intellectuals believe insight and understanding lead to change.

Directives

Action must happen if change is to happen. Nondirective therapy is actionless. Therefore nondirective therapy is traditional therapy. In fact, the therapist takes pride in not telling the client what to do. With a strategic approach, it is assumed that conversation does not lead to change. Action must be taken if change is to happen. With a strategic approach, the therapist must prescribe a directive, either direct or metaphoric. Where does one learn such directives? It is difficult to find training in giving directives.

A Unique Plan for Each Case

With the complexity of our social life these days, one cannot apply one method to cases. There are just too many differences among situations. To use the same intervention in many different cases is traditional, not strategic. The competent therapist learns to design a therapy for each case. The therapist presents the case in training, and the supervisor, therapist, and group devise a plan based on what the case brings in and how it develops. The one-way-mirror supervision facilitates tailoring therapy to each case.

Learn to Deal with Colleagues

One of the necessities for a strategic therapy is the need to deal both with colleagues on the periphery of a case and with any ethnic groups involved. Therapy is not simply private. The therapist must involve the probation officer in a case in a positive way. Negotiating medication with a psychiatrist on the case is an important skill. A therapist must have good judgment about when to hospitalize a case so that it is not done too soon or too late. Dealing with court cases takes skill. In the case of a violent family (see chapter 5), there were six professionals working separately on the case with individual family members. The success occurs when the family therapist persuaded the others that she had to deal with the whole family. She accomplished this by taking all of the other professionals into account.

The Normal Situation

When you accept the idea that the client is responding to a social situation, it is best to arrange a situation as normal as possible and as quickly as possible. For example, to be able to work and make a living is essential for all of us. If an adolescent responds to a difficult situation by staying home, it is best to get her back into school and away from home. It is best for young people to be functioning in a normal situation. In a case of a psychotic couple presented in chapter 10, the supervisor's suggestion is to treat the couple as normal and perhaps to expect them to go to work.

Hierarchy

When two people get together there is a communication structure and, so, an issue of power. A strategic approach requires the exploration of hierarchical structures since the communication is in that form. A symptom indicates a problem in a hierarchy. To resolve the symptom can require a change in structure. The trainee must learn to assume what family structures are typical. For example, the obvious ones are that parents should not form coalitions against each other or mothers-in-law should respect structural boundaries. Such simple ideas are woven through this book. In the case of an African-American family (see chapter 7), a primary intervention is having mother and sons respect the stepfather, thereby raising his position in the family hierarchy.

The Evolution of Live Supervision in Strategic Therapy

The one-way mirror that we take for granted didn't just appear out of nowhere. I was in the Bateson project in Menlo Park, California in the 1950s (Bateson, Jackson, Haley, & Weakland, 1956). We were just beginning to see whole families, and I heard there was a psychologist seeing families in a juvenile hall in San Leandro. So I went over to see him. There were only a few therapists in the country that I knew were seeing whole families for therapy. So it was always interesting to find another person working with families. I met Dr. Charles Fulweiler (Haley & Hoffman, 1967) and found he had a one-way mirror that he used in training teachers for the psychological testing of students. The teacher sat behind the mirror watching somebody test. He said he began to do therapy with the mirror. So I asked him how did he come to do that. And he said that he had a family come in with a delinquent girl—she was found out in the valley somewhere drunk and was brought in to the juvenile hall. He tested her with psychological tests, and she came out with no neurotic problems, so he assumed that she had none. If the tests say it, it must be true. So he turned her loose. He told the parents she was normal. Two or three months later she showed up at a bar in town drunk again. So they brought her back. Now he was curious to discover how this testing could be off. He wondered for the first time what kind of family this problem girl came from. So he brought the family in, and he put them in the interview room while he went behind the mirror. He watched the family together, and he saw them behaving in very banal fashion. The father said to the girl, "Can you get cigarettes here?" And the mother said, "What do they let you wear?" This was a daughter with some serious problems. Fulweiler was a very intense guy. He went around to the door into the other room and pulled the father out into the hall and he said, "Do you love your daughter?" And the father said, "Yes." Fulweiler said, "You go in there and tell her so." So the father went in, and it took him about 10 minutes but he said, "I love you." Everybody then got emotional, including the father. The mother began to cry, and the girl began to cry. The mother said, "Where have you been?" Fulweiler was so pleased with the interaction that he asked them to come back and do this again. Then he began a series of treatments. At first he put the family in the room and pulled the members out one at a time to talk. Then he began to go in himself and join them. Now everybody does a therapy that fits the therapist's personality, but at the time Dr. Fulweiler's procedure was unusual. He didn't want to be so intense with that family, so he stopped going in and stayed behind the mirror. He would then call one of them out and send them back in. He did various things with this mirror. After talking to him, I returned to our project, and we put in a one-way mirror. Through it I could see a family for the first time actually dealing with each other, and we did not have to use expensive film for teaching. We began to have a lot of visitors. All the visitors admired the mirror and thought that working behind the mirror was what family therapy was. So, people put in mirrors around the country.

At once a problem arose: How was the therapist going to communicate with the trainee in front of the mirror while she was interviewing a family? One alternative was for the supervisor to knock on the door and call the trainee out for consultation. This often rescued trainees in difficulty while permitting discussion of the situation outside the presence of a client. However, interruptions were disruptive. The next innovation in this process was to install a telephone in both rooms, the therapist and the supervisor's. The supervisor used the telephone primarily to make suggestions in line with a previously determined plan. While observing through the one-way mirror, the supervisor could call the trainee and make a suggestion. When the telephone in the therapy room lit up, the trainee would pick it up, listen, and go on with the interview. There would not be an exaggerated response to the call. Therefore calls needed to be brief and to the point.

Another intervention was the "bug in the ear" (Neukrug, 1991). With a small earphone placed in the trainee's ear, advice could be given without the client knowing that any suggestions had been made. If mishandled, the arrangement could be like instructing a robot. The trainee needed to attend to both the client and the supervisor while hoping that she didn't develop glazed eyes in the process.

In many of the cases presented in this book, a computer monitor is the principal means of supervision. In general, a monitor is placed in the interview room where the therapist can see it and the clients cannot. The clients are informed that the purpose of the monitor is to receive suggestions from the room behind the one-way mirror. This is acceptable to the clients because they cannot see the messages. The directives need to be short and clear. Computer-monitor supervision developed using a strategic approach that is based on giving active directive supervision and not passive listening (Scherl & Haley, 2000). In summary, the different techniques of live supervision are not mutually exclusive and were all used in this therapy series. Sometimes a succinct computer-monitor suggestion is not always possible and a supervisor will need to talk at greater length to a trainee; he will then call him or her out of the interview for consultation.

What Is Diagnosis?

There has always been a confusion about diagnosis in the field of therapy. The goals of therapy and the ways to define them have always been unclear. As ideology changes, the ways to label what is wrong might change. For example, the goal can be to provide insight, or it might be to provide a growth experience for the client. What is that? How does one measure it? What is the outcome the therapist must list as failure or success? These questions have plagued the field since the 1950s. They cannot be avoided. Here we can specify the type of diagnosis appropriate for strategic therapy. There are several issues to be clarified.

The problem can be one person, two persons, or three or more persons. For example, a woman seeks therapy because she cannot stop eating. That is her problem. The quarrels with her husband make this a two-person problem. Her mother blames her husband, and there is a three-person problem, etc. It is the same woman. The choice of unit will have a decisive influence on the therapist's way of thinking about diagnosis.

As another example, a 12-year-old boy is diagnosed as depressed and he won't go to school. He is the problem. When father insists he go to school, the boy becomes more depressed and the mother fights with the father. The triangle can be seen once again.

The problems of diagnosis can be illustrated with another case. A social worker was given the responsibility for a five-year-old boy who set fires. He not only set fires at home and at school, but he walked through the agency tossing lit matches into wastebaskets. The worker protested that she did not know what to do with a fire-setter. She was advised that the case would be staffed and she would be helped with the problem. A few weeks and a few fires later, a staff meeting was called, and everyone discussed the case. After a while the director of the agency said it was obviously an oedipal problem, and he stood up and dismissed the meeting. The social worker sat down and cried. She had not heard a word about what she was to do. A therapist passed by and asked her what was the problem. She told him what had happened. He said, thinking like a behaviorist, "Well, let's see, to light a fire you have to light matches. We can arrange that." He said to give the boy a penny for every 10 matches he brought in unlit. "Could you do that?" the social worker was asked. She said she would try anything. She arranged the plan with the parents, and the boy was delighted to make money. The parents were delighted that someone gave some help. The boy stopped setting fires.

Traditionally, diagnosis was a set of ideas that was used to classify clients for *administrative* purposes. What was needed, and still is, is a diagnosis that is designed for *therapy*. Obviously, it would be a practical set of categories, easily understood, that would guide the therapist into taking action that would make a successful therapy. That simple idea still awaits a therapist to provide it.

How to Give Directives

Skill in the use of directives is essential in strategic therapy when one understands that action causes change and conversation does not, unless there are directives in the conversation. For clinicians who are uncomfortable about telling clients what to do, one should note that one cannot *not* give directives. Ray Birdwhistell, the body-movement authority, estimated that two people in a conversation exchange 100,000 messages a minute. That's how complicated an exchange of communication is. Carl Rogers, who preferred to call his directives nondirective, seemed to be giving evident directives when he talked with a client. In fact, he seemed to be giving evident directives even when he said he did not want the client to expect him to say what to do. The therapist cannot be neutral.

In the age of nondirective therapy it is difficult to get training to select and give directives. Often people are opposed to directives because they do not know how to give them. One source of directives is Milton H. Erickson, M.D. (Haley, 1973, 1985, 1993). As an example, a woman brought her 50-year-old son to Dr. Erickson and said the son was helpless and dependent on her. She said, "I cannot even read a book because he constantly bothers me." Dr. Erickson did not help them understand their mutual dependency needs. Instead, he told the woman he wanted her to take her son out in the desert one mile. Then he was to push the son out of the car (he could see mother was stronger). She was to drive one mile and park the car. Then she should sit in the car in the air conditioning and read her book. The son would walk in the heat back to the car, and it would be good exercise for him. Mother liked this idea. The son did not. They came in the next week, and she had done the mile walk three times. The mother was pleased. The son was not. The son said, "Couldn't I do some other exercise not out in the hot sun?" "What do you have in mind?" Dr. Erickson asked. The son said, "I could go bowling, and while I'm doing it, my mother can sit in the place and read her book." That was agreeable to everyone, and other tasks were given that helped to disengage the son from the mother.

Milton Erickson used hypnosis to change the past and did it pretty well. Did you ever hear of the "February Man?"

That was a case where Dr. Erickson changed the past. A woman came to him saying she was lonely and had always been lonely. She was afraid to have children because she didn't think she would raise them properly because she had had such an unhappy past. So he hypnotized her. He took her back to childhood and had her imagine she was a child again. A man came to visit her father, and she let him in. Her father was away at the time, so she started talking to this visitor. She called him the February Man because he came in February. So she had a nice time with this gentleman and remembered it as a very pleasant time. Then Erickson took her forward to a few years later, and the February Man showed up again. And he took them through an experience where they played games together and she enjoyed their times together. Then he took her forward again two or three years to when she was older, and he took her up to adulthood and woke her up. She began to enjoy what her experience had been. She said, "I really didn't have such a bad past." Now it is questionable whether what Dr. Erickson had done was ethical or not. Should you change s client's past or shouldn't you— even though the change might relieve her mind? So those kinds of questions come up—once you start taking action to change people with directives. Now that's the only man who deliberately set out to change the past and did it hypnotically to see how extreme you could do it.

Hypnosis provides nice training in giving directives. Even if you don't use it, it teaches you to listen carefully, because you are going to do something carefully and it teaches you to be precise. If you say to a subject, your hand will get heavier and heavier and feel like lifting up, he will never lift the hand, because he wasn't asked to lift the hand. You asked him if he felt like lifting the hand. Once you get that kind of precision in your directives, you get better results. A nicely defined symptom is often resolved pretty quickly with hypnosis. It teaches you to think more broadly about things— more metaphorically. You think of things you haven't thought before. It is a curious phenomenon. It's also a phenomenon that is mysterious in some ways. Sometimes you have remarkable success with it, and you don't always know why. One of the things that began to be tried was hypnosis with the whole family, and it never really took on, although with couples it did.

Types of Directives

One way to classify directives is to divide them into straightforward directives and indirect ones. When the therapist has power, a straightforward directive can suffice. When the client needs to work indirectly, the indirect type can be used. For example, if a man drinks and beats his wife, he can be told to stop that. If he stops, a straightforward directive has worked. If he drinks and beats his wife harder than before, an indirect approach is needed.

Straightforward directives include giving advice, coaching, setting up ordeals, and exacting penance. Directives do not start with the directive itself but with the establishing of a trusting relationship. Directives start with saying hello, being empathic, being concerned, and joining, all of which arrange that clients want to do what you say. Haley had a case of a couple with a little kid who was two years old. They wanted to find out if the therapist thought the kid was intellectually prepared for nursery school. She examined the kid with and without the parents in the room and concluded he was ready for nursery school. The parents could not go to their parents for this advice and the therapist gave it to them. You can coach a wife to win back her husband or coach adolescents to get along better with their parents. In an ordeal (Haley, 1984) the therapist directs someone to do something that is harder than the symptom, whereupon they give up the symptom. You set it up so that every time they have the problem, they do something that is good for them.

The technique of the ordeal was devised by the Master Milton Erickson. An insomniac came in to see him. Maybe, he said, he would get two hours of sleep at night, and he was exhausted at work. He asked Erickson for help to get over it. Erickson asked the client what he should do more of. He said he should read more books. Erickson set it up, saying, "I want you to go to bed tonight, only do not go to bed. I want you to put your pajamas on and prepare for bed. I want you to read those books all night long, and since you might fall asleep sitting and reading, I want you to stand at the mantle all night long and read the books." The client did as he was told for three nights. Each night he thought he'd lie down and rest his eyes a minute. He fell asleep. He slept the whole night and woke up to begin his work day at 7A.M. He then felt guilty that he owed Erickson a night, and he decided he would prepare himself in case this ever happened again. He went out and bought himself a set of Dickens's works if he ever didn't sleep. It's harder on him to read Dickens all night long than go to sleep, so he goes to sleep.

Another straightforward directive is penance. You give someone a penance that is helpful to others. You get people who feel awful and guilty for what they did, and they talk about their guilt. You need to give them something to do that handles this. A therapist had a call from a woman who said she had an 18-year-old son who was going to kill himself, so they put him in the hospital. They took him seriously when he said he would kill himself on the date his brother killed himself. The therapist suggested that they draw him out and tell the parents to talk about all the nice things the other boy would have done if he had lived. He was a Boy Scout. The parents and the 18-year-old were delighted. He knew exactly what his brother would have done, so he wanted to get out of the hospital and do those things. The family all felt so guilty and the therapist gave them something to do.

Indirect directives are used when therapists lack power in the situation. Examples of indirect directives are restraining people from changing, advising them to remain the same, imposing a paradox, metaphoric communication, absurd tasks, and doing nothing, thereby causing frustration. A colleague, Neil Schiff, provides an example of an absurd directive. A woman was referred to him by her pediatrician. Her son wet the bed and had always wet the bed. Neil said what a directive therapist would say: "Are you willing to do anything to get over the problem?" She said, "Yes." Dr. Schiff said "I want you to give your son $50 every time he wets the bed." She said, "All right." The boy made $150. He wet the bed three times and then stopped. The mother was talking to the pediatrician who said, "That man is crazy. You don't reward a kid for a symptom you are trying to get rid of." The mother replied, "Well, I don't care. He stopped wetting the bed." The task overwhelmed them it was so absurd.

Paradox

Strategic therapy is known for its interesting use of paradox. Again, paradox is simple as an idea but it is difficult to carry out. It requires training. Usually, there are two types. One is to restrain the client from improving. For example, the therapist says to a client, "I think I can help you to get over this problem, but I'm not sure you are ready to do so yet." You can say, "What are the consequences if you change?" "What will the husband do if the wife becomes more self-assertive?" You get into a posture where, instead of you pulling the people to change, they are pulling at you to change. Then various delays can be used until the client is insisting on therapy. The second, and usual, paradox procedure is to encourage the client to have a symptom when he is there to get over one. When done well, the procedure has a curious effect. The same approach can be used with couples in distress. You can schedule a couple to bicker. Have them pick a night and a time, say from 8 P.M. to 10 P.M., so they will not be interrupted and they can argue at length. They usually will not do it.

Another case of Haley's illustrates a paradoxical intervention that had a confrontative outcome. "A man brought his housebound wife to me. She could only go out of the house with him or her mother. He wanted her to be changed. I saw the couple together, and I told them I was going to ask them to do something silly. I told the husband that I wanted him to tell his wife the next morning as he left for work to stay home. He knew she wouldn't be going out, but I wanted him to tell her that anyway, and I wanted him to do so every morning until I saw them the following week. The couple seemed amused by the suggestion, and the next morning when the husband told his wife to stay home, they both laughed. The second morning it was not so funny. The third morning after he told her to stay home, the wife went out to the local grocery store alone for the first time in seven years. In the next interview, I had a very upset husband who was worried about where his wife would go and with whom she would go if she started going out alone. The wife acknowledged that she had often stated that if she left the house, she would leave with her suitcase in her hand."

STAGES OF A PARADOXICAL THERAPY

1. *Establish a relationship defined as one to bring about change.*
   This is usually implicit in the framework when someone asks for therapy and pays for it. It should be emphasized by discussing explicitly how the person wants to get over the problem.
2. *Define the problem clearly.*
   The more precisely defined the problem, the simpler the procedure is to follow. (An exception is when the problem is ambiguity.)
3. *Set the goals clearly.*
   The clearer the therapist's goals, the less probable is distraction along the way. It is possible that the therapist agree on a goal with the client while also having a different goal in mind.
4. *Offer a plan.*
   In setting up the framework to offer a paradoxical directive, it may be necessary to provide a rationale to make it reasonable. Sometimes one should just go ahead and leave the plan implicit to avoid debates, but generally guidelines should be offered. For example, a deconditioning framework is appropriate for the client who thinks in terms of learning theory.
5. *Put down current authority on the problem in a graceful way.*
   It is important that this not be an antagonistic put-down but a benevolent one defined as having the purpose of being helpful.
6. *Reemphasize the framework as one designed to bring about change.*

7. *Give a paradoxical directive.*
This directive is essentially to remain unchanged. It can be to encourage the usual behavior, structure, and sequence. It can be implicit, as in encouraging a symptom, or explicit, as in asking someone to "pretend" to have the problem. If explicit, the client can pretend to have the overt problem, such as child being afraid at night, or covert problem, as when the mother and not the child is the one who really is afraid.
8. *Observe response and continue with encouragement of usual behavior.*
Therapist should not relent for rebellious improvement or for upset but reemphasize the plan. Define change as not cooperating. It might be necessary to offer a new rationale for continuing usual behavior, such as encouraging a relapse because improvement is too rapid.
9. *As change continues, the therapist should avoid taking credit for it.*
Accepting credit risks a relapse in relation to the therapist. Even though it might be more pleasant to "share" with the client what the procedure has been, it is risking a relapse for one's own comfort. One way to avoid credit is to be puzzled about why the improvement occurred.
10. *Begin to disengage, perhaps by recessing, and as change stabilizes the therapy will terminate.*

The cases in this book illustrate all kinds of directives from the most straightforward, "Write a letter to your father," in a case of family therapy at a distance, or "Bring father into therapy," to the more indirect as "Can your spirit guide protect you?" or telling a fighter "to take turns at being bad" with his nonfighter brother.

Stages of Family Life

Individuals can slip unobtrusively from one stage of development to the next. In many societies becoming an adult is accompanied by a ritual that is formal, compulsory, and performed repeatedly, often in a religious context. A goal of therapy is getting people through the stages of family life that are difficult. Therapists attempt to move the client into the next stage. Haley developed this framework in *Uncommon Therapy* (1973) to present the therapy of Milton Erickson. There is a transition from birth to infancy to childhood to school to adolescence to leaving home to being a parent to being a grandparent and dealing with old age. Often a client is blocked at one of these stages and must be helped beyond it. Usually a symptom indicates a stage-of-life problem and guides a therapist to an approach. Psychological problems do not occur randomly in the life of a family. They cluster at certain points. One way to think about the cycle is as stages of commitment. During courtship one can always think divorce is possible. With the arrival of a child there is more commitment to take care of it and agree how to do that. Childbirth has its special problems. The husband may develop pregnancy symptoms known as *couvade* during his wife's pregnancy; it has been reported in many societies and our own. In other cultures a ritual deals with moving a man from marriage to marriage with a child. One task of therapy must deal with having him assert his paternal rights over the newborn. Serious problems may occur when someone moves into a family. Women can have severe problems at this time. When the child attends school, it is beginning to disengage from the family. Next is adolescence, which is the most ambiguous stage. It is halfway between being at home as a child and leaving home as an adult. The goals are to live outside the home and support oneself. Leaving home is the most difficult stage. A child can have many functions in the family that change when the threat of leaving home occurs. There are different stages of leaving home (Haley, 1996). Some are positive. But serious problems often occur when a child leaves home after being a bridge between parents for many years. All the relationships get revised when the child opens a space in the house by leaving home. The therapist and parents often face an upset child and an upset parent who is watching the child leave. When Jay Haley was testing family relationships, they were looking for a normal family to try the test on. A neighbor volunteered. On the day when the family was supposed to come for the test, they called and said they were no longer a normal family. Their daughter was going off to college, and their house was in chaos. (When the child is leaving home and collapses—so that he cannot leave—his collapse is intended to keep the home stable.) The goal is to establish a family and produce one's own family, and the parents survive it. Finally there is retirement and old age, with all the handicaps of old age.

A case illustrates how moving on to the next stage can normalize a problem. Haley had a case of a young woman with a trembling right hand. It shook irregularly, and neurological tests failed to show a physical cause. She was referred to him for hypnosis. He asked her what would happen if the problem got worse. She said, "I'll lose my job." He asked, "And what if you lose your job?" She said with a sigh, "My husband will have to go to work." The parents protested the daughter's supporting the husband and tried to break up the marriage. The girl got pregnant and stopped working, and her husband had to go to work to support the family. The parents who wanted their daughter back didn't want her back with a baby. They began to support the marriage instead of tearing it down. This happened in the natural stages of becoming independent. The family went from one stage of marriage to birth of a child, which normalized the problem.

Many alternative household arrangements exist today, and therapists must work with single-parent households, blended families, gay families, integrating stepparents, and managing the multiplication of grandparents in families in crisis. This book illustrates some of the strategies used.

Ethical Issues

Ethical issues are a special concern with strategic therapy since the therapy is brief and directive. The therapist taking this approach is effective and at times intense. A therapist sitting passively and saying, "Tell me more about that," is not risking action that must be controlled. It is perhaps helpful to outline some basic ethical issues with this therapy.

1. The therapist will do no harm. Only those therapy procedures will be used that the therapist is willing to experience or have his wife and children experience.
2. There will be no diagnostic labels that damage a person's social reputation.
3. No therapist will ask a client to undertake any harmful, immoral, or illegal action, even as a directive or paradoxical intervention
4. No therapy intervention will be used that has its origins in the therapist's desire for revenge.
5. Therapists will not do therapy with anyone they define as incurable.
6. The therapist is responsible for the results of the therapy and cannot blame others for them.
7. Therapy should not be confused with medication used for social control.
8. A therapist will not attempt therapy in a social-control setting, such as a psychiatric hospital or prison, when discharge is in the indefinite future and there is no therapy plan.

Ethnicity

The world of clients and therapists has changed. Ethnicity is represented in schools. A local school had an Ethnicity Day. One hundred and eighty-seven different ethnic groups were represented. A percentage of them would ask for therapy.

There are at least two ways to approach ethnicity. One way is to involve oneself, understanding, penetrating, and expressing therapy ideas in the client's framework. This means trying to adapt the ethnic ideas as a way of joining the family. For example, when families migrate to the United States, they face the problem of confusion in the family hierarchy—who is in charge? Discipline and abuse may be confused across cultures.

The other way is to assume that families of all cultures are at least partially alike. The therapist seeks universal aspects. In taking this approach you do not focus on cultural differences. Rather, you focus on the structure and shared ideas of families, no matter what the ethnic group, that lead to change in a specific problem. There are factors that should be taken into account in dealing with an ethnic group.

1. Is the case court-ordered?
2. Does the upbringing of the parents affect the upbringing of the children.

Some cases are so unusual that you must make a plan for the individual case that has nothing to do with the family. For example, a man arrived in an emergency room in the Northwest and he spoke no English. The staff sent for a translator to find out why he was so upset. A translator arrived and was introduced to the patient. The translator was angry and refused to speak to him. The staff finally learned that the translator was Vietnamese and the patient was Cambodian. The Cambodian would not speak to the Vietnamese. The medical problem was difficult to deal with because of a problem that had nothing to do with the family but with war.

Cultural sensitivity is politically correct these days, and cultural exploration may often prolong the therapy rather than make it be better. When to utilize belief systems and when to minimize them is a decision that the therapist must confront in almost every case where therapists and clients come from a variety of backgrounds. In general, regardless of the ethnic group or the diagnosis, courtesy and respect for cultural differences is necessary.

Training programs these days have clients and therapists who are very diverse. Clients range from middle class to homeless. They come from many ethnic groups. Those who do not speak English require a translator. The cases presented in this book were chosen on the basis of being good training cases that bring up issues relevant to the field. The cases are organized to give a step-by-step strategic approach to the case. They include how to deal with marital problems, children's violence, delinquency, court-ordered cases, drug and alcohol abuse, living in shelters, conflicts in couples from different ethnic groups, spirit possession, psychotic behavior, and making a diagnosis. Strategic therapy is an active therapy, and when it is successful, it is the most interesting form of therapy to the client, the therapist, and the supervisor.

REFERENCES

Bateson, G., Jackson, D., Haley, J., & Weakland, J. (1956). Toward a theory of schizophrenia. *Behavioral Science, 1,* 251–264.
Haley, J. (1973). *Uncommon therapy: The psychiatric techniques of Milton H. Erickson, M.D.* New York: Norton.

Haley, J. (1984). *Ordeal therapy: Unusual ways to change behavior.* San Francisco: Jossey Bass.

Haley, J. (1985). *Conversations with Milton H. Erickson, M.D.* (Vols. 1–3). New York: Triangle Press/Norton.

Haley, J. (1993). *Jay Haley on Milton H. Erickson.* New York: Brunner/Mazel.

Haley, J. (1996). *Leaving home* (2nd ed.). New York: Brunner/Mazel.

Haley, J., & Hoffman, L. (1967). *Techniques of family therapy.* New York: Basic Books.

Neukrug, E. S. (1991). Computer-assisted live supervision in counseling skills training. *Counseling Education and Supervision, 31,* 132–138.

Scherl, C. R., & Haley, J. (2000). Computer monitor supervision: A clinical note. *American Journal of Family Therapy, 28,* 275–282.

2

Ethnicity Issues in Strategic Therapy

Today therapists must not only learn to understand the variety of personalities and psychopathologies entering therapy, but they must also deal with a surprising variety of ethnic groups. Displaced families are flooding mental health systems around the world and many urban areas in the United States are now made up of a collection of minorities. With over a hundred cultures migrating to the United States today, many of them with families in crisis, therapists cannot be expected to understand all the customs, styles, symbols, and standards of behavior, especially the beliefs and practices relating to health and illness, but they are expected to deal with them nonetheless.

Therapists cannot be totally understanding of every culture and must decide what ethnic material is relevant to therapy. Should academia focus on training therapists in ethnic differences as a priority? Can a therapist bring about therapeutic change with a client without working in his belief system? Does ethnicity count when it is a court, not the culture, that dictates how a person should behave in his family, for example, in relation to domestic violence? The court system is designed to enforce the rules of the dominant culture, even though today it is sometimes not clear who is dominant. Should therapists share in social-policy advocacy?

To make the problem more complex, therapists are not from a single cultural group. In supervision programs, it is not unusual to see trainees from around the world take on cases from around the world. On a typical day Richeport-Haley observed German, Philippine, Argentine, Puerto Rican, and Israeli trainees deal with Central and South American, African-American, and Japanese families. Therapists everywhere today must deal with cases of cultures different from their own. As an anthropologist working as a mental health consultant in the United States, Puerto Rico, and Brazil, I have always thought it important to describe cultural differences in detail, assuming that the information would enhance the communication between health professionals and their clients (Richeport, 1975, 1984, 1985a, 1985b, 1985c, 1988, 2002). However, observing this family-oriented directive therapy afforded me another point of view. Although it would be ideal for therapists to be experts on different cultures, as well as experts in all other areas of therapy, is it practical?

Ethnicity can be defined as Weidman (1978) does: "Ethnic affiliation is based primarily upon enculturation into a culturally provided cognitive and behavioral meaning structure which is transmitted in an enduring way from generation to generation. . . . It can be determined by taking into consideration linguistic terms, marriage patterns, ethnic friendship networks, socialization in established ethnic enclaves, and self definition in certain instances" (pp. 16–17). Ethnicity differs from race, which "is a category of persons who are related by a common heredity or ancestry and who are perceived and responded to in terms of external features or traits." Ethnicity refers to "a shared culture and lifestyles" (Wilkinson, 1993, p. 19) that often cross racial boundaries.

This therapy minimizes a focus on ethnicity as an essential factor for bringing about change in therapy. Haley (1996) concentrates on the structural changes in the family. These changes can be similar across ethnic groups. Therapists with this approach focus on immigration issues more than cultural differences. They encourage families into mainstream society through actions, not through reflection on their roots. The therapy is not an insight therapy. It is a problem-solving therapy rather than an ideology-changing therapy.

Therapy with different groups in the immigration situation makes it possible to think about what cultures have in common in reactions to social change. Repetitive patterns can occur that are related more to migrating reactions than to ethnic beliefs. For example, a wife can arrive in the United States and become more upwardly mobile than the husband when she can get a job and the husband cannot. The hierarchical status of the husband becomes uncertain, and the change sometimes leads to a depressed husband or a violent one, who is brought into therapy. This sequence is common to a variety of quite different cultures. Coalition situations are evident across cultures. In most cultures, a mother-in-law, or grandparents, have the power to disrupt a marriage. One of the opportunities brought about by this situation is that we can determine what seemingly different cultures have in common from a structural view. For example, though an East Indian father and a Nicaraguan father had quite different belief systems, they presented the same problem: each beat his wife and was arrested and the court ordered him to therapy. In both cases the family had moved to the United States, and the wife found work and began to assert herself more like an

American woman. The husband, unable to find work and finding his status demeaned, beat up on the wife. When arrested he learned that it is against the law in this culture to beat a wife. The therapist's task here is not to understand the cultural differences but to know how to intervene so that the violence ends and these problems are handled differently. A goal can be to bring about a rise in the husband's status and for the wife to have a richer life than she had in the past as she obtains the rights expected of women in America, her adopted country.

A structural organizational approach to family therapy makes it possible to resolve problems when there is minimal communication between therapist and client. Haley recalls the training experience of an Italian psychiatrist who hardly spoke English and who treated an African-American woman who spoke a dialect of English that was difficult for him to understand. Live supervision made it possible to offer suggestions to clarify misunderstandings. In the process the child problem was resolved, and the two adults—client and therapist—came to enjoy each other. The mother's problem with the child arose partly from the fact that she and her mother could not agree on how to raise the child. The therapist helped the two women resolve their differences since he understood aspects of their problem from his experience with similar conflicts between his own mother and grandmother in Italy. When the focus is on the family, cross-cultural similarities make treatment possible by a therapist whose culture differs from the client's.

Another age-old difficulty is the generation gap created by migration situations where children become ashamed of their parents and become more influenced by their peers and teachers. Parents are unable to discipline their children and may resort to abuse. Abuse differs from discipline in ways that are not uniform across cultures. Not only can cultures be different from each other, but within any culture there are intraethnic variations such as differences in geographical location, religion, social class, and gender. It is difficult for therapists to be knowledgeable about all of these differences.

Courtesy and respect are minimum requirements for therapy. Haley (1996) also believes that therapists must adapt to certain basic premises of a culture. If a husband will not sit down with his wife and treat her as an equal, the couple can be seen separately and their problems worked out. The goal is not to make members of the client family behave like members of the ethnic group of the therapist but to respect the clients' culture and still resolve their problems. One can ask the family how a particular issue would be dealt with in the country of origin.

Alternate Belief Systems

Alternate belief systems refer to nonmainstream sources of treatment. Cultural problems of immigrants entering the United States may involve some type of belief in spirit possession, which is one issue that illustrates dealing with different ethnic groups. Spirit possession is the most common explanation of problems throughout the world. Healing through spirit possession is practiced around the world. Specialists, or mediums, act as intermediaries between the living and the dead. Often they divine and heal through possession trances. Anthropologists differentiate ritual possession from sick possession (Richeport, 1975, 1985b, 1985c, 1988). Examples of ethnicity issues in this chapter involve problems that come up in relation to alternate belief systems and violence and the strategies used in the cases.

A Central-American Family

A Central-American couple presented the problem of violence by the husband. The couple accepted the idea that the husband had an *espiritu burlon*, a mischievous spirit that caused him to act violently. Juan and Rosa, in their late 30s, had been in the United States for eight years. They were sent to therapy by the court. Rosa had a part-time job, and Juan was unemployed. They had two young children. Privately, Rosa reported that Juan threatened to hurt her and "to take her eyes out." Rosa was made even more fearful by the three dots that Juan has tattooed on his forearm. For her they reinforce his alliance with malevolent forces. Rosa is also upset with Juan's extramarital affairs, and she says she wants to separate. During the birth of their first child, Juan was with a girlfriend. The goal of the therapy was to prevent any future violence and bring about a more amiable relationship between the two.

FOUR ALTERNATIVES FOR DEALING WITH THIS CASE

Therapists may choose among four alternatives when dealing with a case involving an alternate belief system. These may not be mutually exclusive: (1) The therapist can minimize the alternate belief system and treat the case structurally. (2) The therapist can utilize aspects of the alternate system to further therapeutic goals. (3) The therapist can refer the client to a healer in the local healing system. (4) The therapist can collaborate with the healer. In the above case the first alternative was chosen.

The therapist can minimize the alternate belief system and treat the case structurally.
    Interventions. The supervisor of the case was unsure how to read the violence threat and consulted the Hispanic therapists behind the mirror. (The therapy was done in a one-way-mirror room with a training group behind the mirror taking turns going in to see the families). They felt it was

dangerous for Juan to remain in the house. The therapist was empathic with both husband and wife and discussed with them their past and present difficulties. The strategies suggested to the trainee included persuading one of the spouses to move out of the house for one week. Juan moved out. It was suggested they get help from a family member. The wife's mother was brought in. Her presence proved counterproductive because she was so critical of Juan. The positive attributes of each spouse were to be emphasized. They reviewed why they were attracted to each other in the beginning. Juan was to take Rosa out for the evening. It was suggested the therapist arrange for them a fond farewell since they are going to separate.

Not only was the supernatural explanation of Juan's behavior ignored, other cultural variables were also ignored. These include ignoring the Hispanic value of *respeto.* This covers the English word *respect,* which means deference to the male, to authority (Paniagua, 1994). The very fact of bringing Juan to a therapy session to discuss his personal life with a therapist, and a woman at that, challenges the essence of his masculinity. The therapist assumes the male role, even if a female, as authority in the family and tells him what to do. The therapist ignores paralinguistic and nonverbal behavior. For example, the therapist might have misinterpreted Juan's lack of eye contact with her as resistance, not paying attention, when in reality when a man makes eye contact with a woman, this may denote a pass. Suggestions to the wife also violated basic traditional values of submissiveness, obedience, and dependence, such as the directive to accompany her husband to a bar, which she refused.

In summary, the therapy plan opted for thrusting the family into mainstream American reality in which they must deal with the legal system that sent them for therapy. The therapy sessions gave them the opportunity to rehearse new behaviors and to challenge major cultural patterns, such as machismo, by minimizing them. Juan's resorting to witchcraft was interpreted as an attempt to exert power over his wife in this low-status relationship he found himself in as a migrant in the United States. Even though the therapeutic goal was to increase his self-confidence, and utilizing the client's belief in witchcraft might have served that goal, the priority was to end the violence. No utilization of his alternate belief system was attempted, as in the case examples that follow.

The therapist can utilize aspects of the alternate system to further therapeutic goals.

An East-Indian couple believed that an evil spirit was following them around and took control of them. They demonstrated this to Milton Erickson in a table-tipping session. Erickson, who did not believe in spirits, knew more about table tipping than they did, having studied it in relation to hypnotic phenomena. In the process of coaching them in the correct way to do table tipping, he helped them discover weak good spirits. Although weak, when added up, they exceeded the strength of the evil spirit. Mirroring the couple's belief in spirits Erickson was able to acknowledge and utilize features of that belief system to change the meaning of the spirits from evil to good (Richeport, 1985a). Haley reported that in cases of *ataque*, or a transient hysterical seizure-like state among Puerto Ricans, a young psychiatrist at Bellevue Hospital, who did not believe in spirits, learned enough Spanish to perform a Spiritist ritual that led to the prompt discharge of several patients.

In another case treated in the directive family-oriented approach, a South-American mother married an East Indian who died. She had a 21-year-old son who was diagnosed as autistic even though he went to school and drove a car. She interpreted all of her problems as due to a Cuban "witch." The mother had never returned to her native country, and her family had never met her son. Since she believed that a shaman in her homeland could cure her son, the goal of the therapy was to have the mother and son return to visit their family. The strategy to accomplish this goal became to suggest that the mother return to her country to find a powerful native healer to counteract the black magic. In the directive approach, the spiritual was utilized only to bring about an interpersonal solution. There was no exploration of the belief system as a cause of the problem, just as there would be no exploration of the past to explain the present. When the belief system is very strong, such was the case with another East-Indian woman who interpreted all her suffering as a result of "karma" (past lives), Haley recommended entering the client's system by doing a past-life regression under the therapist's control. When therapists utilize alternate belief systems there is no discussion or insight offered to the client. Utilization of clients' beliefs is paradoxical in that what you want to change is elaborated on.

The therapist can refer the client to a healer in the local healing system.

In our fieldwork in Bali, Indonesia, a 15-year-old boy was brought to a *balian*, or healer, because he was suffering from seizures for which the doctors found no physical cure. The balian suggested that the boy, Nyoman, and a family member live with the balian's family so that he could observe the seizures. Nyoman's father had died, and Nyoman had remained in the household of his father while his mother remarried and lived with her new husband's family. The balian performed many rituals with the boy. He also referred him to a medium with whom he collaborated on cases. Possessed by the spirit of Nyoman's dead father, the medium revealed that the family had not performed the correct house ceremony when they moved. The balian arranged to perform the correct ceremony, which required extensive preparations; the entire family had to attend, including Nyoman's mother. Haley interpreted this case in the same way he interprets most problems. By bringing the family together, the problem could be resolved and the elaborate rituals could lead to interpersonal solutions. (See Richeport-Haley & Haley, 2003.)

Another example illustrates the adeptness of a faithhealer in creating an ordeal to resolve the bitterness after one spouse has had an affair. A man brought his wife to a faithhealer in New York and said his wife had had an affair and he did not want to kill her. Could something be done? The healer saw the wife alone. He then reported to the couple that she did not have the affair. A spirit of the man's first wife had the affair. The problem was to do something to prevent this from happening again. The healer provided a ritual. The couple were to take a bus to another state and go to a particular town. They were to walk one mile to a particular tree and go through a ceremony to exorcize the spirit. Then they had to walk back to the bus and go back to New York. According to Haley, the spirit was utilized to save face, and the travel and ceremony solved the problem because the investment was large enough to get over the bitterness (Haley, 1994).

The therapist can collaborate with a healer

In many countries therapists who understand their culture use informal healers as resources. (For case examples, see Harwood, 1977; Lambo, 1966; Richeport, 1979, 1985a, 1985b). An example of collaboration between therapist and healer is the case of a Puerto Rican client, Paul Lebron, a 25-year-old schizophrenic, chronic undifferentiated type. His psychosis was manifested in the belief that he was possessed by a demon that he first saw when he was 6 years old. His mother took him to a spirit medium who advised to take him to a doctor. She, however, relied on spirit mediums until he was 23 years old, when she took him to a psychiatrist. Paul used the Spiritist explanation to explain his feelings of detachment, handwashing compulsion, and refusal to touch people. He dichotomized the forces within himself into good and bad, with himself in the middle trying to keep the bad from predominating. To prevent the bad from taking over, he walked compulsively for hours and therefore could not hold down a job.

After Paul had spent 2 years in psychotherapy, the psychiatrist felt he could produce no change and referred him to Dr. Hilton Lopez for hypnotherapy. Paul continued to see Spiritists at the same time. Paul returned to work and college. Dr. Lopez felt that "despite his progress, and since Paul was seeing mediums anyway," he would use a medium as a consultant to help banish Paul's demon. Dr. Lopez called on Carmen, a former patient, whom Lopez had guided into replacing unwanted spirit possessions into spirit mediumship, which brought her prestige. Lopez directed the interaction and then transferred the direction to Lao-tzu, Carmen's spirit guide. Lao-tzu located the "evil" in Paul's left hand and the "good" in Paul's right hand. Paul appeared very expectant as Carmen clasped his hands together and then tore them apart sharply. Paul began to tremble in a contest between Paul's possessing entity resisting departure and Carmen's "vital fluid" working to push out the entity. Lao-tzu told Paul that he was "good, intelligent, and a normal man."

Dr. Lopez resumed the direction of the interaction. As he thanked Lao-tzu for coming, Carmen, slowly recovering from trance, asked what had happened. Lopez used the remainder of the time to reinforce the idea of the expulsion of the demon. Since then, Paul has been working full time for many years and has girlfriends.

Problems may arise when therapists and healers collaborate as in the above case, because it gives the healer a great deal of power. Montalvo and Gutierrez (1989) strategically use humor to show the misuse of cultural beliefs in cases of spirit explanations.

PROBLEMS OF VIOLENCE

In the following cases the primary problem was violence. There was no alternate belief system involved. The three families, Spanish, South American, and Japanese, were all ordered to therapy by courts. The main interventions ignored cultural variables and dealt with the cases structurally, with utilization of cultural patterns as a minor strategy.

A Spanish Family

A working-class mother from Spain beat her teenage daughter for dating. The family believed in the custom of virginity at marriage. The girl reported her mother to the authorities and the mother was arrested. The court ordered the mother on probation for 8 months before a hearing would be held. The family was ordered to therapy, each member with a different therapist. Although the family had been in the United States for 10 years, the parents did not speak English whereas the daughter spoke it perfectly. The girl was placed in a foster home that offered her many material things her parents could not. This made the parents feel even more inadequate. In the sessions the girl would yell at the parents, tell them she hated them, and threaten suicide if she was forced to live with them.

The goal at first was to get the daughter to go back home to her parents. The goal changed to having the daughter establish an amiable relationship with the parents without living with them and to helping the parents survive the relationship so contrary to their culture.

Interventions

There was division among the trainees regarding this case. The Hispanic trainees felt sympathy for the parents. They objected to a system in which a foster home would be selected that was of a higher class than the home of the parents. One young trainee sympathized with the daughter who was trying to Americanize. It was suggested that the foster parents be made godparents or members of the extended family, a tradition common in their country. The sessions consisted of listening to the parents talk about their humiliating visits with their daughter and complimenting them on their efforts. The court had disempowered these parents, and the strong values of parental respect and obedience were lost. An ethnically oriented therapist (Moitoza, 1982) might have attempted to thrash out cultural issues, most importantly the preservation of the honor of the family through the daughter's virginity at marriage, parental obedience, chaperonage, proper dating practices, and religious orientation. There was none of this. There was no effort to have the daughter accept her roots, nor discussion of ethnic values and traditions. The therapist encouraged the mother in her part-time work and schooling. The goals achieved were that the mother and father got along better. The mother began to work part-time. The daughter continued a relationship with the parents that was more amiable since she was not compelled to move back with them.

A South-American Family

A son in his early 20s was court-ordered to therapy for repeatedly possessing and dealing marijuana. He would be imprisoned if this happened one more time. The mother, who only spoke Spanish, and the eldest son, who translated for her, came to therapy. The goal was to get the boy off marijuana. The intervention was to have the family come up with a strong consequence if the youth relapsed. Once the family realized that they could do something, they had a lengthy discussion of what to do. They decided that the consequence would be to ostracize the son from the family for 3 months and to shun him if he took drugs again. The son has not gone back to drugs. The therapist did not need to understand the strong bond of a Latin-American family and the difficulty it had in banning a member. The goal of therapy, regardless of ethnic group, was for the family to take charge of its member and make a serious consequence rather than have the community do so.

In contrast to this directive approach, a culturally focused therapist would have explored the importance and positive functions of a close-knit family. It would emphasize the values of forgiveness based in a religious charity ethic. In keeping the communication style of this ethnic group, the therapist might have been authoritarian and told the family exactly what to do rather then letting them decide. Haley opted to make it as brief and directive as possible with the law involved.

A Japanese Family

A Japanese brother and sister were court-ordered to therapy after he beat her. They lived together, and the parents sent him money from Japan to go to school. He was depressed. He failed at school. The sessions consisted of Hiroshi's complaints against Toni, his elder sister, because she would come home from her bartender job and talk on the phone. He said he needed to relax and to sleep and that she kept him awake. He also complained that she drank too much. Toni insisted that she was a "strong" drinker, but it was not explored if she meant that she was a heavy drinker or that she could hold her liquor. The goal of therapy was to negotiate the house rules so that they could get on better. The interventions used to accomplish this were (1) Have each one think positively about the other. Toni admired Hiroshi's attention to details and perfectionism. Hiroshi complimented his sister on her friendliness and that she was not detail oriented. (2) The therapist concentrated on their relationship, not on her drinking problem, and on having them equally negotiate the house rules. In one session, however, the therapist asked Toni to give up drinking for 2 days. They ended up getting along much better, and the physical abuse ceased. Traditional cultural hierarchies, loss of face, and indirect communication styles were ignored in this court-ordered case.

This book describes a brief strategic family-oriented approach that can be used as a way of working when dealing with a variety of ethnic groups. If you avoid cultural immersion, you can be briefer. The following discussion refers to the premises and techniques in the initial phase of the therapy that proved to be successful.

Challenging Ethnic Values

In a family-oriented strategic therapy, patient expectations, cultural mores and values, paralinguistic cues, and traditional hierarchies might all be minimized. The therapist implicitly challenges a central culture pattern, such as Hispanic machismo, Mediterranean "virginity complex," and Asian loss of face. Because these patterns were maladaptive in a new country, and brought the family to the attention of the authorities, a therapy approach was used that did not discuss these insights but created directives to change them. In addition, this directive approach has the premise that just because you understand a problem, a belief, a culture, a symptom, that does not mean it will disappear. Therefore, this therapy does not help people become more aware of anything, including their roots. Erickson (Haley, 1985) said, "I think therapy is primarily a matter of getting people to function adequately within a reality framework. The reality framework is that of eating and living and responding today, in today's realities, in preparation for tomorrow" (Vol. II, p. 8).

Several of Erickson's cases show the maladaptive behavior of hanging on to old ways. He would do an acculturation therapy and might even recommend that the client not see any member of his ethnic group (Richeport, 1985a; Zeig, 1980). Margaret Mead discussed families who preserve a timeless continuity with the past and do not change, which causes a great deal of stress (Danna, 1980).

Experiencing Different Roles in the Interviews

A directive therapy approach provides families the opportunity to practice alternate roles, in a concerned supportive setting, which are more compatible with everyday reality. Juan must listen to a female authority talk about his personal life and endure his wife criticizing him in front of strangers. Doing so, he is rehearsing an alternate role that is more adaptive in the United States. Rosa rehearses being more equal with her husband, which is acceptable in the United States, but not as acceptable in her own country. The Japanese siblings practice being equals who negotiate house rules. These new behaviors are given a trial run as the family walks through assignments in the sessions that can later be transferred to everyday life. Erickson (1967) commented on the power of rehearsal that results from the belief that an action that has already been achieved by symbolic actions provides a "new psychological orientation of compelling force, affecting a new organization of thinking and planning" (p. 1389).

Making Use of Culture

Knowledge of the culture increases options for planning strategies for problem solving. Therapists must have knowledge of cultural complexities if they want to utilize the very behaviors that are maladaptive. Rather than ignoring the behavior, the behavior is made use of paradoxically. Making foster parents godparents in the Spanish family and performing a ritual to exorcize a spirit are examples of utilizing behaviors to further therapeutic goals. Although it is not practical for therapists to understand the culture of hundreds of groups migrating today, utilization is a powerful approach. Erickson encouraged therapists to learn anthropology and to utilize beliefs and practices as he himself did. In the case of a Prussian soldier who was the victim of a stroke and was paralyzed and unable to speak, Erickson called him a "dirty Nazi pig" among other insults. Although seeming harsh, he was familiar enough with Prussian culture to know that this would make a proud and self-inflated Prussian so angry at him that he would overcome an eight-year paralysis and begin talking again, as he did (Haley, 1973). In spite of the directive approach's lack of focus on ethnic issues, it is, paradoxically, an approach that is more culturally appropriate than other approaches that have focused on ethnicity issues. Strategic therapy fulfills the expectations of many cultural groups: (1) The family and or social network is included in the therapy. (2) Therapy does not stress exploration nor insight. (3) It is action oriented, not discussion oriented. (4) The therapist maintains a position of expertise and authority. (5) The client receives concrete advice. (6) The therapist maintains a posture of courteous concern. The goal of the therapy becomes acculturation of the family to new rules and to giving up their maladaptive ways.

In the chapters that follow, the strategies for dealing with cultural issues are not mutually exclusive. In chapter 4, a depressed Middle Easterner who hangs on to the expectations of an authoritarian father figure who is paralyzing him is challenged and encouraged to become an equal with his father, since they have the same career. Chapters 5, 7, 8, and 10 deal with cases of violence in ethnically diverse families. An effort is made to use their culture as well as minimize its influence and focus on practicalities. In an African-American family, utilization of playful language patterns and hip-hop are utilized. However, there is no attempt to thrash out issues of racism in the white neighborhood where they live to explain their fighting behavior. Court-ordered Pacific Island teenagers are dealt with in a U.S. court system rather than stressing the informal court system of the extended family that handles misbehavior. In the case of an abusive Brazilian woman with Spiritist beliefs, first an attempt is made to utilize these beliefs. When unsuccessful, practicalities of functioning in everyday life are stressed. The briefest approach is usually taken.

REFERENCES

Danna, J. (1980). Migration and mental illness: What role do traditional childhood socialization practices play? *Culture, Medicine, and Psychiatry,* 4, 25–42.

Erickson, M. (1967). Pseudo-orientation in time as a hypnotherapeutic procedure. In J. Haley (Ed.), *Advanced techniques of hypnosis and therapy. Selected papers of Milton H. Erickson, M.D.* (pp. 369–389). New York: Allyn & Bacon.

Haley, J. (1973). *Uncommon therapy.* New York: Norton.

Haley, J. (1985). *Conversations with Milton H. Erickson, M.D. Volume I: Changing individuals: Volume* II: Changing couples. *Vol. III: Changing children and families.* New York: Triangle/Norton.

Haley, J. (1994). Workshop on Directive Therapy. New Orleans, May 12, 1994.

Haley, J. (1996). *Learning and teaching therapy.* New York: Guilford Press.

Harwood, A. (1977). *Rx: Spiritist as needed.* New York: Wiley.

Lambo, T. A. (1966). Patterns of psychiatric care in developing countries. The Nigerian program. In H. R. David (Ed.), *International trends in mental health.* New York: McGraw-Hill.

Moitoza, E. (1982). Portuguese families. In M. McGoldrick, J. Pearce, & J. Giordano (Eds.), *Ethnicity and family therapy.* New York: Guilford Press.

Montalvo, B., & M. Gutierrez. (1989). Nine assumptions for work with ethnic minority families. *Journal of Psychotherapy & the Family,* 6(1/2), 35–52.

Paniagua, F. A. (1994). *Assessing and treating culturally diverse clients. A practical guide.* London: Sage.

Richeport (Michtom), M. (1975). *Becoming a medium: The role of trance in Puerto Rican Spiritism as an avenue to mazeway-synthesis.* Ann Arbor: University of Michigan Press.

Richeport, M. (1979). The psychiatrist as a culture broker. The hypnotic techniques of Hilton L. Lopez, M.D. *Svensk Tidskrift, 5,* 16–19.

Richeport, M. (1984). Strategies and outcomes of introducing a mental health plan in Brazil. *Social Science and Medicine, 19*(3), 261–271.

Richeport, M. (1985a). The importance of anthropology in psychotherapy: World view of Milton H. Erickson, M. D. In J. Zeig (Ed.), *Ericksonian approaches to hypnosis and psychotherapy* (pp. 371–390). New York: Brunner/Mazel.

Richeport, M. (1985b). *Macumba, trance, and spirit healing* [16mm film]. New York: Filmmakers Library.

Richeport, M. (1985c). *Terapias alternativas num bairro de Natal: Estudo na antropologia medica.* Natal, Brazil: Editora Universitaria.

Richeport, M. (1988). Transcultural issues in Ericksonian hypnotherapy. In S. Lankton & J. Zeig (Eds.), *Treatment of special populations with Ericksonian approaches* (Ericksonian Monographs no. 3 (pp.130–147). New York: Brunner/Mazel.

Richeport-Haley, M (2002). An anthropological view of Jay Haley's work. In J. Zeig, (Ed.), *Changing directives: The strategic therapy of Jay Haley.* Phoenix, AZ: Milton H. Erickson Foundation Press.

Richeport-Haley, M., & J. Haley. (2003). Family therapy in Bali [30-minute video]. New York: Insight Media.

Weidman, H. H. (1978). *Miami health ecology report: A statement on ethnicity and health.* Miami: University of Miami.

Wilkinson, D. (1993). Family ethnicity in America. In H. P. McAdoo (Ed.), *Family ethnicity strength in diversity.* Newbury Park, CA: Sage.

Zeig, J. K. (Ed.). (1980). *Teaching Seminar with Milton H. Erickson.* New York: Brunner/Mazel.

3

Strategic Therapy with Couples

M arriage therapy is interesting and rewarding because it arouses one's personal involvement in marriage. After all, nearly everyone is married or going to be married or ending a marriage. It is hard to be objective when actions touch one personally. It is frustrating as well because there does not seem to be an agreed-upon set of ideas. There is no orthodoxy in marriage therapy.

Marriage therapy has had many intelligent people applying themselves to it over the years. It should have produced a new ideology but seems to have borrowed ideologies of the time. This happened with psychodynamic theory, behavior therapy, and family therapy.

In the psychodynamic period, spouses were seen individually. The past was largely the focus. Symptoms were held to be unconscious expressions of the individual, and therapy was insightful. In the 1950s, marriage counselors began to be revolutionary by interviewing spouses together. One question was "What is an ideal marriage?" Two ideas were offered. Conflict-free marriage was one possibility. Healthy conflict was another, and spouses were taught to fight and express themselves.

Behavior therapy brought the use of conditioning ideas to marriage therapy. Family therapy brought in the concept of systems and organization.

How the problem arrives can make a difference. With a child problem, a child can improve, and then the parents have a conflict. With family therapy, the triangular unit leads to the theory of coalitions. One can see a therapist is siding with one spouse against the other, triangulating the marriage.

The focus is on the present situation, not the past. If a woman is having a sexual problem with her husband and was abused as a child, strategic family therapy would focus on the relationship with the husband and not on the childhood abuse. The motivation of symptoms of a spouse can be

31

seen as protective and helpful. This is opposite from the theory of repression, which is a negative theory. Today positive is the fashion.

Today therapists must deal with a variety of marriages, not just a simple couple. They recognize differences in culture, class, age, gay and lesbians, romantic or arranged, separated or divorced, living together or apart, and multiple divorce.

Each case is unique. No one method has been developed. The result is a lack of focus for a general view, but it is necessary to have unique therapy for each couple.

This chapter illustrates techniques that can be used with marriages in distress. To use a strategic approach, it is best to hypothesize that marital relationships are based upon sequences of behavior that follow rules. These rules can be inferred from observation of repetitive behavior by a couple. They are pervasive in a couple's interaction, and they range from small issues to major crisis. For example, a husband will routinely behave irresponsibly. The wife will behave responsibly, and she will complain about the husband being irresponsible. They will follow this rule whenever they communicate. A rule like that is evident even when they visit the therapist. The wife will responsibly bring them into therapy when they are in trouble. The husband will come reluctantly—not taking responsibility for their problems. Symptoms are the expression of a conflict of rules. A couple can follow rules that lead to pleasant experiences or they can repeat rules that are appropriate for distress. Behavior causes how people feel. The rules of relationships are difficult to change and the intervention of a therapist can be necessary to change the rules and so relieve their distress.

Difficult interchanges are not often relieved by insight, since being aware of a rule doesn't change it. For example, a therapist might say to a wife, "Have you noticed that you followed the rule that you complain and your husband will defend himself in almost everything you say." The wife says, "That's true. He never pays any attention to me." The husband responds, "She complains and is dissatisfied no matter what I do." The communication interchange is complete. She complains, he defends himself, and then he withdraws. A goal of the therapy is to change these rules and so the distress. The goal is not to stop following rules, which is impossible, but to stop following those that are stable and cause misery. Since some viewers are unfamiliar with the power of rule-directed behavior, a more subtle version can be described.

Spouses can have a pattern in which the wife initiates what happens and the husband responds. Or they are reversed and the husband does the initiating. Nothing happens unless the wife initiates it. The husband is willing to respond but not to initiate something happening. Sometimes this pattern has its origin in courtship days. At that time a wife courts a man and makes everything interesting. The man responds, pleased with the girlfriend's making things happen. After marriage the wife feels the burden of initiating everything that happens. She wants the husband to initiate what happens. But he follows the rule that they had established, by which he is only to respond. She becomes frustrated, and he is exasperated, feeling his contract with her is being violated.

Other examples of couples behaving according to the rules can be described. A couple can communicate and always escalate a disagreement. (They behave as equals.) Or the spouse follows the rule that one spouse takes care of the other. (They behave unequally whatever they do.)

A case will show some rules that couples are trapped in, and it will emphasize the therapy interventions that can help. The techniques will include paradoxical interventions, which can be effective in changing distressing rules.

PLANNING THE FIRST LIVE INTERVIEW

A working-class couple in their 30s came in angry at each other and unhappy. The man, Jose, was Mexican American and the woman, Rose, was a tall blonde of American descent. So there were ethnic differences. They were not married but living together and planning someday to get married. She had a 10-year-old daughter living with them. They had a history of both being addicted to drugs and alcohol. They went through the 12-step program and now were clean but still thought of themselves as addicts. The supervisor began with the therapist by asking her how she usually started a first interview. The therapist answers, "How would you describe what brought you here?"

HALEY: Well, it's always nice to try something different. You can ask him, "What would your wife say if you ask why you are here?"

Assuming it's a marital problem or heaven knows what problem this is, often couples come in with such bad feelings that when you ask each of them what the other thinks is the problem you get two different responses.

THERAPIST: I haven't gotten the opportunity to try that technique yet, so I'll probably try that.

HALEY: Maybe you don't have a case really, except for the first interview. Which would be nice, I think. Every therapist should shoot for one session.

OBSERVING THE FIRST LIVE INTERVIEW

The supervision is "live," with the trainees watching behind a one-way mirror and taking turns going in to do therapy. Suggestions from the supervisor to the therapist are sent to a computer monitor in the therapy room. The therapist can see the messages sent on the monitor, but the clients cannot.

The supervisor thought the couple could think of themselves in a more positive way if the therapist asked the couple to imagine that they had never had a problem with drugs or alcohol. Neither could imagine being cured.

Computer Suggestion: Ask them what problems they would have if they were normal not ex-addicts.

The context in which the rules of the couple were expressed was the framework of thinking of themselves as defective because they had been addicted. They believed that they were not normal like other couples. Their in-laws encouraged that view because of their addict history and were not helpful. The woman complained that she was having trouble with their relationship. This is what brought them in. She said he didn't communicate, didn't want sex, and didn't show her affection, and he made her very jealous. The man complained that the woman constantly complained and didn't recognize that he was busy. He was a construction worker and also a musician, so he worked night and day.

To do something about the woman's complaining, a paradox was proposed. It asked them to do what they were already doing. It was evident that the rule they followed was that the woman complained about the man and he defended himself. That was the rule imbedded in their relationship.

Computer Suggestion: Ask her to complain and him to defend himself.
Computer Suggestion: Ask him to criticize her and ask her not to respond.

This was a direct suggestion to the couple to change their rules. It was not paradoxical. Then they began to argue about issues like normal couples do around the house. He said she would be less overwhelmed if she went back to school or got a job. Both seemed overwhelmed at the idea that they were normal.

A paradox was given to this proud couple. They were avoiding sex, and to help them get over this problem, they were instructed to avoid sex.

Computer Suggestion: Say to get a better understanding of your attitudes about sex, it's forbidden to have sex this week.

The first interview ended with the therapist suggesting they expect more from each other since normal couples do that. They seemed relieved to be normal.

DISCUSSING THE FIRST INTERVIEW

The trainee is applauded as she returns behind the mirror to the group. She expressed her uncertainty to the group.

THERAPIST: At the end I was a little worried that [they would say] they weren't going to come back. Even though they hadn't given me any indication, they convinced me they were coming back. I mean they will be here next week. Because I said, "Well you have the number if anything comes up," Just saying stuff like that and he's like, "Oh, well, we don't have any excuses. We'll be there."

To the chagrin of the therapist, the group suggests that the client is flirting with the therapist. Haley reframes this as positive and brings in the therapists' attributes to aid her therapy.

TRAINEE ONE: I've decided that he was flirting with you.

THERAPIST: Was I?

TRAINEE: No.

THERAPIST: Good

HALEY: Why is that good?

THERAPIST: Because I would feel really weird about that. It's not my style. It would surprise me if I was being flirtatious with someone.

HALEY: When working with couples, all you have is yourself.

THERAPIST: Okay. Well, I'm not attracted to him. How about that?

HALEY: Well, you don't need to be attracted to him, but you could say to him, "I'm sure you know how to please a woman."

THERAPIST: Well, I said I'm sure you know how to please her.

HALEY: Right. But you could put the male into it by adding that.

THERAPIST: That's true.

HALEY: Whatever you have you use. If you are a pretty girl, you use that. If you are an older woman, you use that. If a male, you use that with males. If you're a girl 19 years old dealing with couples 50 years old, then you get helpless so they'll help you to achieve results.

HALEY: *Neutrality can be inappropriate.* The rule that you should be neutral is a real handicap in therapy—or that you shouldn't side with either one against the other.

I remember a case of a couple who came to therapy because they couldn't decide whether to stay together or separate. They were both dissatisfied and unhappy, but neither was willing to initiate a change. The therapist was experienced in doing traditional therapy with couples. He had been taught that a therapist should be neutral and not side with one side, with one spouse against the other. By behaving in a fair way with each spouse, the therapist was unintentionally legitimizing the rules of the relationship.

In the conversations behind the mirror, the supervisor's task was to change the behavior of the therapist so the couple could change. I asked the therapist if he could be unfair. Could he choose one spouse and say that one was entirely wrong, and the other was entirely right?

What helped was the supervisor saying that other therapists could be unfair. It was decided [that the therapeutic would] side against the husband. The wife could have been blamed, but the husband, being the responder, would be more appropriate. It was also easier for that therapist to join the man against the wife. The therapist said to the husband, "You are in danger of losing your wife. I think what you are doing is absolutely wrong, that you are doing things to turn her off by not talking to her, by not being aggressive, by not courting her." He told him to get her a present, go to a show, and get her flowers. Once committed to the marriage, the couple could negotiate differences safely. Both husband and wife were able to accept blame in a way they could change their behavior by influencing some of the rules of their relationship.

Haley showed the video of this case to the group at a later meeting. [For a more complete discussion of how to unbalance a couple see Appendix A (Haley & Richeport-Haley, 1998).]

THERAPIST: Well, I felt like I was being genuine, and I felt like I was being true to myself. [The supervisor had suggested she see each partner alone, with the man first.] When she came in, I kind of wished you could have been in the hallway still. She was so pissed when she came in the room from being out in the waiting room alone. I mean, you should have seen her coming down the hall.

TRAINEE: She was steaming, huh?

HALEY: She's a jealous woman.

THERAPIST: Did you see that it was a little hard for me to send her out first? So, I was glad you suggested that I do that, because I would have had her stay just out of my own comfort.

HALEY: There is also a reason for that. You know every couple has rules they follow. And this one follows the rule that she complains and he defends himself. And that was discussed. So, she expects to come in first and complain and then he can come in and defend himself.

THERAPIST: Right.

HALEY: If you are trying to break up that pattern. . . .

TRAINEE THREE: You have to do the opposite of what you are used to.

HALEY: You do whatever you can.

It is often difficult for therapists to judge what is the right thing to do. Haley usually recommends doing something they would not ordinarily do.

THERAPIST: So, for me, with my being kind of intuitive, and that's kind of my style, I should basically sometimes just go flip my intuition, right? That's what I mean. Not that I would always ignore my intuition, but if I had. . . . My sense was I would have kept the wife in the room [and seen her first]. So I was aware of the rule.

HALEY: Every couple has rules they follow. For them to change *their* rules, you've got to change *your* rules. It's an interesting problem. If you study the tape of that—the way they turned everything into that rule. I mean you ask him to criticize her, and he makes a brave try and she makes a brave try to restrain herself, but then she complains and then he defends himself.

THERAPIST: Yeah. I really tried to hold her back. It was hard. So, what is their problem?

HALEY: Well, that's it.

TRAINEE: The way they relate.

HALEY: Or at least that is something you want to change because it makes them miserable. If they were happy with that, it wouldn't matter.

THERAPIST: She says, "I want him to talk," and as soon as he does, she can't stand it. She just has to start her part.

HALEY: She has to complain.

THERAPIST: Yeah. And I feel like, wow, we are a long ways for them to even be able to hear each other at all. I mean of all the other couples I've seen, I would probably say they are the least able to hear each other. (This statement indicates the negative feeling the therapist felt in this first interview compared to the positive outcome.)

Haley brings up the triangle of the mother-in-law's involvement in the case and the fact that the couple is not married.

HALEY: Whenever a couple gets mad at each other, there usually is a third person playing them off.

THERAPIST: Oh, that's right.

HALEY: Particularly with a couple with ethnic mix, usually it's the mother-in-law.

THERAPIST: Well, then, the other thing was, "He doesn't want to marry me. I'm not good enough for him to marry me." You know, that whole thing is in there. So you would just bring it in to talk about it or you would invite the relatives in?

In order to push for a problem to come out, the supervisor uses the question, "What would you be worried about if this was our last session?" In the interview the woman said, "He would talk to me, he'd look at me, he'd trust me." He said that she would respect and trust him.

PLANNING THE SECOND INTERVIEW— A WEEK LATER

HALEY: What's your plan?

The group discusses the possible reactions to the paradox to abstain from sex given last week.

THERAPIST: Actually, I feel like they are just going to come in and tell me about the sex—whether they did or didn't, because I told them to abstain. That's what I had hypothesized would happen.

HALEY: You don't want to hear it, is that it?

THERAPIST: I just think that they are just not going to have been able to resist the fact I told them not to and they are just going to have sex.

TRAINEE: That's real progress if they have had some good sex. That's great.

THERAPIST: Yeah. I'm still kind of surprised about the reaction, even though I understand theoretically how it works, but still they just did exactly that. They just went against me like that. It was great.

HALEY: If you wanted to carry that on, you could start by saying, "One thing I'd rather not talk about this week is sex because that is a person's private life. So let's talk about something else."

THERAPIST: And then what? You think they would resist that?

HALEY: Well, they would try to talk to you about sex. It's the same principle.

Built into the therapy interview is the disengagement of the therapist and client. A good subject to bring up is "Therapy is for people who can't solve problems for themselves."

HALEY: What do you think you have to solve to be done with them?

THERAPIST: Well, that's what I was wondering about too, because I remembered that sex was one of the main issues. The only other issue that they really presented were the criticisms. They didn't call it that, but he called it shutting down. He would shut down and not talk, and she would say he won't talk to me. That was the only real thing that they really put out there that they don't like about their relationship, besides the sex. So I just have to figure a way to go with that. Or ask them to, again, if I spend the first period of time with the sex issue saying, "Let's not talk about that," but then they do. . . .

HALEY: What you don't want to do is reward them for cooperating with you about sex by just dismissing them.

THERAPIST: What do you mean "just dismissing them"?

HALEY: Well, if you say, "Don't you have any other problems?" like you are through with them after they have just done what you wanted them to do.

THERAPIST: So what would be a good response?

HALEY: You could go into it a little differently and say that therapy is for people who can't solve problems for themselves, and you solved this. You could probably solve other things yourselves. So you are talking about them doing better rather than you rejecting them. But I think it is helpful to have clear goals. One of the clear rules was she complains and he objects and then withdraws. The goal of therapy is to change the couple's rules. It cannot be done by simple directives.

THERAPIST: I saw that he could function differently when I had told him to complain and I expected him not to do very well at it. He was quite good at complaining to her. But that's not the way they normally interact.

The supervisor offers protection theory in order to reframe the therapist's negative view of the couple, whom he sees as wallowing in self-pity and selfishness.

HALEY: I don't think that is a good way to think about it. You should have a different theory.

THERAPIST: Okay. What?

HALEY: I don't know, but a better one than that. That's very negative, that they are both selfish.

THERAPIST: What do you mean when you say worse off?

HALEY: Well, I mean, who do you think may not make it home tonight or should I see them alone because they seem really troubled or something like that? I think that a better theory is something to do with protection. That when she begins to fall apart, he does something that makes her angry and complaining, and then she pulls out of it and she's human again for a while. I think she is unhappy in her life, generally, more than he is. And I think he helps her by misbehaving.

THERAPIST: Because it gives her something to focus on?

HALEY: That's not necessarily true. You need a theory to operate from, but it doesn't have to be a true one. These days there are no truths. So you just need a good operational theory. I think that if she developed a career or something, he would relate to her differently because he wouldn't have to hold her up.

THERAPIST: Because I think her following him to the club to hear him play music is. . . .

Protection theory is extended here so that both therapist and clients can view each other more positively by reclassifying motivation.

HALEY: *She can think of him as an artist deserving respect instead of only being irresponsible.* He responds to being called an artist.

THERAPIST: And you just found that artist works?

HALEY: Well he's an artist if he's a drummer. You can do the same thing with a kid. Now he's 12 years old and you can't expect the same things from a 12-year-old you would a 13-year-old or 11. So you have to treat the 12-year-old in a special way because he is different from other kids.

THERAPIST: I see what you are saying.

HALEY: I mean you just reclassify him.

The supervisor encouraged the therapist to try to empower the woman, who needs more satisfaction outside the home. He suggests asking the man to help the therapist help the woman.

HALEY: I would just say to him, "You seem to be doing very well. What about your fiancée? What could she do more to make herself happier?" Do it very straightforwardly. Because if you have a hypothesis that he is holding her up and it is distressing the way he does it to her, then you think of some other way she can get held up. You use yourself for one thing. She will think of you as a professional career woman. You've got to use that without putting her down but while stirring her up that women these days are doing all sorts of things that you would never expect. Most women are dissatisfied unless they have something that really occupies them outside the home. Just keep in mind she hears you saying that.

THERAPIST: Right. I understand.

HALEY: And that you don't want to put her down by saying I did and you are not. Are they here?

OBSERVING THE SECOND INTERVIEW

The therapist saw the couple together and also each alone. The supervisor suggested in the session that they imagine they had no addiction problems. The couple began to complain that they could not think of themselves other than as addicts.

Rose did not complain about Jose but talked about the difficulties of life. They began to discuss her fears of being overwhelmed and relapsing by becoming an addict again. Jose was asked to complain, and Rose to defend herself, as a way of changing the rules.

Computer Suggestion: Ask him to complain and her to defend herself.

DISCUSSING THE SECOND INTERVIEW

The group expresses amazement at the couple's changes. To the surprise of the group, Rose went thirty minutes without uttering a complaint against Jose. The discussion leads into the competing therapies of family therapy and the 12-step program. (See page 45 for a more complete discussion.)

HALEY: But she was just not complaining. Actually, it was when "Could they be curable?" came up that she began to complain.

THERAPIST: Well, he complained pretty darn harshly when I said, "Imagine that you don't have drugs or alcohol as a problem." And he said, "Well, that's who I am." Well, I understood what you were saying, but he really took a stand on that more than I have heard him take a stand on some other topics.

TRAINEE ONE: Usually with a dedicated 12-stepper you are really attacking their value system.

TRAINEE TWO: Right.

TRAINEE THREE: You really are.

HALEY: But the problem is that it's two competing therapies. There are different ideologies, there are different expectations, and there's a different approach. And it's like having a cotherapy with somebody that has a different ideology.

TRAINEE ONE: No. I think if you take what they bring and use it, I think you can work it.

THERAPIST: What I am struggling with is I don't know that 12-steps or whatever is the only way to get from A to B.

Ethnicity Issues

Two Hispanic trainees in the group were exasperated with the man's communication. He both offered to help Rose and at the same time made it seem like he was doing her a favor.

HALEY: Well, that's a question whether you should discuss Hispanic males to him.

THERAPIST: What's it like for him to be one?

HISPANIC TRAINEE ONE: With his Hispanic background to have to deal with her points of view being American. Because I guess she didn't grow up thinking the woman has to do this and that.

THERAPIST: She said she did grow up thinking that women have to take care of the home. That's why I got the feeling she's pushing harder to be that traditional role as the woman in the home than he was.

HISPANIC TRAINEE TWO: This man is saying, "I'll do the dishes." He was just saying, "I'm not going to take control of the house and tell myself to go do it, but if you tell me to do it, I'll do it."

HISPANIC TRAINEE ONE: I actually think he was saying, "I'll do you this favor every once in a while if I am in a good mood." I mean that's that mindset—is that you are not going do it but every once in a while I will do that favor.

HISPANIC TRAINEE TWO: That's what my dad does. Once a month he'll do the dishes, and we have to applaud him. . . .

TRAINEE: Exactly.

HISPANIC TRAINEE TWO: . . . then he tells everybody I help out around the house.

THERAPIST: I have a husband like that. No, he's not Hispanic, but he's got a cultural thing going there—traditional.

HALEY: But it is a question whether to bring that up as an explanation. She must have put some thought on this too—that she's involved with a Hispanic.

THERAPIST: So I wonder where I am going.

HALEY: Being Hispanic makes him a special person, and she can't take it as personally as she does. When he does certain things it's just a cultural thing.

THERAPIST: So we are trying to build more acceptance in each of them?

HALEY: Sure. To make her more tolerant of him because it isn't a response to her—it's in his nature.

THERAPIST: Right.

HALEY: If you decide to go that way.

THERAPIST: I didn't put it in words that they could relate to. I wasn't clear enough.

HALEY: You want them to expect more of each other by expecting less of each other.

TRAINEE: Yes.

THERAPIST: Expect more of themselves. Yes. But I couldn't get that across in a way that they got ahold of. I got a feeling they left really confused.

HALEY: That's okay. You know one thing they responded to very well was you being positive—about them improving.

TRAINEE: Oh, their body language showed that.

HALEY: She looked delighted, really. She took it like a personal compliment. And I think she is thinking therapy is a place where you go to improve, and I think he thinks it is place where you go because she says to go.

THERAPIST: Well, once he said, "I don't think you can ever please a woman, but if this will do it, okay."

TRAINEE: That's right, he did say that.

TRAINEE: "You can never please a woman." That was funny.

HALEY: Is that Hispanic?

HISPANIC TRAINEE ONE: Oh my gosh, no.

HISPANIC TRAINEE TWO: Isn't that male? (*The group laughs.*)

THERAPIST: Was there anything different that I could have said? You know, was I sitting okay?

The supervisor suggests bringing in relatives.

HALEY: Who has a mother?

THERAPIST: She does.

HALEY: And the mother lives where?

THERAPIST: I didn't ask. But she said, "We went walking." [This has been previously suggested for weight loss.]

HALEY: It's a question whether to bring her in.

THERAPIST: Oh, into the session?

HALEY: If it's not going the way you would like it to, you could bring somebody else in. But I think it is going well. You could do without it. But if you want to get further into a complicated cultural marriage, then the mother might help. I don't know whether he could tolerate having both women in there jumping on him—and a female therapist at that.

TRAINEE: He would be out of it and looking down.

HALEY: Well, let's not bring in others next time. But I think they are improving. I was impressed with her lack of complaining. It was extraordinary.

TRAINEE: It's a big change.

HALEY: I think it was good to bring them together complaining, in the sense that it came around to what is a very important issue, that is whether they are curable or not. Or whether they could ever be comfortable about being overwhelmed. I mean that was a good way to put it—that if she gets overwhelmed she would turn to drinking. Because then she talks about all the ways she gets overwhelmed. But there is something that he doesn't expect of her because she might blow it [take drugs or drink]. And I think it's the same with her. Once they are defined that way, they're not going to expect as much.

PLANNING THE THIRD INTERVIEW— DISENGAGEMENT

HALEY: I would start with them in some way to find out if this is their last session. And one way to do it is, is the classical, "What if this was our last session, what would you be worried about?" And if they get upset and say, "My last session?" then you say, "I didn't say it was your last session. I just said what if it was." But people go right to a problem, usually, if you do that.

THERAPIST: Yes we saw that happen.

HALEY: It's a classic. But if not that way, then you try to think of some other way to give them a chance to be normal. You could say, "Well, let's have a session on how normal you are."

THERAPIST: We did that. Remember they couldn't get into that normal concept very well. They identify themselves as recovered drug addicts.

HALEY: Oh, that's the problem.

TRAINEE: They are proud of that being their identity, because they have overcome that. So, the whole normal thing was there.

Differences in Theory between Family Therapy and 12-Step

HALEY: I don't know whether your clients will have this difficulty. I'm not an enthusiast for an approach that says somebody is incurable and that they are going to be diseased the rest of their life. I don't think that is a good thing to impose on people, but it's the common way to treat addicts—the 12-step program and all. I would rather not work that way because I think they are helped without being indicted. I mean, if a father in a family says, "I'm an alcoholic," and you ask him when he had a drink last, and he says, "Fourteen years ago," it means his family has been with him as a damaged person for 14 years—which I think is a thing you shouldn't impose on people unless you have to. There are some alcoholics obviously that live with it day to day, and you hold them up and that's it. But most of them can have a good outcome if you do something about their social situation—their families, their friends, and so forth.

Now, with the issue that came up here—even if they could be perfectly normal, they are always going to be considered abnormal. And that's a problem because when [the 12-step] is successful, that's fine, but it often is not successful and you just have an unhappy person who feels they're hopeless and they can stay off booze but they are hopeless to ever do anything about it.

Anyhow, that's a therapy of it's own that has a separate set of ideas and principles and steps. When you mix it with family therapy, you have a problem—you drink because you are involved with somebody in family therapy theory. The drinking is a product of the social situation— not just the individual's weaknesses. And that's a very different way of looking at it. It's an awkward thing to collaborate. But you can do it. If somebody has stopped drinking and had difficulties stopping and is pleased to have stopped, the fact they call themselves diseased—I would let go. I mean, why not? Your goal is to keep them from drinking, really, and ruining their lives. They keep talking about the difficult life of the addict. But the fact is they've got wives and they've got children and they've got in-laws and all the social situations of addicts. Family therapy has been pretty successful to date. I like to turn people loose when they are normal—as far as the problem they came in with. And this is the problem with them, because they can't think of themselves as normal, apparently.

THERAPIST: Right.

HALEY: So I am sure that one of you people has a solution for this. What do you recommend? What would you say to them if this was their last session?

THERAPIST: What they are doing is, both are in need so that one can take care of the other one. She's very verbal about . . . that her needs ought to be met. I'm not sure if that's just to keep him with somebody that needs him. And she still seems to be complaining, although less, about him.

HALEY: What if they do say they need help and they want more therapy and they are not getting along? What's the next possible step?

THERAPIST: And there is a daughter in the picture that we have never even discussed.

THERAPIST: And there was the marriage issue. She mentioned that, too. You know, that they're not married and that her mom wants her to get married. It was real similar to that first case. So, there's a lot of stuff still out there.

HALEY: I would just say, if they are still having problems, that you would like to see some more of the family. If one of their mothers comes in and advises you on how to help them.

TRAINEE: Tell them that.

HALEY: Yeah.

THERAPIST: Oh, cool. OK. Well I'm going to go see. They are probably here. They are usually pretty prompt.

OBSERVING THE THIRD INTERVIEW— DISENGAGEMENT

Computer Suggestion: Have them talk about the commitment to each other.

HALEY (*behind the mirror*): Whatever they say is the problem, you should deal with it.

THERAPIST (*to clients*): So your relationship . . . You guys are still talking about the relationship on whether it will continue?

Computer Suggestion: Say to them you will have to convince me you need therapy.

The therapist was surprised that the couple reported that things were going so well. After the discussion she suggested they come back in 6 months, which was agreeable to them.

DISCUSSING THE THIRD INTERVIEW— DISENGAGEMENT

The group discusses how to make a judgment on ending therapy. The supervisor relies on the impulses of the therapist. In this case she told the clients to return in 6 months while letting them know they could call at any time if necessary.

TRAINEE: (*The therapist comes back to the group behind the mirror smiling after the couple left.*) Very good.

HALEY: Let's talk about it.

TRAINEE: That was exciting to see how much they were changed.

HALEY: It was extraordinary, really.

THERAPIST: I'm amazed. I mean they still did some of their same stuff. But I mean she's backed off, and he's stepped back. How did that happen? It was so different. I mean, you should have seen them before. She was crying all the time. I mean, it was just completely different. I mean, they were smiling and everything. None of that—he was mad and she was crying and . . . I'm trippin', I am. I'm just amazed that they were so happy. That was great. Thank you. And that (*pointing to the computer*) works great.

HALEY: You liked it?

THERAPIST: I do. I wouldn't have thought that I did, but it was so easy. And then I could just insert it [the computer monitor suggestion] like right in the moment where it's easy.

HALEY: Yeah. There was one suggestion that was just in the flow of what you were saying.

THERAPIST: Yeah. It worked really good.

HALEY: What gave you such confidence in 6 months? How were they behaving that you liked?

THERAPIST: I don't know. Did I think of that on my own?

HALEY: You said 6 months. I was thinking 3 weeks.

TRAINEE: Because we were all surprised.

THERAPIST: I don't know where I got 6 months from.

HALEY: Well, I would trust it.

TRAINEE: Maybe you were thinking in relation to how long you would be here in the program.

THERAPIST: Yeah. Well, I guess I was thinking that their faces would contort if that . . . I didn't want to make it too short. So I'd rather make it long and make them go "Oh" or something.

HALEY: Six months is really a cure.

THERAPIST: That is a really long time. It was obvious. You know what I mean? It wasn't like I had to force them.

HALEY: Well, it was not obvious here, but it's an example of how the mirrors screen things out. You get a different picture back here than in there.

TRAINEE: And that's why Jay said you should decide, because he said you're getting a different emotional reaction from us behind the mirror.

THERAPIST: Well, I threw it out there, and she was, like, "We'll call if we need you."

HALEY: It's the correct thing to do. He was a little hesitant. He was willing to come in 6 months. I think he likes you.

THERAPIST: I liked them. I thought they were nice people.

HALEY: And she gets along with you very well, too. I mean the transformation has been considerable. But anyhow, you can always give them a call in a week or month or 6 weeks or whenever you feel like it.

THERAPIST: Really? I don't usually do that.

HALEY: You should. Make sure things are okay. Sometimes they are okay and you have them in for one session or two and send them out again. You should always do a follow-up to keep a record of your successes.

THERAPIST: I just don't want to feel like I was putting myself in their lives.

HALEY: If you see them in 3 months, they will be having trouble remembering you. Or if you see them in 6 months, certainly.

THERAPIST: Oh, I don't know. I mean, do you feel like I kicked them out too soon?

HALEY: No, no. I think you should always follow your impulses, and I think you were correct. I would have done it because of some other theory, that you should do it from 2 or 3 weeks then a month and then

3 months. But when they change, you take advantage of that. It must make them feel more successful that you said 6 months instead of 3 weeks.

Therapists Should Be Generalists

HALEY: One of the things about therapies these days has changed. It used to be you should specialize, like, in child therapy and never see an adult. But nowadays, because of the economic situation (that's one reason) you really have to be able to handle any kind of a problem. And you should be able to handle kids' problems and the parents' problems and marital difficulties, and you should be able to do some sex therapy. It doesn't mean you have to be an expert on it, but you should read up on it to be able to participate with them in doing something that will start something a little different. That is, you shouldn't just assume you refer. We used to refer everything. Everybody was a specialist, and you referred everybody to that specialist. But now you have to be a generalist.

THERAPIST: They did want me to tell you all thank you.

HALEY: Well, good.

DISCUSSING THE OUTCOME

HALEY: Take each case and say what is the outcome. Have I succeeded with this case or failed with this case? Or, on the scale of zero to ten, are they at zero and need improvement or are they at ten? And it's fair, if you brought a case in, through the course of the case to either succeed or fail or halfway fail. But if you see them just once and you don't see them again, it has to be a great interview. But I just thought you might be interested in looking at your own work and seeing how complicated it is to do a simple study—with whether somebody got over a problem or didn't get over a problem. I think what's happening in therapy, as you all know, is there is much more focus on problems and solving them in brief therapy. The research was complicated on the outcome when it was deep therapy that went on for months or years. They didn't formulate a problem, so how could they study it and decide that there had been improvement? And now you are forced to focus on the problem. You have to formulate it, you have to make an intervention, and you have to see if you've got a change. The outcome research is changing now.

THERAPIST: Changing to what?

HALEY: It's changing to a briefer...a better possibility of doing an outcome study because you formulate a clear problem, hopefully. You see them for a short period of time, so it isn't a long period so that you have forgotten what they came for.

THERAPIST: I think because it was the only case that I have had that was that brief, sometimes I still feel weird about it.

TRAINEE: They looked so happy.

TRAINEE: I know.

TRAINEE: And they chose 6 months to follow up.

TRAINEE TWO: If she was hurting, she would have called you. She would have been on the phone.

TRAINEE: She said, "If we need something, we will call."

THERAPIST: I don't know.

HALEY: It's up to you.

THERAPIST: Oh, man. I'm trying to think about the outcome. They were having sex again, they were talking positively, she was smiling not crying.

HALEY: That's a big step.

THERAPIST: I know. They were joking with each other and I...guess I would give them a....

THERAPIST: So I've got to give him like an eight or a nine. Okay, nine....Eight and a half.

TRAINEE: All right, we are up to nine.

HALEY: When's the next one?

Summary of the Case

What has been presented here is the planning and carrying out of therapy by a supervisor and a training group. It shows a supervisor at work and the trainees expanding their ideas and skills, hopefully. The goal is to change therapists as well as to change clients since the therapists must learn how to change people in distress.

This training case has illustrated different intervention techniques within a social context. The couple came in with a history of being addicts. They were now recovered but were influenced by that addict history. One effect of the scars of addiction included a fear that if they got upset they could relapse and be addicted again. Therefore they did not provoke each other to an extreme. Within that framework the therapy took place.

The couple was seen together as well as individually. The therapist planned to see them briefly and began to disengage from the first interview.

She completed the sessions in three interviews. This plan was based on the extensive therapy they had experienced, which contributed to their idea that they were defective in some way because of their therapy history. They could not think of themselves as a normal couple.

The therapy focused on the rules of the relationship that the couple followed, rules that left them exasperated with each other. The focus of the therapy was on changing those rules. The simple rule they followed was that she complained and he defended himself. She protested that he neglected her, and he defended himself by pointing out how hard he worked. She complained he was irresponsible. He said she was too responsible. She said he was avoiding her and neglecting her. He said he was too tired. The basic motivation of the couple was assumed to be protective. For example, the wife would become depressed and the husband would act up, and she would feel that he was at fault and so she would feel better. The interventions were simple and included both direct and indirect directives. The wife responded with jealously when the husband was seen alone with the therapist. A directive was used that was direct. The husband was asked to criticize the wife, and she was to defend herself. In a paradoxical variation on this intervention the wife was asked to criticize the husband and he was to defend himself. This was the rule that they came in to get rid of, and it was paradoxical to ask them to do what they wished to stop doing. Another simple directive was built on their avoidance of sex. The therapist told them that sex was forbidden this week. Thus they were asked to avoid what they were avoiding. They responded appropriately.

The rules in this case were simple ones, and the interventions were simple. Improvement was measured in the last session. The therapist was pleased with the outcome when the couple reported their changes. They were having sex. They were talking more positively. Rose was smiling, not crying. She recessed them for a period of time. The changes apparently continue.

At a 6-month follow-up the couple had not returned.

REFERENCES

Haley, J. (1996). *Learning and teaching therapy.* New York: Guilford Press.
Haley, J., & Richeport-Haley, M. (1998). *Unbalancing a couple* [35-minute video]. La Jolla, CA: Triangle Press.

4

Family Therapy at a Distance

A Case of Depression

*D*epression is a misery to experience and difficult for a therapist to cure. Each case is unique when one takes into account the social situations and the possible biological causes. There are many medications to choose among and debate. Therapists can have different theories for the talk therapies they do. Families can be in the session, or it can be only an individual client depending on the theory.

In many cases a family is not available to be in the therapy, but that does not preclude doing family therapy. The situation arises with migrant families when the family remains in a foreign country, with individuals who refuse to bring in other family members, or with a family member who is in jail or detained elsewhere. The issue is not geography. It is communication. An innovative therapist will think of ways to incorporate the family even when members are not present. The client can write a letter or send an e-mail or telephone a family member from the session. You can get the client to complain about family members to make them angry enough to come in to the session to correct the client. You can insist on the family's calling a meeting to deal with the crisis on their own. When families refuse to come together, you can focus on the individual and assume this will affect the family organization.

In this case a young depressed man, Abdul, is brought in as a consultation since the therapist trainee was treating him elsewhere and wanted special help with him. His family was living in the Middle East. A group of 10 students were gathered for the training. The therapist described his case.

THERAPIST: He's been like that for about 12 years, since he came over here to America. Basically, he left his family to come here when he was about 18 to pursue medical school. And he was doing pretty well. He got good grades for a while, but then he started to get depressed and that started to knock his grades down. He lost his motivation. He started seeing a psychologist. He's been in and out of therapy for a long time.

HALEY: Why don't you say what are the problems you are trying to solve with him.

THERAPIST: He wants to be able to alleviate his depression.

HALEY: The presenting problem is being depressed.

THERAPIST: He doesn't have many friends. He spends most of his time at home. He doesn't leave the house. He plays computer games—three card games all day and he has sexual fantasies.

HALEY: If he failed, who would react?

This was to determine who was most involved with his success.

THERAPIST: You know we talked about that. He seems to say he just doesn't want to be a failure in his family's eyes, so I guess his father, not his mother, would react to that. Yeah.

   His father is a physician. Women are more oppressed there. They wear veils, and he just wanted to come to America and be able to date and pursue medical school.

HALEY: You're doing very well. I would assume this guy is failing in relation to the family. You have no access to the family. Therefore, you have to do something that's by mail or by telephone to make connection with the family in such a way that there's a change. What have you tried to do with him?

It is important to find out what was previously tried so one doesn't repeat it.

THERAPIST: Well, one thing was, he spends so much time indoors. He won't leave the house really at all. Two weeks ago we recommended that he go outside for a while. Just go outside no matter what it takes. Go outside for 20 minutes. Just go for a walk and be right back. And he puts up a lot of resistance because he seems to have tried everything.

HALEY: It sounds like previous therapy has been at work.

THERAPIST: Oh, the man is a basketful of "ism's" and all sorts of lingo. I mean, he's definitely been in therapy, but nothing has really helped him.

He was just under the impression that you come to America and there's women everywhere. You know, the land of milk and honey. And there are. It's true. But like he said, he was shot down a lot. He'd ask women out, and they'd say, no thanks, or they'd say OK and they wouldn't last past a first date.

HALEY: I think that you could observe that he knows what you are going to say and he knows how to undo it. If he's had a lot of therapy, he's got more insight than he knows what to do with about why he does what he does and how it's related to childhood and all this. But it has nothing to do with getting over the problem.

THERAPIST: He did follow through on the intervention in terms of going outside the house.

HALEY: For how long?

THERAPIST: He did it every day last week, actually.

HALEY: Oh, well that's very good. Doing the usual things, but he's been through that. So you've got to do something unusual.

THERAPIST: So you are talking about a little paradox in there. Just saying, you know what, that might be the case. You are going to go the next 40 years of your life stuck in the house playing those games.

Give the Client a Task That Activates His Relationship with His Family

HALEY: If you could, challenge him in such a way that he does something helpful for himself to prove you wrong rather than because you ask him to. If you said, I think you should write your father and say that you are getting quite interested in women here. And what will he answer if you do that? And I don't know what he will answer, but he'll say either he will be pleased, or he'll put you down and say it's not true. And you say that isn't what he's going to do at all. You are going to be very surprised at his response. So why don't you write him a letter and I will help you write the letter. You don't have to lie and say I have a date, but you have to say, I am becoming more of a person who admires beautiful women in this place.

THERAPIST: I don't know how that will go off in the Middle East.

HALEY: Well, I don't know either, but he would do it if you persuade him that his father will love that. His father will say that's wonderful. I'm so glad you are enjoying yourself with this woman. He will say that isn't what my father will say.

THERAPIST: Right.

HALEY: You say it is.

THERAPIST: You just want me to insist on that?

HALEY: That's right. I know your father better than you do.

TRAINEE: So he'll write the letter to convince you that you are wrong.

HALEY: That's right. You want him to do it. Then this father is going to get the letter saying I'm enjoying myself with a woman. The father's got to respond to that. Now he's either going to come against it or with it or say to his wife, our son is going bad. It will make some action. If his father is a physician and he keeps failing as a medical student, you could have him write a letter saying that I decided to be more successful as a physician than you are. I think I have learned more in the last few years and I can go to medical school and succeed.

THERAPIST: Right now he would fight me tooth and nail on it, saying that he feels like a total failure and he doesn't really have plans to go on at this point. He feels he's too old to begin again.

This is characteristic of depression.

HALEY: But what do you think he should be doing?

THERAPIST: I think he should be pursuing what he wants to do.

HALEY: I know, but what do you want him to do? Do you think he should go back to medical school?

Abdul is too depressed to have a clear goal, so the therapist has to help him with it.

THERAPIST: I mean if that is truly his goal.

HALEY: Well, he put some time in there. It's the only thing he's put some time into. He has a rule that he has to fail, and your problem is how to change that rule in such a way that he doesn't fail and that you don't fail with him.

But I think that he's not going to change until he behaves differently.

THERAPIST: Right. But he can't get himself to behave differently at this point.

HALEY: And talking to him about why he doesn't behave differently only makes more talk about why he doesn't behave differently. You've got to get him to do something, and he's not an easy one. I mean, to get that guy to do something you ask is a problem.

THERAPIST: But he did. . . . He did go out the door.

HALEY: Well, you've got to start him doing something. One of the ways to think about depression is that they sometimes come out of it when they get angry.

THERAPIST: If they're motivated enough, you mean.

HALEY: If you can get a depressed person angry to prove you wrong or something like that, you got a fair chance. You got him started at doing something, and this guy could use some anger. I think he's probably mad at the world at the moment. Think about how you should be, as far as you are concerned. He should be in medical school; he should be having dates with girls he likes. And what else? He should have a job to support himself.

THERAPIST: These are all the things that he wants.

HALEY: Yeah. And those are your tasks or your goals to get him to do those things.

THERAPIST: Well, his number one goal is to alleviate the sadness.

HALEY: We used to hypothesize there are unconscious desires for failing or something like that. Now it's because there are consequences in an organization if you fail or if you succeed. And what consequences there would be we don't know because we can't see his family, but it must be his family. It must be his father if he's gone to medical school and his father is a doctor. I mean the connections are obvious. The way you describe the guy I would think of saying to him, I have a plan that will solve a lot of your depression because you try things and they fail.

THERAPIST: Well, he allows them to fail. There's something in him that sabotages him as he sees it.

HALEY: Well, you say that there's something that sabotages you, and becoming a doctor is an example, that you just didn't make it as a doctor. Why don't you become a nurse? Take nurse's training. You got your ambulance experience. You got the doctor's experience so far. Be a nurse. You can make a very good nurse. I mean this guy's not going to be a nurse.

He is from an upper-class family and too proud to take a lower-status job, particularly in the health field.

But if you insist he ought to be a nurse, you'll make him mad.

THERAPIST: (*Laughing*) That's funny. It's funny because I'm trying to picture him getting mad at me. I mean it would be great if he did. That's for sure.

HALEY: I would think about doing something that he does to spite you. I know that you don't think of that as the way therapists behave, but in therapy what you do is you make a relationship by conversations flowing. And you set up the relationship in which you can give a directive and then he'll do it. And that's the purpose of the conversation, really to set up that relationship so that you can introduce an action that will make a change. And that they'll do it. In this case this guy's a professional at not doing it. You can tell from the way he resists. So you got to do it in some funny way, a paradoxical way.

THERAPIST: Will that alleviate his depression?

HALEY: There's a chance of it if you make him get mad.

THERAPIST: I mean, that will somewhat alleviate it for good?

HALEY: Well, you don't know. You do the next thing. I mean if you get a day that he's not depressed because he's arguing in his head about you, then that's one day, and maybe you can get 2 days. But I think you need to connect him to his family so that he describes himself in such a way that they hear that he's succeeding or that he tells him, I've decided that I'm going to graduate school. Leave it open on the doctors. I'm going back to graduate school.

THERAPIST: Just leave it open?

HALEY: Leave it open, or say, I think they wouldn't believe him if he said he was going to go back to medical school. You've got to put some thought on how to get him to do something positive. And when you put the thought on that, you keep coming back to yourself; that he does it in relation to you to prove you're wrong, or to prove you're right, or because he's your friend. I mean there're two kinds of directives. There're those where you tell him what to do and that's it, and those where you get paradoxical in some way and restrain them from changing. And it sounds like you did the straightforward one last week to get him out of the house for that long. It's a triumph with this guy, and I think you should pursue that track.

THERAPIST: Well, my idea behind it was that if there is indeed this subconscious evil villain that's trying to hold him back. . . .

HALEY: Something happens with them [parents] when he succeeds. It's taken for granted in family therapy that's the situation. It's just complicated here because he lives far from them and he's living alone and unhappy. But that's why it's important to connect him with the family and make some hypothesis like failing in relation to them. Because the individual approach of him being here and having unconscious ideas just hasn't worked, and only discussing his family won't work.

HALEY: There's got to be a letter to them or a phone call to them. Assume that his failing life must have something to do with those parents and then set up a letter to them saying, I'm succeeding, and see what response he gets. He'll have upset parents. It's the hypothesis.

THERAPIST: I don't think so?

TRAINEE: I'm wondering when we make a distinction between environmental and start making referrals because there is a concern for organic origin. He's on antidepressants?

THERAPIST: He's already gone to county mental health. But like my supervisor said, you know, the doses are really low. In fact, they are below the standard. There's no real enjoyment, and he considers this depression very painful.

HALEY: And with the only son, they are going to be divided over how to raise him, how to deal with him, what is to be expected of him. I can see why he got out of there. But he didn't get out of there. He's still psychologically with them.

THERAPIST: He talks to them on the phone a couple of times a month.

HALEY: I don't know what the letter might be. Well, it should be something that you predicted happens in a certain way because you know about families, and he says, not in my family that won't happen, and done in such a way that he's got to write the letter in order to prove you are wrong.

THERAPIST: I know what you are getting at. I just wish you would give me the direct answer.

HALEY: But I don't know the letter. I mean, that's something you have to devise.

THERAPIST: I need a little more information about the family.

HALEY: Should he write the father or the mother? It should be a letter that says that he's doing well, that he's succeeding, or that he's found an interesting woman.

THERAPIST: Even if it's not true?

HALEY: Well, look among these women and say, were any of them interesting? I'm trying to get him to say something positive about a woman, so it won't be lying when he writes and says that there's something positive about this woman I met. He probably wouldn't write. He would telephone. I am sure he would say, Father is disappointed, and therefore he could write the father and say, I'm sorry I disappointed you.

THERAPIST: Do you have to wait until the father gives a response or say in that first letter, say I know you are disappointed in me but I forgive you.

HALEY: That's complicated enough so the father can't answer it easily.

THERAPIST: Yeah. That will throw him off a little bit.

HALEY: Anyhow, I think you should think about how to communicate between him and his parents on something that frees him some from this failure business on the hypothesis that that's related to them and he's helpful to them by failing. I mean this is one of the discoveries of family therapy, too. Kids help their parents by having symptoms themselves.

But you have to set it up so he makes a change at long distance, which is hard. Whatever ideas he's putting into this letter is a change, because he's going to say something in relation to his father that is different than he usually does. But the best choice would be to have him send a letter.

THERAPIST: And so the letter should be somewhat confronting.

HALEY: It should be that he's successful or going to be successful or finally decided that he's had enough and he's now thinking seriously about going back to school. Just anything that his father would say, My God, he's changing. And the mother would say it's not your fault.

THERAPIST: I definitely will follow through on something like that.

ONE WEEK LATER

Caught in the Middle of Two Supervisors Who Disagree

When supervisors are in conflict over what to do with a client, it is the same as a clinical situation in which parents are in conflict over a child or other triangles that form in a family. The therapist is in trouble and often has difficulty deciding what to do. In this case one supervisor had a more psychodynamic orientation while the other had a strategic orientation. They tried to combine the supervisors' two orientations

HALEY: OK. You were going to present what you did.

THERAPIST: Let me tell you what I did in the case of the depressed man. I wasn't able to implement what we had talked about, the letter, because we didn't talk much about the family. My other supervisor wanted me to hone in on his emotions. He's dissociated. This is what I prescribed because I wanted to do something that was somewhat in the strategic realm. Now there's a situation where he was talking to one friend of his, this girl, and when he calls her it doesn't cost anything, but when she calls him it turns out it's a toll call. And he told her to call him and she called and this phone bill ended up being two hundred dollars. He told her that he would pay the whole two hundred dollars. But I told him, I said, "But under no circumstances are you to pay two hundred dollars on that bill, all right." And the other thing is I told him, "I want you to really focus on your emotions when you're weighing the two and what emotions come up when you think about paying absolutely nothing and telling her that, or giving her three hundred dollars." Because my other supervisor wanted me to really help him focus on his emotions.

HALEY: I am not an enthusiast for bringing out peoples emotions on the assumption that it is related to change in some way. It's different if you provoke him to get mad at you. Then you're working out a relationship with him. But I don't see the positive nature of him paying an extra hundred bucks unless it's a woman who's very tight with money, or there's some special issue around him and her and the money. What has she said about the phone call?

THERAPIST: She tells him, "I can't afford it, and you are the one who told me to call you." But he didn't know that there was a toll call, so she should at least accept some responsibility, but she's not willing to.

HALEY: This is one of the differences when you get focused on emotions. Often you get into the emotional situation that doesn't involve an organizational problem. And the idea of writing the father is an organizational problem. Whether he fails or succeeds, if it's in relation to his parents, it's important that he relate to them in such a way that he can succeed, if you give a task in an organizational arrangement. With this one giving an extra hundred bucks I don't see how it affects him organizationally unless he's trying to break up with this girl or get together with this girl in this way.

THERAPIST: He was trying to get together with her, but now he can see they are not close. They don't know each for that long, maybe a month or two.

TRAINEE ONE: Well, it doesn't matter. If you want to have a relationship with me, and you ask me to call you, I'm not going to pay for it, you have to pay for me.

HALEY: What will it do to your relationship when you cost him an extra hundred dollars?

THERAPIST: A hundred dollars isn't an astronomical amount.

HALEY: But I mean in relation to you?

THERAPIST: I know he'll probably look at me as a different type of therapist who's willing to confront him or challenge him.

HALEY: You'll be less predictable, you mean. Do you have a prediction, which he'll use?

THERAPIST: Well, maybe that it's—the three hundred.

HALEY: Will we know next week?

The group bets on which amount the client will pay.

HALEY: But ask him what his father would have done in this situation if you want to get into the family a little more.

THERAPIST: That's good. This last time, when I really started asking him questions about emotions and things like that, he definitely sparked up and was intrigued if nothing else.

TWO WEEKS LATER

HALEY: Do you want to tell about the latest report.

THERAPIST: I guess in a nutshell he still hasn't committed what he's going to do.

The trainees discussed the different possibilities.

Parallels Between Supervisor, Therapist, and Clients

HALEY: Well, I could use you as an example. There's some argument that trainees behave the way that the supervisor has them deal with the clients. If you find a trainee that has very great difficulty getting a directive over, to get it delivered, then usually the client has a great problem of doing what the therapist says. I think it's interesting what a struggle you had over writing that father a letter.

THERAPIST: Well, it was because I didn't really know what to focus on. I really wasn't sure if the things that we talked about were an issue.

HALEY: And so, it's the same with him. He doesn't know what's really an issue, particularly, with his family I think. But anyhow, you're going to have him write a letter. Right?

THERAPIST: Oh, yeah. It will be somewhere along the lines of how much a success he is here and how happy he is or something to that effect. And now I have this issue about his parents pushing him to come here to live. He also acknowledged in this session, though, he knows that he is lazy.

This is the first statement that his parents may come and live with him if he is not depressed.

HALEY: I'm sure he knows it.

THERAPIST: But he said, "Look, let's face it, I know that I'm lazy. You know it's pretty clear that I'm somewhat lazy, but I also have this depression and I'm not sure where the two meet."

HALEY: He's trying to analyze it.

THERAPIST: Oh. You don't understand. This guy analyzes a bug on a flower. I mean everything is analyzed to the deepest level.

HALEY: That's the past therapist's responsibility, really. If he writes a letter, the answer back will give you a lot of information about that family. One new thing is what you need with this guy, because he's so ready not to have anything new. . . .

THERAPIST: Then we go around in circles forever.

HALEY: That depends on you.

THERAPIST: Yeah. I mean I'm working with my supervisor there and with you here, and he just keeps trying to figure out why he feels this way.

HALEY: So you're caught between two different ideologies really.

THERAPIST: Oh, in some sense.

HALEY: Well, most trainees are.

THERAPIST: But you can help them.

HALEY: You can negotiate them as long as they are not completely incompatible. But if you felt you were really failing with this guy and he's not changing, we can get the other supervisor to come in with you and the three of us will talk if you want to do that. But that's only if it's not going well. At the moment, it's uncertain.

When you have a problem with conflicting supervisors it is best to bring them together to resolve conflicting issues.

THERAPIST: If he follows through with the schooling, I will see that as a positive move forward, because the guy is not getting out of his house.

HALEY: Sure, that would be. If he became a successful older son in the eyes of the family, I think that would change a lot of things.

PLANNING THE FIRST LIVE SUPERVISION

HALEY: One other thing that I thought we ought to deal with tonight is the letter. He's a guy who doesn't improve, apparently, in therapy very much. He has had a lot of therapy. He is avoiding living normally and doing a career like he ought to do. So that he needs something that gets him started differently. And I think one of the things he's doing is assuming that he can go to therapy forever. If not this therapist, another therapist, because he's been doing that with a number of therapists. That logically leads to one possible directive, and that is to tell him you want him to agree that you're his last therapist, that he'll never go to see another therapist again.

TRAINEE: Wow! That's possible?

THERAPIST: Even if that means he has to see me for 3 years.

HALEY: Whenever. The rest of his life. The rest of his life, he can't have another therapist. If 2 years from now he gets depressed, he's got to call you.

THERAPIST: Even if I live in Antarctica?

HALEY: That's right. He can deal with you on the phone. But you do get people who hang out in therapy forever. And they learn the language and they learn the ideas like he apparently has. Do you think you can say you want to be his last therapist?

THERAPIST: Oh, sure. I'll say that to him. I'll bring that up.

The group is looking forward to seeing this client for the first time.

HALEY: We hope he's coming in tonight. You start by saying I have something that's going to be very important that I want you to do and it's going to mean a basic change in your whole attitude about yourself. And I want you to agree you'll never go to another therapist after me. That you'll finish with therapy with me. I mean you want to put it as positive as that. The temptation is to make it tentative. What do you think of the idea?

THERAPIST: Right. You don't want to give him an out. You want me to pursue the letter as well?

HALEY: Sure. Is he going to bring it?

THERAPIST: No. We haven't mentioned it. I was going to bring it up tonight.

HALEY: You haven't. . . . (*amazed*) You didn't talk to him about the letter before?

THERAPIST: No. No. Actually, I did mention the letter last time. I'll tell you the truth. I did mention the letter, we didn't pursue it for too long. So I want to go back to it.

HALEY: That's something you would have to set up with some care if you want him to do it.

THERAPIST: And the running theme would be that he would say something positive.

HALEY: And lead him. I wouldn't make it too long, you know. He should say, "I'm going to be successful." It should be, "I've decided it's important that I be successful" or more tentatively like that. You need to collaborate with him about the letter on what his father would think when he sees it, and how would his father understand it. I mean, you treat it like the father is there or he's just a letter instead. I'm sure an older son with a father who is a physician is a big family issue. (*The son became depressed in medical school.*) Then it's a question of how to manage it so he can succeed no matter what his father does. You should get some kind of action involved, because he knows already that if he succeeds, he's going to have to bring his parents over.

THERAPIST: Well, what can I do?

HALEY: Well, you can just say "Where would you have your parents live if you were successful?" You put it like, well, they might expect something of you. They might expect you to support them and have a place to live. Is there a place in this city where you would like to place them.

What Abdul is worried about is that he can't say no to his parents.

THERAPIST: We talked about that, and he had indicated that they would be living with him. He is going to be calling me for the next 10 years of my life.

HALEY: They have to answer this question. Do you want them to answer in a letter or on the phone? I think they will be back on the phone when they get the letter. So you have to anticipate what you are going to say on the phone.

He's going to say they'll be pleased that I'm doing well. You need to say they won't be pleased. They are going to be upset and negative about it. And he's going to say I know my parents better than you do, or words to that effect. But he's got to prove it to you that you are wrong, and then if he writes it and they get it, they are going to call and he has to find that negative something in the call.

THERAPIST: But then what does he do with that?

HALEY: Then you're right. Then you are in the position of saying maybe he can succeed just a little bit and they wouldn't be so negative about him. Then you say, you begin to work on improving on being normal. You could have him succeed secretly. He signs up and he doesn't tell his parents that he signed up for medical school or whatever. Because why does he have to tell them everything? You are doing anything to get that guy to begin to succeed.

THERAPIST: Yeah. He's really down about the medical school because he wants to do it and go but he doesn't have the money to apply. So he's using that as an obstacle now.

HALEY: But if he settles for less, like being a nurse. . . .

THERAPIST: I haven't brought that up yet.

HALEY: His father is the physician.

OBSERVING THE LIVE INTERVIEW

The client comes into the session looking sad and pensive, looking toward the floor as he analyzes all his reactions. The trainees watch from behind the mirror as Haley transmits directives to the therapist on a computer monitor that the therapist can see and the client cannot. The therapist, contrary to Haley's advice, spent the beginning of the session on the phone call.

Computer Suggestion: Have him draft the letter.

THERAPIST: Getting back to the letter. I want us to come up with a rough draft.

Computer Suggestion: Would your parents be pleased if you succeed?

THERAPIST: You are going to say something to the effect of "I'm confident now about the future. I'm doing things now to put my life in a better position where I want to be in, and I'm very hopeful that in the future I'm going to be very successful." What do you think he's going to think when he reads that? What's his response to that?

The therapist used a directive style in the latter part of the session after Haley repeatedly asked "What happened to the letter?" The session focused on the client writing the letter and not really wanting to.

DISCUSSING THE LIVE INTERVIEW

HALEY: You got the letter drafted.

THERAPIST: We started to fight tooth and nail on it. I needed more information.

HALEY: You need practice phrasing things as possibilities that make them sound like they're an actuality. And he's a nice candidate for it. Did you think he was more cheerful at the end of the interview?

THERAPIST: Yeah. His affect picked up.

HALEY: He can say, "It might not be true, but I'm feeling so much better I may succeed."

THERAPIST: See, I didn't think he would allow that in the letter. I thought that he was going to be very emphatic and, like I said, self-assured.

HALEY: Well, you know what he did wrong to start with in his letter. He took away all credit from himself. He said, "I'll improve with therapy and medication and I'll be happy."

HALEY: But I think you ought to write another letter with him about him being with a woman.

THERAPIST: To his parents?

HALEY: To his parents, saying, "I have met a woman I'm fond of." You can say that.

THERAPIST: But he hasn't.

HALEY: Well, he can say, "I've been thinking about a woman lately." I'm sure he has, you know.

THERAPIST: Well, I don't know if he's going to like this pattern of now he's sending letters to his parents and he's going to obviously stay up all night trying to analyze and figure out why the heck I asked him to do it.

TRAINEE: What else does he have to do?

HALEY: Well, there're also two things in his life. His career and women right at the moment and his family as a background. So you work on what is most relevant. You make most active whatever he is most involved in. Conversation alone doesn't do it. It takes some action of some kind.

THERAPIST: That's what I want to bring up. How he really didn't do anything with what I had suggested before. So if I go through like 10 different ideas or interventions and he doesn't implement any of them, well, then. . . .

HALEY: You don't go through 10. If he doesn't do the next one, you handle it there. I would see this guy every two weeks at least, not every week, to give some time for something to happen in between sessions. But I thought you handled it very well tonight.

THERAPIST: Thanks for saying so. I felt like I was working.

HALEY: But keep in mind your goal in therapy with this guy is to get him independent of you. That's a major goal. And so, if you can get him to spontaneously do something that you haven't recommended, you're on your way. One of the things you can do is when you say, "If you're courageous, you can do such and such." Then if he does such and such, he's done something courageous. But anyhow, he's a difficult guy. I mean he's a very experienced patient. Most of what you would try with him, he's had tried with him. Therefore, you have to come up with something new.

THERAPIST: His real key is that he's trying to find out where his depression is coming from.

HALEY: How do you explain his lifelong depression like that? You should name it something else.

THERAPIST: He calls it sadness.

HALEY: Sure. Sadness would help. Or homesickness can help. I wanted to throw that in there, which might have happened to him at that time.

THERAPIST: How do we change the social situation?

HALEY: You're doing it. You are changing the relationship to his parents. I mean, even all the way home tonight he's thinking, What am I putting in this letter and will my father do this and will he not do that?

THERAPIST: Or he's also thinking, What is this going to accomplish? He even said that.

HALEY: Oh, a better answer than you gave would be to say you'll find that out when you do it. You'll be surprised what the reason is.

THERAPIST: You saw him. He covers all the bases.

The group made some suggestions to counteract Abdul's negativism.

HALEY: Well, he's had 12 years of therapy trying to find the cause. To shake that is very hard.

THERAPIST: But that's the whole thing. I mean he will not allow himself to just not be depressed anymore.

The therapist's continual negative reactions to Haley's suggestions is paralleled by the negative reactions of the client to the therapist's suggestions. If the supervisor succeeds in making the therapist more positive and decisive, the therapist will succeed in making the client more positive and decisive.

PLANNING THE SECOND LIVE SUPERVISION

HALEY: I would pick something like getting a job and he has to have that job by a certain date. A month or two months or whatever, and everything in the session is organized about meeting that date. I think you can activate him to even name a date to step forward.

THERAPIST: But the main thing that's going on here is he has this sadness, this depression, that keeps him from doing anything.

HALEY: Do you think he took seriously that you were his last therapist?

THERAPIST: I don't know.

HALEY: If you wanted to do something more obscure, you would say, "I want you set a date for when you'll go to work. And it should be to go to work at a job that you won't like."

THERAPIST: He's going to say, why? You know what he does.

HALEY: He says why because you say why. I can see you have a lot of enthusiasm for these suggestions. Have you got two ways to handle it if he wrote the letter or if he didn't?

THERAPIST: No. I hadn't, and I didn't really plan it out.

HALEY: You should think about it. What you might do is if, in the middle of the interview, you're feeling hopeless about him, I would just ask him to wait outside and come out here and we'll help you be more hopeless. I think he's the kind that brings out hopelessness in therapists. He's been doing it for 12 years.

OBSERVING THE LIVE INTERVIEW

The trainees are free to comment on the interview from behind a mirror as it happens. The instructions were unusual. Almost all the suggestions sent on the computer involved persuading the trainee to persuade the client to write a letter to his father. It's important that the man do something, not just talk about it. Just as it is important that the therapist do something not just talk about.

Computer Suggestion: What about the letter????? [sic]

THERAPIST: Did you think about the letter that we talked about last time? Did you write a letter? What did you do with it?

Computer Suggestion: It is supposed to be a positive letter about the future.

THERAPIST: Let me ask you this. What will your parents think about this in terms of success or how would they look at it if you talk about going back to school?

Computer Supervision: What would your parents think as positive?

Computer Suggestion: What are you going to do with the letter?

Computer Suggestion: Have him write down the letter and read it.

THERAPIST: I assume your parents will probably call you after they get the letter or you'll just speak with them shortly thereafter. All right, so, is that a plan?

The client agrees to write the letter to his parents.

DISCUSSING THE SECOND LIVE INTERVIEW

THERAPIST: All right. I've done it.

TRAINEE: That was great.

HALEY: I think you handled it very well. I mean, you got to the letter and you had it written.

THERAPIST: Got it to say what we wanted it to say. I mean, I was very pleased about that.

HALEY: You presented your differences with him very well.

THERAPIST: He did it. I was astounded. I really was. I did not think he would follow through because he questions everything. And, you know, after trying to figure out why, either way, whether he figures it out or not, he's still going to do something.

TRAINEE TWO: He's really followed through with everything that you have asked him to do now.

TRAINEE THREE: You expect him not to do it, but he does.

HALEY: He just questions it and then does it. Well, that means he's going to mail it.

THERAPIST: Yeah. He's going to mail it this week.

HALEY: This is the kind of difficult case you often get in private practice with those who've been in therapy for years.

THERAPIST: It's a good one to cut my eyeteeth on. That's for sure.

HALEY: It is. He'll educate you. One other thing you might have done to make it more intense would be to have him do that whole letter, get it all set, and then tell him not to mail it.

THERAPIST: After all this?

HALEY: After the work you did—and just tell him it was only for his own education to help him out of his depression. He would be angry.

THERAPIST: Yeah. He would be angry because we've already discussed what the purpose was—to discover what the reaction is from his parents—and maybe he's eager to know what the reaction is.

THERAPIST: Well, should I not have him mail the letter then?

HALEY: Oh no. I was just saying that's another alternative. You want to get him mad, because this guy needs to get mad about something.

THERAPIST: His affect was the brightest I've seen. You know, what did you guys think about the going back to school and he kept belittling it? I was really struggling with that because that is a humongous step for him. I mean, I saw that as a real positive development.

HALEY: He came in more cheerful. With most patients you are pleased when they come in more cheerful. With him I would think he's avoiding something. So he'll act more cheerful so that you'll ignore a directive, like the letter he may not have to write if he's cheerful about going back to school.

I would just assume he's interpersonally very skillful. He's sacrificing himself for his parents but at the same time resents it and is in conflict with them. But that doesn't mean he isn't doing himself in for their sake.

This is part of the problem working from here to the Middle East, and you can't get the parents' reaction to something he does. That's the problem. It's stable if he fails. So he's got to let them know regularly that he fails.

THERAPIST: Intellectually, he would argue that that's impossible. His parents would want him to succeed.

OBSERVING THE THIRD LIVE INTERVIEW

The strategic technique with a client who will not easily change is to concentrate on one topic or on getting him to do one thing. In this case it is to mail the letter to his parents. The dialogue underlines the family therapy at a distance because it is as if the parents are in the room as client and therapist ponder their possible reactions to the letter when they should receive it. The therapist is pleased in the improvement in the client this week. He is signing up to go back to school. The supervisor is also pleased.

ABDUL: I am going on a date this weekend. I have been feeling more energetic, excited, like when I did experiments at the lab. I think I am getting better because of the medication.

ABDUL: Can I put in the letter that I ask them for praise of my successes?

THERAPIST: Nothing is going to keep you from being successful. Congratulations for coming up with that.

THERAPIST: You have been more proactive now than you have been lately. What do you think? What will your father's response be when you say I am confident about the future?

ABDUL: My parents want me to be successful but I am rebelling against their wish to be successful. They don't believe that I will be successful.

THERAPIST: It is essential to send the letter to see their response. What are some of the other ways you could rebel against their wishes which are less destructive to you?

Abdul responds with three principal kinds of rebellion—that he doesn't believe in God, that his girlfriends are not from the Middle East, and that he came to the United States, all of which his parents were against, but they are not necessarily destructive to him.

ABDUL: I look at the letter as a tool as what is happening in their mind.

THERAPIST: What consequences should I impose if you don't send the letter? I have an idea. I will send your father a letter that you will fly them here for Christmas. This is immaterial because you are going to mail the letter. We can't progress in this area unless the letter is sent.

ABDUL: I will send it express mail.

THERAPIST: You theorize that your father is going to have a positive response. I don't think so.

The supervisor had told the therapist to do something to which Abdul would have to respond to prove the therapist was wrong.

ABDUL: I can pick up the phone tonight and tell them.

THERAPIST: It is much better to have it in written form so they can read it a few times. Are they going to crumple it up, throw it away, or ponder it?

Abdul takes a deep breath, puts his head in his hands, and tries to visualize his father's reaction when he receives the letter.

THERAPIST: Of course, you know, you don't want to improve too fast, I guess. Right? Do you want to take it slow, inch by inch, or do you just want to snap into it one day.

Computer Suggestion: Ask him when he'll send the letter.

ABDUL: Tomorrow morning. (*They discuss all of the peculiarities of mail going to the Middle East.*)

DISCUSSING THE LIVE INTERVIEW

HALEY: Do you think he's going to mail the letter?

THERAPIST: He said he wanted me to apologize to you guys because he just didn't realize that you guys really would have wanted to know what the response was right away. But, he said he would have mailed it sooner.

HALEY: Would you believe him if he said he mailed it?

THERAPIST: Yeah.

HALEY: I would too, but there was some vote in here that he might lie.

THERAPIST: Well, I don't see that at all, but I guess anything is possible. But I'll tell you I am hopeful. First of all, you saw his affect. He was not down and depressed. I mean, he was energetic. He was engaging.

HALEY: He was even joking once.

THERAPIST: Right. We were laughing. So I'm feeling kind of cool but that's because I was under the vent. It's like he said, it's not familiar to him to feel this warmth, this happiness. And I'm happy for him that he's been able to experience that. I mean to get him back enrolling in school next semester. I mean, that's a humongous accomplishment.

HALEY: What you are really doing is turning the man's life around. With a guy like that, you worry about him improving as a temptation for the therapist and then collapsing so the therapist is disappointed. That is, there are people who do disappoint their therapist. But I don't think he's doing that at all. I think he's coming out of whatever he was in. It might be the medication.

THERAPIST: Yeah. But medication or no medication, I mean, he is getting more and more proactive. What about the letter? Like, all right, let's get the darn letter already. So I think it's more the computer, not me.

HALEY: You did very well this time.

THERAPIST: Well, thanks. A professional does the job that has to be done, no matter how they feel, right? So I just went in there and said, look, I've got to give this guy my best. I can't just go in there and just kind of, you know, fake my way through it.

HALEY: President Truman was the man who defined therapy. He said that if you can't stand the heat, get out of the kitchen. You've got to be able to stand it and not say it's just too much for me.

ONE WEEK LATER

THERAPIST: He mailed it and his parents haven't received it yet. It's going to take three to ten days for them to get it. So he gave me his e-mail address. If any of you want to e-mail him back for the results of the letter, he said that he would be more than happy to e-mail them to you.

At this point, Abdul confided to the therapist that he was engaging in risky sexual behavior, meeting people on the Internet. That also explained why he spent so much time on his computer. He looked for submissive partners who wanted someone dominant. He revealed other sexual fantasies as well. The client prefers the explanation of being molested as a 12-year-old than being depressed in relation to his parents.

THERAPIST: I asked him this week about the molestation when he was 12 years old. And he told me the entire thing again, like he didn't recall that he had told me the whole story before. He cruises out on the Internet, looks up the S&M sadomasochistic ads and things like that, and he's always looking for submissive people who want a dominant. We talked about fantasies he has in terms of sex and what type of sex appeals to him. He likes the hair pulling. This is getting really bizarre. He likes the idea of slapping a woman once before they have sex.

TRAINEE ONE: And he wonders why he doesn't have any girls coming around?

THERAPIST: But he's engaging in dangerous or risky behavior. He told me about 3 months ago he got together with this woman off the Internet [a bondage woman] and they had sex and totally unprotected. And one time he got together with a transvestite from the Internet and he said they had sex. He said, "First, I spent a lot of time talking." He's like counseling the guy. They were talking about this transvestite's past and all the tragedies behind that and they had sex, but he said it was horrible. He said, "It was a sick thing that I did." You know this whole thing has taken a whole turn. I mean, talk about deviation. This is just a whole different ballgame now. He hasn't mentioned it to anybody else. I spent a lot of time telling him how much I appreciated the trust. Well, I did kind of half make him promise that I would be the last therapist he would come to. This is about nine sessions down the road, or nine weeks.

HALEY: It sounds like it is more elaborate than that. I mean it wasn't just a trauma. He's got a way of life involved. He will have to undo his way of life to have some goal of normal living.

THERAPIST: And look at it. All the women that he hangs around with are like 18, 19, 20 years old. He's the teacher.

HALEY: It's a gift in therapy with him when he tells you these things. It's depressing. It may not be one you have enthusiasm for. I think he's unhappy with the way he is, and he got a therapist who got him to write a letter to his father. That probably brought all this out.

TRAINEE TWO: Well, yeah, very well may have. Absolutely. Because, in part, you're doing things with him that have never been done before. You've asked him to be his last therapist. You got him to write a letter to his Dad, which who knows what that stirred up, but I suspect he's seeing you differently than he's seen other therapists. You've got more leverage.

HALEY: It is better to focus on current behavior so that he does not get carried away with that trauma at 12 years old.

THERAPIST: But that could be the ideology—at least of the depression. I'm convinced that at this point even if he found the key to his depression, that's not going to change his behavior.

HALEY: And if he can remember that incident in detail, then it won't necessarily affect him and what he is doing with people now. I think you are fortunate if you can get a case like that—a multiproblem, strange case within an ethnic group. I mean, if the guy goes to work and begins to do something that gives him some self-esteem it would be nice. I think a lot of this stuff then drops away. One thing that I think is important when you are thinking about a strategy of therapy: You can either decide that that traumatic incident in childhood caused him to do what he is doing today with a guy. Or you can say that he does this with a guy, and when he wonders why he does it, he remembers that incident and the trauma helps him explain why he has these feelings now. But it doesn't mean remembering the trauma is the cause of his present behavior. It means it is an expression of the trauma.

THERAPIST: It is a cause. Well, isn't it?

HALEY: If you accept that the past causes the present, then it is the cause.

The father was casual about the letter. The son even had to ask whether he received it. A 6-month follow-up revealed that the client was going to college. He had left therapy after 4 months.

In this case there are a variety of brief therapy interventions made. An issue was dealing with a client who had had years of therapy. It was necessary for the therapist to be unpredictable and extreme in certain ways since the client had experienced years of insightful traditional therapy for depression.

A second issue is the parallel between therapist–client relationship and therapist–supervisor relationship. If the supervisor is reflective with the therapist, the therapist will be reflective with the client. If the supervisor is firm with the therapist, the therapist can be firm with the client. In this case the supervisor attempted again and again to persuade the therapist to arrange the letter to the father. When the therapist did what the supervisor said, the therapist was able to get the client to do the task. The letter writing was the vehicle for the action. This was why it was so important that the therapist take action. The father's disinterested response was as important as an angry response, since either way the client could shift his family relationship in his own behalf. When dealing with depression, you need action and not only reflection.

Although the strategic approach of giving directives is culturally congruent with the patriarchal hierarchical structure of the family, it also challenges both the psychodynamic and culturally sensitive approaches. In this case Abdul was rebelling against traditional cultural values that he should follow his father's advice and stay in the homeland, date ethnically similar women, and lead a clean lifestyle. The directive to write the father a letter saying that he was doing well was a paradox leading to change because he was challenging his father but doing so more positively. The strategic approach also challenged the cultural value of expressing one's feelings. Abdul had spent years analyzing and talking about his sadness. The strategic approach forced him to take action.

NOTES

This case has stimulated discussions among colleagues on the possible theories of change. Braulio Montalvo (Personal communication, June 2002) has offered some interesting hypotheses.

1. The insistence on writing a letter provided the depressed young man with an opportunity to share his gutter lifestyle. He had fallen on bad times and felt like an undeserving sinner. He was lonely in his deviant lifestyle, living on relationship scraps and feeling no one was interested in him. The therapist was interested and nonjudgmental, providing a ladder out of the gutter and a second chance, the chance for absolution and reconnection socially.
2. The insistence on writing and mailing the letter revealed to the young man a therapist in distress who needed to deliver for a community of colleagues behind the mirror. The young man did not want the therapist to fail and stretched to deliver. He had finally related generously and competently with someone nice! He felt good about it. The sense of succeeding at this snowballed and lifted his depression.
3. The insistence on writing a letter afforded the young man a chance to make the tug-of-war with his father into a tug-of-war with the therapist. He stalled, dodged, opposed, procrastinated, but the therapist outlasted him, and the conflict was resolved by producing for the therapist. Since the conflict was over, the sense of relief at having broken a stalemate created a lift out of the depression and a chance to repair his lifestyle.
4. The insistence on writing the letter as if he cared about a woman or going back to school surfaced his belief that his father had intense expectations regarding other or both of these two areas of accomplishing. When the father responded in a moderate or "I don't give so much as a damn" way, he discovered, despite the letdown, that he was free to not fail if he wanted to. He could move on. The paralysis had no function and was not needed.
5. A combo theory: He really had a father who didn't care much while he wanted the father to care more. He was, by failing, trying to get the father "pissed off," angry and reactive to him, but the nonresponsive father was so unreactive that the young man had to escalate by falling deeper into paralysis and into a gutter lifestyle, which further depressed him. The therapist acted as if everything this young man did was important and worthy of his reactions. If the young man didn't do something, it mattered, it was very important. Even writing a letter was important. This changed the young man's sense of helplessness into helpfulness and a wish to reciprocate by lifting his depression.

6. All those above social interactive sequences facilitate and move along with mysterious neurotransmitter changes brought about by his medications, clicking in just in time for the depression to lift, responding to both social and biological interventions.
7. The social shifts are not as decisive in producing the observed depression lift as the obscure effects of the powerful medicines he was taking.

5

Changing a Violent Family

In this age of violence, therapists can be saving the community from violence instead of exploring personal discontent. To accomplish therapy, they find themselves working with attorneys, law enforcement personnel, social workers, 12-step sponsors, psychiatrists, and so on. The quiet reflective interview is replaced by dealing with violence among the family members. Abuse laws are designed and enforced. Time and again, the strategic family therapist is called upon to see one individual in the family with the other members parceled out to other professionals. The lack of communication in a case among the professionals is illustrated in this case of a violent family. Strategic techniques provide direction to prevent serious abuse, resolve family conflicts, and increase, collaboration among the professionals.

Training to deal with abuse can be done in various ways. For this case, a group of six trainee therapists are gathered with a supervisor to learn how to do strategic therapy. Trainee therapists take turns going behind a one-way mirror with a supervisor observing and commenting on the action by sending messages to the trainee therapist through a computer monitor or calls him or her on the telephone to guide the action. The supervisor on this day is Haley. "Tell us about this case. Is this your first interview with this family?" Haley asked.

THERAPIST: No, but it's my first family therapy session with them. In this family, the mother had a boy about 10 years old. The relationship with the father didn't work out. She then got involved with another man and with him had twins. I think they are 8 years old. This past year she left the children home with the twins' father. He apparently lost his temper and beat the 10-year-old boy to the point where he had to be hospitalized. This father of the twins went to jail. I'm not sure if he's still in jail or out of jail, but it was considered a criminal child-abuse charge. All

79

the children were removed and put in foster homes. Mom has all the children back now.

HALEY: (*Impressed*) How did she do that? (*This is the goal of many mothers to get their children back from foster homes.*)

THERAPIST: She went to counseling, went to parenting classes. She did everything that Child Protective Services told her to do. The children were all placed in counseling, and everybody had a different counselor. I saw Ellen, who is eight. You will see her in there. Somebody else saw Judy, who is eight. And somebody else saw Anthony, who is ten, the victim. And then somebody saw the mother, Maureen, outside our agency.

HALEY: This occurred after she had them all back?

THERAPIST: No, this occurred before she got them all back. She just got all the kids back.

HALEY: What happened in therapy with the multiple therapists when she got the kids back?

THERAPIST: It was a mess.

There were five therapists in this case, four attorneys, a probation officer, and three supervisors.

THERAPIST: There's a lot of fighting going on in the home, but the main fighting—I mean physical punching each other—goes on between the kids. So from week to week, if my patient [Ellen] was improving, following the rules and going to bed and walking away from conflicts, then Anthony would be worse. And then the next week Judy would be better and my client would be beating the hell out of everybody. When mom tries to discipline them, they don't listen to her.

HALEY: Is anybody else living in the home?

THERAPIST: Well, that's funny you mentioned that, because she doesn't have a phone. Apparently there's a guy named Joe in the home.

HALEY: (*The supervisor wants the therapist to define the goals.*) What do you want in the ideal situation to solve this problem? How would you like the family to look when you are done with it?

THERAPIST: I would like no more punching out and no one having to go to the emergency room.

HALEY: One of the goals you should have, I think, is to clarify a hierarchy in the family. To have mother in charge of the boy, who is in charge of the twins. Twins are always a problem when they have difficulty. They have difficulty with each other and nobody knows how to treat them when they are two people acting like one person. It's very complicated. I don't know how people raise the threes and the fours. Anyhow, I would keep in the back of your mind that you would like the twins to accept the boy being in charge, or being helpful, and at the moment I gather they don't.

THERAPIST: No

Haley normalizes the issues by emphasizing that twins are special problems and suggests to the therapist to ask the kids what it's like to be twins, if they ever saw another family with twins, and elicit a description from the kids of what their family should look like.

THERAPIST: So, what should I do when I go in today? Should we just talk about what do they see as a problem?

HALEY: I would start with what do they see as a family that has a mother, has a father. Sometimes mother isn't there, sometimes father. But some kind of description that can be drawn out of them.

GROUP OBSERVES THE FIRST
LIVE FAMILY INTERVIEW

The therapist brings in the family composed of mother, 10-year-old son, and 8-year-old twins. They discuss raising twins as well as their special problem of violent hitting each other. The supervisor must come up with a plan to stop the hitting. The mother says she is thinking about giving at least one of the twins back to Social Service because of the hitting. This would be tragic. since this mother had worked so hard to get them all back from foster homes where they had been put when father was arrested for beating the stepson and putting him in the hospital.

Supervisor calls the therapist out of the interview room and proposes a plan to prevent the hitting. The plan is to pay the kids for not hitting. You have to get the family to agree that if they are violent, nobody gets the money, thereby creating motivation for peace.

Paying Kids to Get Rid of Symptoms

HALEY: No hitting for a week. Nobody hits anybody. And if they don't hit anybody, you give them each a quarter.

THERAPIST: (*surprised*) I give them a quarter?

HALEY: Everybody gets a quarter. But if they lay a hand on anyone once, no quarter.

THERAPIST: OK. I'll do that.

HALEY: They need such motivation.

THERAPIST: Well, let's up the ante a bit. What about a dollar?

HALEY: That's too much.

THERAPIST: A quarter?

TRAINEE ONE: A dollar would be pretty good if I were 7 years old.

HALEY: That's too much. You can make it a dollar if you want, but you are going to contribute this if it goes over a quarter.

THERAPIST: (*The therapist returns to the interview room and relates the plan to the family in a playful way*). Now, guess what?

ELLEN: What?

THERAPIST: You know what?

JUDY: What?

THERAPIST: If everybody here, including Mom, can make it one whole week, can make it 7 days, with no hitting, everyone gets 50 cents. Is that a deal? (*The kids look at each other excitedly.*)

THERAPIST: Deal?

Computer Suggestion: Ask what is a hit?

THERAPIST: (*Therapist defines a hit.*) So in this family a hit would mean body contact, head, body, foot, and also an intention to hit. What if some hitting went on and you weren't in the room, Mom, and somebody comes and says, Mom, Mom, they hit me, but you didn't see it, would that count?

ELLEN AND JUDY: (*The twins respond in unison.*) No.

THERAPIST: So Mom has to see the hit?

ELLEN: Yes.

Computer Suggestion: Make it firmer. No excuses.

THERAPIST: No hitting. No ifs, ands, or buts. There is no hitting. No hitting in this family.

JUDY: Period.

THERAPIST: If you hit, you don't get the 50 cents. You lose the game.

ELLEN: Who gives us the 50 cents?

JUDY: Her (*pointing to the therapist*).

THERAPIST: I'm giving it to Mom, and Mom will give it to you next week.

You are doing two things here. One is motivating the kids to stop hitting. Secondly, you are reinforcing a hierarchy with mother more in charge.

GROUP DISCUSSION OF FIRST FAMILY INTERVIEW

Haley asks the group, "What do you think about the morality of paying kids to behave themselves?" There was disagreement among the group. Haley defends the strategy as a way of making a different process clearly defined. They'll behave the way they behave only around something clearly defined. The therapist questioned whether the son who is older should get more money. Haley said no. They either all get the same payment or none of them gets any. The misbehavior in the family is related with the more general Durkheimian theory of deviance. A deviant serves a function by showing people how not to behave, because they don't know the rules on what not to do until somebody breaks the rules and then they know. So each group, in order to be stable, has to have somebody break the rules and act strangely. Often when the rest of the family begins to stabilize, one of them takes action, and that has to be dealt with.

Another trainee questioned Haley about why he does not emphasize feelings in therapy.

Haley replies, "It's not only that bringing out emotions don't produce change, it gets in the way of the therapy. I mean that to encourage people to express their emotions is based on the idea of the theory of repression that came out of the nineteenth century—that everybody should express their emotions and then they would be healed and express their ideas and their unconscious ideas. I haven't seen it to be very effective at all, and it usually interferes with the relationship, because they get off into metaphor when they talk about feelings. And if you want the metaphors that's fine, but if you don't, it gets in the way of the therapy."

PLANNING THE INTERVIEW—A WEEK LATER

Haley anticipates with the therapist the possible consequences of paying to lose the symptom of hitting.

HALEY: What if they hit each other again?

THERAPIST: I'll be very disappointed.

HALEY: You've got to anticipate and think about what you would do, whatever happens. They had the choice. They didn't hit each other or they did hit each other and you have to do something with it. Or everybody was happy and not telling the truth about who hit. The question for you is, Are you going to end up giving the money to them even if they hit each other?

THERAPIST: No.

HALEY: OK. That's clear.

THERAPIST: Maybe next week then.

HALEY: You could postpone it. That's right. Say, I'll give you one more week to get the money.

THERAPIST: That's a good idea.

HALEY: I know there is always a compromise of some kind.

THERAPIST: Now, last week I think we left off where we were trying to put Mom in charge and the oldest boy sort of second in charge and then we were trying to reframe the behavior as more of a twin problem.

HALEY: That's right. You did that very well.

THERAPIST: Oh, well, thanks. I think we should continue with that theme because I think Mom heard it but I don't know if she believed it.

HALEY: Well, she kept on finding it hard to raise twins after they were about 6 months old. Nothing happened from then on.

HALEY: So, think about this. You have to deal with the 50 cents because they are going to come in eager for their 50 cents. You either have to do something with it at the moment or you can say to them, Before this interview is over I'm going to be offering 50 cents to those who didn't hit each other, but I'm not going to do it now. That is, you can stretch it out if you want or put off the decision unless they are really eager to know if they made 50 cents.

THERAPIST: OK. Now, why would we do that—have it at the end instead of the beginning?

HALEY: Because it's a climax to pass out the money first. Everything else is kind of minor. Well, it's probably because you raised the 50 cents from 25. That made it real money and possibly you can buy something with it. Twenty-five is like a symbol a token, but 50 cents is serious. And I would take all of the advantage of it as you can to find out more about hitting or what they think of hitting or whatever you want to explore and you explore with them cooperating because they have something coming.

TRAINEE: OK. Sounds good.

HALEY: Just say that you'd like to talk to her alone. Can you send the kids to the waiting room? You need her permission is what I mean. I would assume the kids are reflecting her state of mind and her relationship to you.

The therapist spent much of this session getting the mother to say that she will not give up the children. Mother shouldn't threaten abandonment of children if they don't behave, particularly when they have been in foster homes, and their homes have been temporary.

The children hit and the therapist chose not to pay the 50 cents. Then a compromise was reached: they could have the 50 cents for effort because they tried to stop hitting. The family was pleased with it. The session ended as the mother passed out the 50 cents, reinforcing the hierarchy. Paying a child for good behavior can be like giving an allowance.

DISCUSSING THE SECOND INTERVIEW

THERAPIST: I'm glad that you did the effort thing. Although Anthony hit, he did volunteer to do dishes three times that week. So, when you guys did the effort thing, everybody got 50 cents and it equalized everybody. Mom started talking about all the good things that they actually did.

The follow-up discussion centered on the importance of the mother's reassuring the kids that she will not give them up to Social Service again, which she had been threatening to do because of the hitting. "I think it's best to just sit the mother down and say, Tell them you're never going to give them up. You are going to keep them forever, no matter how they behave, and so on," Haley emphasized to the group.

HALEY: Many times kids are strung out in Social Service. They get back with their families, and because they have been moved out before, they make trouble to see if they will be kicked out again.

THERAPIST: And in this family it's a possibility because Mom has gotten to the point where—and that's why we wanted the family therapy— where she's ready to get rid of Ellen. You know, everything is always blamed on her, but I thought she was one of the most well behaved.

Bring In More Family Members

Haley begins a discussion on bringing in more relatives because of the obvious triangles in the case.

HALEY: There are two fathers involved or not involved, and they must have mothers. There're mothers-in-law, and grandmothers of these kids. They must be involved in some way. Usually, if the kid is really troubled, there are two adults in conflict over how to deal with him. It's the classic arrangement. And still they misbehave. So, there has to be somebody else in there. Naturally, the one mother-in-law is a little angry because the boy's mother put her son in jail.

THERAPIST: Well, he's the one that beat the kid, and the kid even went into the hospital. It was that father's mother that's not talking to her. She blames her. She was not even home. She was working when he beat him up.

HALEY: People who hadn't seen the family together think they are awful, and then when they see the family, they say, Well, they must be misdiagnosed; they're behaving like reasonable people. And I think that's so here.

You do need a goal. *Picture in your mind how you would like them to be when you say goodbye.*

THERAPIST: OK. That's good.

HALEY: Well, OK. I thought that interview went well.

TRAINEE TWO: It did. Excellent.

PLANNING THE THIRD FAMILY INTERVIEW

The Twins Take Turns at Being Evil

Haley proposes a paradox to solve the misbehavior and to reinforce a proper family hierarchy by putting mother in charge of the paradox. Since the therapist has been referring to the girls as the good and evil twin, he begins by exploring that language. The playfulness of the therapist's delivery of the paradox is made into a game with the children.

HALEY: Is the evil one given that name?

THERAPIST: No, that's a term. Mom keeps saying how bad she is.

HALEY: Her characterization is what?

THERAPIST: The evil twin.

HALEY: They do say that?

THERAPIST: Well, no, but she says all sorts of stuff—"Well that's the one that acts up". . . .

HALEY: A possibility would be to say that the evil twin has had this burden too long—being evil. And it's the other twin's turn to have it sometimes.

THERAPIST: OK.

HALEY: And pass it over and see how well she can behave equally like her twin. You can then criticize the good one for not being evil enough.

THERAPIST: Yeah, let's do it.

HALEY: To see if you can make sure that you give everybody something to do, you give the boy the position of saying whether it's working or not. How well is she doing—the evil twin?

THERAPIST: OK. He's like a referee. Right?

HALEY: The referee.

THERAPIST: OK. Got it.

HALEY: And Mother's the supervisor.

THERAPIST: OK.

HALEY: You can start by just chatting about how they are doing or you can ask them to predict whether one twin could be acting like the other one.

THERAPIST: Mom is like a manager of the baseball team, and the brother is the referee, and then the twins are the evil twin and the good twin.

HALEY: The fielders.

THERAPIST: (*laughing*) The fielders. OK. And they're to feel this way.

HALEY: And then to be able to go 5 minutes this way.

THERAPIST: OK, 5 minutes. Oh, I don't even have my timer.

HALEY: Somebody else in there should be able to keep the time. There's no clock on that wall.

THERAPIST: Well, I'll give them my watch.

HALEY: You better watch that.

THERAPIST: Kids are pretty good with my stuff.

OBSERVING THE THIRD FAMILY INTERVIEW

THERAPIST: You've worked so hard on being that evil twin. Now we are going to change your job. OK? And guess who I will give it to, because she's such a wonderful actor and she's going to be like an evil twin for 5 minutes. Say now, Mom, you're the manager. You're going to let the referee, Anthony, know when to start the game and you guys. . . .

JUDY: (*The kids are excited about the game.*) Yes! Yes!

THERAPIST: . . . are going to play. Wait a minute I will put magic dust.

JUDY: (*Screaming like she is changing.*)

THERAPIST: You are now the good twin, and you wore such a pretty dress and now, wait a minute. Woo, poof (*she scatters the powder*) now, you're that evil twin.

ELLEN: (*She laughs.*)

THERAPIST: OK. Now, do you happen to have an evil-twin voice?

ELLEN: (*She yells out.*)

The therapist moves the family's positions. The good and evil twin change places with the boy coaching them to be more good or evil. The mother supervises the argument between the good and evil twins. They change back again. This is paradoxical because the therapist is instructing the evil twin to be evil and the good twin to be good. The evil twin is behaving good when she behaves evil on instruction.

DISCUSSING THE THIRD INTERVIEW

TRAINEE THREE: When she [Judy] said, "cool," she wanted to be the good twin.

HALEY: One of things that was interesting is when the mother moved. The whole interaction just changed.

TRAINEE: The boy got really disappointed when he wasn't getting the money even though he controlled himself.

THERAPIST: I talked to her over phone, and she was very positive. I think it's because of the therapy. We're positive focused and we're helping changes.

What do we do to try to cement some of this stuff?

TRAINEE: How about saying, "Did we have two good twins this week, because I think that's the good goal, like Mom said—"

HALEY: Quite a goal. Just to get them participating with each other successfully.

Haley describes a previous case of twins to the group.

HALEY: I treated twins once. They were about 17, and they said they never competed because they ran the 100-yard dash at exactly the same speed. They swam a 100 yards at exactly the same speed. They both had twin girlfriends. They were working on the car that they each shared, but they really were so competitive that they didn't know they were competitive, but it made their behavior very positive. And these two you can make positive. . . . If you can get them competing on something, in some game or some skill or something.

THERAPIST: Not against each other, but you mean together?

HALEY: Not against each other but improving. What these other two twins did is when one got better at the 100-yard dash, he helped the other one learn how to do it better so that they could be exactly the same. But it takes twins I'm talking about. . . . There's one thing that differentiated them, and that was one of them had a symptom. He blocked when he spoke. He had real difficulties speaking, and that made him different from the other one. And it seemed so obvious when I saw them that something would have to be done about both of them in order to do something about that one, because they really were so alike in every way that this is the one thing that that guy was individual with.

FOURTH FAMILY INTERVIEW—DISENGAGEMENT

Built into the therapy is the idea that it will end. How the therapist can approach this is discussed below.

HALEY: Suppose you said to them, "If this was our last session, what would you worry about?" What would they say?

THERAPIST: I think she would complain about the kids and what's going to happen to the boy?

HALEY: When you say that to them, usually they go into the problems that most worry them. And you know you can always say, I'm not saying that this is our last session. I'm just saying what would you be worried about if it was. But it defines the situation as temporary. The clientele will put off doing things—well, I'll do that later in the therapy sort of thing. And it helps to make it clear that therapy will not last forever.

THERAPIST: We can do that and see what happens.

HALEY: Think about how to terminate, which is one of the more interesting problems in the business, because it's a disengagement that's hard to do sometimes. Because if things are going well, you want to continue and they want to continue, and they'll start making up problems in order to keep continuing. And it's best to make it clear that this is temporary. I think part of the job of the supervisor is to help a client and the therapist to get separated. Because it's not easy. You have a tough judgment of whether the problem is still there and bad enough to continue or are they really over it and just not presenting it that way.

THERAPIST: Now, if you're not sure, can you spread it out or are you better to cut it off?

HALEY: No. The best way to do it is to say, Let's meet in 2 weeks, or in 3 weeks, or how about the first of the month. And then what happens is they get interested in other things, you get interested in other cases. It's for both of you really.

THERAPIST: I didn't realize it was for both of us. That's true.

In addition to termination, in this session the therapist asks the family to say what is positive about brother this week. She asks for other resources such as grandparents and the church. Each family member is asked to name one thing the family needs do. It was clear that the son's father did not want to see him. This information was unknown previously, because the son had his own therapist who followed the rule of not communicating with the others.

DISCUSSING THE FOURTH INTERVIEW

HALEY: Would any of you have done that interview differently?

TRAINEE: That father just doesn't want to see him probably as a revenge on the mother.

HALEY: The most basic thing really is to get mothers to say they'll never leave the kid or the kid will never leave them. They can say it casually but really they have to say it and put it into words. They can think it— but there is a difference between thinking it and saying it. Kids hear what the parents say. They don't particularly watch what they do, but they listen so when a parent says, "I have an awful job and it's a pain in the ass," the kid thinks his father has an awful job when actually the father likes work, but it's a pain in the ass. Those distinctions are hard for a kid.

THERAPIST: Right.

HALEY: He feels it's ambiguous where he is going to be and what he's going to do and who with. It's related to friends, it's related to school, it's related to so many disruptions in his life. So it's one of the most basic things. Parents can treat a kid badly as long as they make it clear he's going to be their kid.

THERAPIST: What did you guys think about when I said, "What if this was the last session together?" And you know she really didn't say anything.

HALEY: No, but it was upsetting to her. She's very involved. And it isn't time for a last session, but it's time to say that it's going happen so she doesn't depend on you to do what she is going to have to do.

THERAPIST: But I thought we were supposed to stay away from emotions. Wasn't that what we are suppose to do?

HALEY: If they come out, you deal with them. You've talked to the father?

Too Many Professionals on One Case

THERAPIST: No, I haven't talked to him. I've been going through the social worker and the social worker thinks it's [stepdad attending the session] a really good idea. It's just that she was waiting to hear from the last two attorneys just to make sure, and Mom said she will give him directions to the therapy.

HALEY: It might help if you call him, if that wouldn't confuse all the other people involved.

FIFTH INTERVIEW

The Father, Jose, Jailed for Beating Stepson, Arrives

Permission was obtained from three court-appointed therapists to bring the stepfather into the session.

THERAPIST: He went to jail for physical abuse. He was there I don't know, 6 months or whatever his sentence was.

HALEY: 6 months.

THERAPIST: He's going to church and they are in a fundamentalist, born-again Christian kind of church, and he sits three pews back from the family. I guess he's apologized even to the congregation and to the pastor. He's already done some things. He's gone to a domestic violence workshop, and an anger management workshop. He's gone through all the parenting classes.

HALEY: He's going to be a professional parent pretty soon. You measure your distance from the family by how many pews back. Is that it? (*The group laughs.*) I think you need to explain to him something about what you're up to, what you would like to achieve, and why you are seeing the family. So that you can work from that because he doesn't really know. He must know they come here but he must know what for. Does anybody have a special way to open this up?

THERAPIST: No, I've never met him.

HALEY: I think it would be nice if you could by the end of the evening have a relationship where if he's upset he'd call you. That he feels you're on his side.

THERAPIST: Really.

HALEY: I think you ought to ask him what he'd like to be doing 5 years from now. So that he has a life that's not just wrapped up with a kid he beats up. I would try to get passed that and clarify with him that the court is out of it and everything is out of it and the family can work out it's own problems now.

THERAPIST: So at what point am I going to bring in Jose?

HALEY: It depends on how far you get with him. I don't know what he has been told, but you should tell him that you want to talk with him a while and then you'll bring the others in. You want to see the two of them without the rest of the family. I would just tell them what the agenda is so that he knows what is going to happen. I would do it without making a big issue and give him some information, because you don't know what he's been told about what's been happening, or if Anthony wants to see him or not. Somebody else have an idea around here?

THERAPIST: Anthony thinks he has to forgive Jose for what he did to him or else he will go to hell.

HALEY: Well, he better do it then. (*Students laugh.*)

THERAPIST: I asked Jose to sit in the truck.

HALEY: Why don't you start with him and bring him in.

THERAPIST: OK, and the social worker is going to help baby-sit or whatever you need her to do.

HALEY: Very good.

OBSERVING THE FIFTH INTERVIEW

The therapist brought the stepfather in. The therapist explored the life of the stepfather and asked why he had beaten the boy. The man said he did not want to use it as an excuse, but he had discovered he had cancer and was very upset. He also lost his athletic ability, which was important to him. This was his only incident of violence. He now was seeing a counselor and a probation officer for 1 year. He had 7 months to go. The therapist guides the stepfather on what should be done.

THERAPIST TO FATHER: This is the deal. OK? I need you to walk out with me, and I need you to be very gentle and apologetic to Anthony. And you can tell him you're sorry if you want to, but say I really need to talk to you, I really need to say something to you, and I really would appreciate it if you would come in here with me.

Jose came in and apologized to 10-year-old Anthony, whom he had beat up. The boy seems to have missed him and enjoyed his jokes from the broad smile on his face. The boy and stepfather were moved and hugged each other having been separated for more than a year. The therapist asks stepfather to give suggestions for dealing with violence. He says, "Never, never hit a girl." The boy says he is sorry. Jose replies, you have nothing to be sorry about because you did nothing wrong. There was no reason for him to do what he did. Anthony, who seems to have a similar anger problem, gives the stepfather some pointers on controlling anger. The boy talks about how he is protecting his sisters, taking on a fatherly role. Then Jose the father of the twins brought them into the room and apologized to the boy in front of them and for having caused the family to break up. They forgave him. The therapist arranged a game she invented called Jellyroll in which the father and the kids held hands and rolled up together hugging each other. Jose brought in the mother and apologized to Anthony in front of her and to her in front of all the kids. She tells him that she loves him. This was a touching interview both in front of and behind the mirror.

DISCUSSING THE FIFTH INTERVIEW

THERAPIST: What did you think about the dad? When we first went in together and he was first talking to the boy, he had tears in his eyes. The child did, too.

TRAINEE: The kid saw it, though.

HALEY: What a contrast from the first interview you had with them, when you went in just to get them not to hit each other.

TRAINEE: We didn't think that that dad was going to come through like that, because, before the boy came in, he was not taking responsibility at all. So we were worried. He seemed to own up to things when the boy came in.

TRAINEE: It was like pulling at my heart when I heard Anthony.

HALEY: He has put a lot of thought in that, I think.

TRAINEE: Well, he feels it's his fault that the family was ripped apart and that he should have been being a good boy.

THERAPIST: Did you see Mom's resistance when I had her take some kind of responsibility [for the abuse]?

TRAINEE: Yeah. Something that helps there sometimes is to say I'm sorry for not protecting you.

HALEY: Oh, I thought you were doing that.

TRAINEE: You did great leading. You were pulling along really well to get her to hold up to it and take some responsibility. That was great leading in that regard. She didn't know what to say.

THERAPIST: I was very careful. I could feel the tears coming. I was thinking whatever you do, don't say, How do you feel? (*The group laughs.*)

TRAINEE: Although you did ask at one point, What did you think about that?

TRAINEE: That was a great way to end a class. I tell you. I mean Anthony's face was worth it all.

The family was seen for four more sessions and terminated successfully. The children were not violent nor misbehaving. The mother was satisfied. In a 1-year follow-up, the therapy was a success despite the number of therapists, supervisors, attorneys, and court people involved.

Summary

In cases of family violence, seeing and communicating with as many professionals and relatives as possible increases your leverage in the case, as illustrated above. This is not easy, since family members are usually on different sides and are represented by professionals helping one individual and not the others in the family. It helps to think of the whole family as your client rather than one individual. The strategic family therapist helped the court-appointed staff by bringing all the helpers together.

In cases of violence, the therapist often needs to do something quickly and unusual to bring about change, because the consequences may be additional violence or the breakup of the family. As in this case, the mother was about to give up the kids to foster care once again because she could not handle them. The therapy focused upon teaching the mother to convince the children that she would not give them up if they misbehaved and to help the children behave.

One technique used was paying kids to give up their symptoms. One would not expect this reinforcement to appeal to many therapists. In this case it helped. The therapist must decide on an amount that is not too small to be unimportant nor too large to be unreasonable. She has to get the family to agree that if one of them is violent nobody gets the money, thereby creating motivation to stop the symptom in a clearly defined way. She must follow up on the symptom to find out if the money was deserved or not. She then had to decide if they had repeated the violence but had tried hard in many ways to correct the undesired behavior, in which case she gives them the benefit of the doubt and paid them for the effort. This was a game to get rid of the symptoms.

Paradox with children seems effective in stopping symptoms. It creates a playful situation that is congruous with the communication of kids. It shows that if behavior can be switched or passed around, it can be changed. In this case, it involved switching places of the evil and good twin. It also reinforces the family hierarchy by placing somebody in charge of the paradox. In this case the mother was in charge and the older son was the referee. (See chapter 8 for a classification of paradox.) The goal of the therapy in cases of violence is to ensure that no harm comes to anybody again.

6

Compulsory Therapy

A Violent Case

*I*n court-ordered cases it is essential to reinforce a family hierarchy in which parents cooperate with each other and are in charge of their children. In the case presented here, there is an attempt to make a coalition of parents in relation to the children. The attempt failed when the father declined to come into therapy to help with the boys' problems. The therapist wanted to bring the father in to join the mother in exerting authority with two violent boys. The father declined to come in for the first few interviews so that the mother was without parental pressure on the boys. The triangle was not complete until the father was brought in to join the mother in relation to the child. This situation is so common that therapists are trained to persuade a father to come in to a family session. The triangle can be both positive and negative. When positive, it can increase authority. When negative, it can solidify opposition against a person.

In this Pacific-Island family the traditionally accepted triangle has the father in charge, the mother joining him, and nonoppositional children. In this case the mother sided with the boys, particularly because she was opposing a common cause of conflict in the Pacific-Island community—racial prejudice, which was the cause of violence and involved the family with the law. The directive family approach used in this case was culturally appropriate and offered solutions to the court's instructions, and the court was flexible enough to adapt to cultural differences.

A family was brought in by a therapist trainee who was in compulsory therapy with him, as ordered by the court. It was a family with seven sons in which two of the sons were arrested for violence.

PLANNING THE FIRST INTERVIEW

HALEY: Tell us what you know about this family.

Therapist: What I know about the case is that the two sons evidently were walking down the street. Somebody, a neighbor kid, yelled some profanities at them, some racial slurs, and the two sons proceeded to beat the kid up. One son nailed the kid to the ground, and the other son kicked him in the mouth and knocked out a tooth. They both hit him and kicked him again. Then the police got involved when the kid told his father. The victim's father pressed charges, which got the boys into the juvenile probation system. This is mandated counseling for them to have to come here. The whole family is supposed to come, at least one parent, and at least the two kids that got in trouble.

HALEY: The two kids here are the ones who beat up the other kid?

THERAPIST: Hopefully that's the way it is. It's a new policy that if anybody presses charges, they automatically have to go through legal hoops and jumps. It's going to, almost, like an extreme now—if any kid brings any sort of a knife on campus they are automatically expelled. Even if it's a little thing that hangs off their key chain. That's what the courts are doing with this now. Any type of violence whatsoever—they are putting them through this big process. . . . Well, if he hit some kid, the court people or the police or somebody has hunted them down.

This is what is becoming a common case in therapy, a compulsory family therapy case. The court has reacted to the boy's fighting by ordering them to probation, community service, and to group therapy for anger management and for family counseling. There are two parents in the home, but the father is often traveling out of town. This leaves mother in charge of seven sons, and she is feeling guilty about her sons' involvement with the police. Father was not at home when this violence occurred. At this time, he is at home and is expected for the family interviews.

HALEY: What are you concerned about?

THERAPIST: One of my big concerns is whether there really is a problem. So the kids beat up another kid. Does that mean that they should be in juvenile hall? I'm also concerned that there are going to be no family problems. I'm not so sure how I would have reacted if somebody spit out racial slurs to me. I might have thumped somebody, too.

HALEY: So you start on their side.

THERAPIST: No, I am going to start neutral and just try to find out what's going on.

HALEY: And who is here? Mother and the two boys?

THERAPIST: Yes. That's as far as I understand.

HALEY: Is there a father somewhere?

THERAPIST: The father, yes. And that's who I would like to try to get in, eventually. I asked about him: "No, he can't make it, he works three jobs." You know, he's constantly busy. I am going to address that in here and find out what it will take to get him in here.

HALEY: Can you find out who decides when the therapy is over?

This question is asked to find out how much power the therapist has.

THERAPIST: For them or for me?

HALEY: For them. There must be a court limit of some kind.

THERAPIST: I decide.

HALEY: You decide, and then the court goes by what you say?

THERAPIST: Exactly. A probation officer evidently has 500 cases that he's just ready to close. He will base his action upon my recommendation. And I do have the power, if they don't show up or are not compliant with counseling, to report that, and the boys will go straight to juvenile hall.

HALEY: And they know that?

THERAPIST: I'm not sure.

HALEY: I think at some point you ought to say you have a problem. That you have so much responsibility in this situation and that you decide what happens to them and say you want to be absolutely fair. That is, you could put it like it's a problem of yours, which it is.

THERAPIST: Yes. It is.

HALEY: Often, when families like this come in, they don't have any idea what they are here for, the details of the situation, who has power over what. So it is best to clarify that.

THERAPIST: OK.

HALEY: I would like you to do the therapy as you would normally do it. Don't try to do what you think I would want you to do until I tell you what to do.

Haley's direction to the therapist intended to provide the steps to a clear solution of the case and establish who has the power and authority in the case, and who needs to be present. It is more in line with cultural expectations than an approach stressing inner processes.

THE GROUP OBSERVES THE FIRST INTERVIEW

The supervision is "live" with the trainees watching behind a one-way mirror and taking turns going in to do therapy. Suggestions from the supervisor to the therapist are sent to a computer monitor in the therapy room. The therapist can see the messages sent on the monitor but the clients cannot.

THERAPIST: So after you nailed him, you went down and then you jumped in and you kicked him in the mouth?
So which one actually knocked out the tooth?
Now, what is going on with your case? Why are you guys here?

This interview focused on defining the problem. The mother came with the two boys and the father did not appear. Both the mother and the boys were quiet, responding only when spoken to. The boys spoke little and sat with their heads down. This reluctance to talk is often what happens in compulsory therapy. Cultural reasons for their behavior of not making eye contact and not talking except when spoken to reveals the discomfort of discussing problems outside of the family and the shame that their behavior has caused the family. The family members behave as if they don't want to be there. It is important to explore hierarchy in the family, particularly when there is violence. The following suggestions explore hierarchy.

Computer Suggestion: Ask the boys about the mother's rules.

THERAPIST: What are the rules in your family? What do you think about them?

We learned that the boys have a strict curfew at dusk.

Computer Suggestion: Since he (older brother) is the oldest, he can take charge of the younger ones.

THERAPIST: And what about the dad coming in here? What's the possibility of getting him in here? Because I want to get his perspective on this too.

Computer Suggestion: Mother needs more compliments. (Mother has seven boys and needs support)

DISCUSSING THE FIRST INTERVIEW

HALEY: Whenever you have an opportunity, you should compliment the mother.

THERAPIST: Just keep praising?

HALEY: Because you have to find something that they did well. But you can see her change. See, she doesn't know why she is here, what it's for. Is it to show she's a bad mother? Is it to show she's really mistreated her children? So, you counter that with a compliment about being a single mother with so many kids. It changes everything and her attitude toward you. You know another way to put it—if you want them to come up with something—is to say that "there are problems that you can solve and there are problems you find you can't solve, and my job is to help you with the problems you can't solve." So you eliminate the day-to-day living problems.

TRAINEE: Oh. That's a good thing to remember.

HALEY: But I thought that went well.

THERAPIST: It was so easy. [She refers to suggestions on the computer from the supervisor.] It was so easy to get ideas and directives as to what to do. I just glanced over, and I tried to read fast so I didn't look like I was staring.

HALEY: It requires me to make a very short sentence.
Who would have done the interview differently?

THERAPIST: We've got to get Dad in here next time to find out (being if he's daddy's boy) how the son's going to react when Dad comes into the room. Then see what happens.

HALEY: That's why I think it would be good to have everybody.

THERAPIST: Yeah. I was getting there, and I am glad that you put that on there. Because I did—I was thinking, well, will I want to try to fit eight people in this room?

HALEY: You were asking the group something?

THERAPIST: I was concerned where to go from here. I'm going to see what they bring back next week. See if they think about what I talked about and come back with a problem or come back with something they want to work on and use this time for it.

HALEY: What was the plan when you went in? We should have discussed making a hierarchy if we knew these kids and knew the problems. But without that you can only probe and begin to get it formulated as the interview goes on—which is, I think, difficult for families like this, who just want to be instructed what to do and where to go. So they don't like to spend their time improvising. But you have to improvise if you don't know for sure where you are going with them.

The cultural expectations of this family are congruent with the strategic approach of giving directives and not philosophizing.

THERAPIST: Well, give me a plan then.

TRAINEE ONE: Yeah. You did a great job.

TRAINEE TWO: I thought you did very well.

TRAINEE THREE: We were amazed at how well you were able to use every single suggestion.

TRAINEE FOUR: Good rapport.

TRAINEE FIVE: You looked relaxed. You used humor. I like that.

THERAPIST: I just tried to forget that everybody was here and just act like it [mirror] wasn't there.

HALEY: But it was interesting to me that several times I started to call you and you had already begun to do the things I had in mind. I thought that went well. And I think if you bring them all together, that's the most therapeutic thing you could do to solve this particular crime because you are going to have seven boys and a father and a mother.
  Because, after the big session, if it goes well and they are cheerful. . . .

THERAPIST: They think they're mandated for 10 sessions, and I said I had the power to make this shorter, and we can address some problems. I hope to have lured them in with this.

HALEY: Let's put the other eight sessions in the bank, and if you get in trouble, you got to come back to the bank. Then say I'll call you in 8 weeks, 10 weeks, or whatever is left and make sure everything is OK. So they know you are in the picture and you are a positive force in the picture. Well, we are running into the next case. Congratulations.

THERAPIST: Great. Thanks, everyone.

TRAINEE: Good job.

SECOND INTERVIEW—EXPECTING FATHER

THERAPIST: I'm going to ask him questions about how he reacted when he heard the news of the fight, what he did about it, how he thought Mom handled it. Hopefully, he feels that Mom's doing a good job and get some strokes for her out of that and also try to reinforce his role as Dad in this situation.

OBSERVING THE SECOND INTERVIEW

The mother focused on the family rules for the two boys. The father did not appear and was said to be working.

Computer Suggestion: Ask the mother if she is worried about the boys doing it again.

THERAPIST: So you are worried about will they do it again?

Computer Suggestion: Ask the boys what they would do if a boy insults them racially again?

THERAPIST: I would like to see Dad alone. What would happen if they insult you racially again?

CLIENT (boy): You have to struggle out there. It's just, you do what you've got to do.

THERAPIST TO MOTHER: Is it the first for them?

Haley tells the therapist to come behind the mirror. They decide to see the mother alone and give her a positive progress report.

DISCUSSING THE SECOND INTERVIEW

THERAPIST: I'm not picking up a problem.

HALEY: There's not any strange behavior there?

THERAPIST: I was looking for some kind of a glitch somewhere in what they were answering or something that I can pick on, and the only thing I got so far is that I still have to test Dad out.

HALEY: You know when I was editor of *Family Process,* I got a Scandinavian paper on the sailor's life. He goes out for 6 months and then he comes back and he wants to take over the family and the wife has got it organized her way. And they get in real battles, and it was a great relief for him to go back to sea again.

THERAPIST: And that's why I was trying to ask if there was any of that in there. Like what's the difference between when he's here versus when he's gone and when he comes back. Everybody just functions the same way.

TRAINEE THREE: It sounds like culturally they just adhere to the hierarchies.

TRAINEE ONE: Dad comes home, he's the boss. He leaves, Mom's the boss. What did you think about the question asked, how will you know when they're cured?

THERAPIST: Yeah. That was good. It gave them a destination.

HALEY: What it is, is a metaphor that people begin to rally around, which keeps you focused on the problem. That's just what you want. I think you would only go into her parenting if there was some evidence that that was related to these kids going wild. There didn't seem to be anything like that.

THERAPIST: I'm not finding that. They have good grades. They seem very respectful. They are not fighting amongst themselves.

HALEY: You are doing very well to fill the time. (*Everybody laughs.*)

THERAPIST: I did appreciate all the suggestions on the computer. I felt like I had to fill 45 minutes worth of time.

HALEY: I think a lot of compulsory therapy cases are like that. If they have to see you and at the time you solve the problem, and you have to go on simply because there have to be 10 sessions and what do you do.

THERAPIST: Call in a colleague.

Those are two big boys. And from what it sounds like, the ones who are even younger are just the same size.

HALEY: I think they get respect on the field.

THERAPIST: I think so.

TRAINEE: Did you know what was said that ticked them off—exactly what was said?

TRAINEE: The racial slur was something they heard second-hand. If you remember, somebody else told them that this guy had made some racial remarks and was talking about his mother, and then they ran into this guy with his friends and some words were exchanged and then they left. Then later on they came back and, obviously, were afraid that something was going to happen and reacted.

THERAPIST: My whole sense of the kids is that they are very warm and open and friendly. I didn't get the sense that they have a violent streak through them. I just didn't get that.

HALEY: Usually, you can feel it in the room if they do. They let you know it, is what they do. If you see just the dad, you are dealing with him man to man about raising kids, particularly, when he is out of town so much. If you see him with the two boys, then you get an idea of his authority with the two boys as well as the mother does.

THERAPIST: I would like to get them all together. I would like to bring them all here and then, as the session goes on, if I need to, ask the boys to leave and him to stay, and go from there.

HALEY: Well, you got the kids out very nicely here. I thought there was no issue about it at all.

THERAPIST: Just have it be the three boys?

HALEY: I'm leaning toward just the men.

THERAPIST: And have the mom stay out of it.

HALEY: I think the mother can stay out of it. He has a relationship with those boys independent of her, I'm sure. And if you see her with him, they will just parent together. You know this is a man thing. This is a man thing when you hit somebody and knock them out.

THERAPIST: Ask him how he feels about that? He's proud.

HALEY: But it could be done with the father alone.

THERAPIST: I would like to do the same thing that I did here where we have it both ways—see the interaction that goes on between the three of them, see the hierarchy that's established, see how they react to Dad's response and how Dad responds to them and then maybe talk to Dad alone afterward. Let's make Dad's presence contingent on their treatment to satisfy the court.

HALEY: You might as well take advantage of compulsory therapy.

THIRD INTERVIEW—EXPECTING FATHER

HALEY: There are a lot of guys overseas who are away that much and their kids aren't beating people up.
    And if they all show?

THERAPIST: I don't know.

HALEY: You could see them in parts or you could see them all together. You know one thing you might do, if they all show, is see them all together and then decide whether you want to talk to the father alone or not or the father and the mother alone. Because what they say about the kids they might not say with the kids there.
    To get some idea of what conflict there is between mother and father, it's often helpful to see them without the kids. You're trying to pack a lot into a very brief therapy on a case where your problem can be

that you find them having difficulty with life like in being away so much when that isn't the issue really, unless it's related to the violence in some way.

If it's a special problem with them (his being away), in this sense, that there may be a way that he could be on shore and his wife would like him to and he would rather not, then you are into an issue of conflict, which may or may not be related to the boys.

The father did not appear at the third interview. At this point it was becoming evident that his presence was going to be necessary. He appeared to be important in the family, who had trouble focusing upon the boys' problem without the father there. The therapist came behind the mirror to discuss a plan.

OBSERVING THE THIRD INTERVIEW

HALEY: Apparently, what you would like to do is make it clear that you can't close the case until you see the father.

THERAPIST: OK. So this might be a short session.

He concluded that he could not advise the court about the case without the father present. Mother told him to personally telephone the father, which he had not done, and he did so. The father came in at the next interview. In the training group there were differences of opinion about whether the boys would be violent again. It wasn't clear there were ethnic issues until the father came in.

DISCUSSING THE THIRD INTERVIEW

TRAINEE: The son was a serious clam when it came to saying anything about Dad.

HALEY: He sure was.

TRAINEE: We were trying to figure something out. Oh, sure, Dad probably came down on his sons but they were afraid they may get in trouble if they said that Dad whipped me, Dad threw me into a wall or something. I don't know.

TRAINEE: My husband would. My husband would say you know that the door wouldn't mean a damn.

TRAINEE: They're not going to say.

THERAPIST: So, it's a cultural thing?

TRAINEE: It's a cultural thing. Dad probably said, Next time this happens you are going to have to deal with me. Right now, your mom is going to handle it, but next time you are going to have to deal with me. And if their Dad has to come down here to deal with this, these guys are in big trouble. But that's why he needs to come here.

THERAPIST: I've got his phone number, so I am going to call him at work. I don't know, maybe there was deception used by me saying I can't close the case up until I see Dad, but in the end I think that really is true.

HALEY: That's clinically good.

THERAPIST: I don't feel like it was a deception because I do now want to see Dad before I close this case.

THERAPIST: We learned that he [the victim] killed a dog and threw it in the back of a truck, and had cans of gasoline sitting outside the kid's house. The dog's owner pressed charges against the kid that the clients beat up and now the victim is in jail.

TRAINEE: It's been a heck of a year for the victim.

TRAINEE: I noticed from Mom right away that you're not picking up that there is remorsefulness. I think Mom sees this as, you know, I've got good kids, we're a good family, here's this horrendous family over here and this was kind of a mistake.

At this point the family found out the boy the sons hit was going to jail for another crime. The group was not in agreement about how to handle the clients. If provoked by road rage or insults, one of these boys might react with violence again. The group was perplexed that this was the only time the boys said they were out after dark, thus breaking their family-instituted curfew of 6 P.M. They also were surprised that the boys had a beeper and were not driving.

TRAINEE FOUR: But the point I'm trying to make is let's generalize it to any situation where they're out in public and somebody casts a glance at them they feel is dirty or disrespectful. When are they going to be able have some internal control to walk away from that or ignore or not acknowledge it?

THERAPIST: Well, they're saying that this experience has given them that internal control.

HALEY: But they are also saying this is the first time it's happened. They haven't been pulled in before on this.

TRAINEE: I'm curious. What do you think about that beeper? These are kids that aren't driving.

TRAINEE: They can't go out after six.

HALEY: I suggest you find out if Father was embarrassed by what they did. We got a little information about it but did not learn much about how Father really reacted to this whole thing.

THERAPIST: I have asked in every session how Dad handled it—how he reacted and what he did.

TRAINEE: Maybe you can ask Dad.

THERAPIST: That's what I've got to do. I've got to ask Dad because I'm not going to get it out of them.

THERAPIST: Start with all four of them again?

HALEY: I would start with all four of them. Sure, and speak to the father first.

THERAPIST: OK.

HALEY: The more you listen to the father, the more power he has. So there is kind of a laying on of hands of power. If you pay more attention to the father than you do the mother, the father will rise in status. So it's not just gathering information. It's a structure in which you are laying hands on. If the father says, I'm just never here, how can I handle these problems when I am away so much, then I would begin to shift and have him support mother handling this instead of him handling this. But it doesn't sound like these boys beat somebody up in relation to the family. You have to make it clear whether you are an agent of the court or the family or both on issues such as what would you reveal and what wouldn't you reveal. And the issues are pretty complex when it's a court-ordered client.

THERAPIST: I told them that the only information that I would give back to the court (or back to the probation officer) was whether they were compliant or not.

HALEY: The clientele should never decide who comes in. You should decide. And some people make a big issue, if the guy doesn't show up they won't see the family. That's it. And other times you will see one in the family and not the rest of them. So you have to have the flexibility.

HALEY: I think the mother will bring him in. Once she saw she had to, she began to activate. . . . Maybe after this terminates, we should make a bet and do a 6-month follow-up if they get into trouble or not. And people have to put their money on the line. (*Everybody laughs.*)

One trainee thought that the boys would get violent again. The others did not.

OBSERVING THE FOURTH INTERVIEW
—FATHER ARRIVES

The relationship of the father and the boys was focused upon as it had been with mother and the boys. It had not been clear there were ethnic structures in the family until this point. The father was seen alone at the end of the family session. Many of the possible explanations of the training group differed when cultural issues appeared in view. Rather than the father being irresponsible for not coming to therapy, he proved to be the authority in the home, with the wife secondary. He said he was deliberately not being involved with the court, stepping aside so his sons would feel the power of the law. He wanted them to feel fear and not be violent again.

Rather than being an abusive father whom the boys feared, he was embarrassed and hurt over the incident. When alone with the therapist he wept. The shame of the boys' act reflected on the whole family, and the father said his name was not respected. Rather than supporting the violence by defending their honor, he had always taught them to walk away from gang-banging and cursing. The rules in the family proved to be strict. He and his wife required the boys to be in at dark and do their homework. The father even wanted to apologize to the father in the other family, but he learned the boy who was the victim was now in jail on another charge.

The father arranged not to travel in the next 2 years so that he would be home with the boys. He expressed his view of what happened by saying, "There is no such thing as a small wrong or a big wrong. Anything that will reflect on the name of my grandfather is embarrassing. I want the boys to grow up to be proud of themselves." (The therapist brought in the whole family after seeing the father alone.)

THERAPIST: Basically, what we have talked about so far is to explain to Dad what this whole get-up was about, what my position is with the court . . . what his reaction was to the incident and how he felt about it and so forth from there. Does that about summarize things? Did I leave anything out?

DAD: No.

DISCUSSING THE FOURTH INTERVIEW

HALEY: Would any of you have handled this differently?

TRAINEE: No.

HALEY: It's one of the cases that might or might not be a case.

THERAPIST: That's true.

THERAPIST: I don't think it was a case [because the family was solving the problems themselves]. (*Everybody laughs.*)

THERAPIST: That was the impression I got. I don't think it was a case.

TRAINEE: I thought you handled it real well.

TRAINEE: So in these three solid sessions you confirmed your hypothesis.

THERAPIST: Yeah.

HALEY: The family could have been messed up in this case. It could have been mishandled and got father mad or they could have refused to come in to sessions and then the court would get down on them, which would escalate those problems.

THERAPIST: And that would have been too bad.

Follow-up

Different from most cases where violence needs to be punished, this case shows that family participation is necessary before coming to conclusions. Also, the family therapist was given the power in this case to make decisions, which is often not the situation, as seen in chapters 5 and 8, in which a number of professionals raise coalition problems. The court dismissed the case when the therapist reported, and in a 6-month follow-up there had been no further violence. If the father had been treated as if he were irresponsible, and the case had been mishandled, it could have been a misfortune to this respectable family. The court personnel were cooperative, which was fortunate particularly in this case.

7

Paradox and Play with Children

The Boy Who Can't Stop Fighting

M others often use paradox without its being called that. When a child is difficult, sometimes mother asks him to be difficult. This can encourage the child to behave. Parents also like the phrase "See if I care" when they do care. Although paradox is found in natural communication, paradox as a therapy technique requires skill. Paradox is also built upon play. In the case example of an African-American family, the playful language patterns of jiving and rap are compatible with the paradoxical directives employed. The family interpreted the paradox as play rather than trickery or manipulation as some colleagues might.

A therapist in training brought in a family for a consultation because of a lack of improvement after a year of individual therapy of one of the sons. In the family were 9-year-old twins, a 13-year-old boy, mother, and stepfather. The therapist hoped a brief consultation with the supervisor and the training group would give the therapy a new start. The case proved to be more difficult than expected; therefore, the supervisor suggested the situation be treated as a new presenting problem instead of a consultation.

The first step in starting a case in this approach is to formulate a presenting problem. The problem should have certain characteristics. It should focus on the present, not the past. It should clarify which colleagues and members of the family are involved. It should involve what interventions had been previously tried.

The supervisor, Jay Haley, asked the therapist, "What is the problem you would like to solve?"

The therapist says it is a boy who cannot stop fighting. He cries and he wants to stop but can't seem to stop. He's driven. We have had him in therapy for a long time.

There are several issues that can make the problem more difficult to solve. One is the way the therapist in training presents the problem as a boy who is helpless and hopeless. A symptom is defined as something the person cannot help. The supervisor would like to lighten the mood and point out that the boy might be capable of something positive.

THERAPIST: You know he doesn't stay in school very long. He is always getting bumped out of schools. So he is a little African-American kid and he has a twin brother who doesn't fight, but they watch wrestling pretty much around the clock. We have taken him out of the last school and put him in a class where there is a bunch of other kids just like him, and they are understaffed. They have one teacher to eight of these wild kids, and they pounce on the teacher. So they have been through eight teachers in this class this year. They leave it quickly, the class is so unruly. And they don't have enough funds, I guess, to have enough aides to handle the class. But we thought that changing schools would solve the problem and it hasn't. He continues to get suspended. His mother works, and he is home alone when he is suspended. He is a very nice kind of depressed kid. We put him on antidepressants, and that did not seem to work, so we were looking at doing Ritalin. He is not ADHD but Ritalin has been shown to help reduce aggression. And we have done so much else, and it's not working. I had the whole family in once. There are the two twins, an older brother, and a stepfather who sleeps all day. They didn't like talking about personal business in therapy at all. But Mom wants to get them all together and try the family route again. Mom works fulltime, stepdad works in the mornings. He only has one arm. She describes him as a dependent personality. He doesn't drive. She takes care of him.

In the last session I said to the boy, "Are we expecting too much from you? What's going on inside? Are you incapable of not doing this?" And again he started to cry, and he said, "I can't help it." So I don't know what to do. He is obsessed with it. He says that he sits in his desk, and if somebody bumps him or trips him, for the next several minutes he visualizes the fight that he could get in with them. He works it all out in his head. And I said, "Then do you act on it?" He said, "No, not always." And I said, "Does it come out the way you imagined?" He loves it, and then he goes home and watches wrestling. And he's not a mean, vicious kid. He's not vindictive. I mean, he's vindictive, but he's a very gentle soul when you see him. He cries and he's a very gentle. His father died when he was 2, and he had lots of issues around that—not really knowing who Dad was and not feeling connected to the stepfather. Dad was murdered, I think. The males in this family die by the age of 25 for the most part. Part of the issues when he came in very depressed was, "It doesn't matter, I'm not going to live anyway."

The supervisor began to suspect that the therapist lacked empathy for the stepfather and told the therapist that it must be hard to drive a car with one arm. The stepfather did not come again after one interview.

Integrating a peripheral stepfather is one of the techniques of family therapy dating from the 1950s. The presence of a stepfather brings the possibility of an "integration of a stepfather technique." This can be a new stepfather or one in the family for years. In this case it has been 8 years. If the stepfather is inadequate in some way, he might be focused upon for improvement along with the problem person. In this case he is depressed and handicapped. The fact that mother talks about throwing him out makes his presence more relevant; something might be done to improve him as well as the son. Since he would not come in after the first interview, empowering the African-American stepfather at a distance involved getting him to do tasks with the boys and getting the family to show him more respect. This special treatment could shift his low position in the family hierarchy. At this point there were two strategic approaches that might be used. One was to use the increased responsibilities given to the stepfather, and the second was to use paradox to stop the boy's fighting. The stepfather has also been negatively influenced by the murders of men in the family.

HALEY: What is your hypothesis?

This question offers the group the opportunity to focus the therapy. In the therapist's hypothesis, the boy's anger was seen as a reflection of the family's need for revenge for having been done wrong by society, and the revenge was expressed by the son's aggression.

HALEY: I don't care for the hypothesis that he is expressing the anger of the family toward the world. I wouldn't know where to go with that. I would assume that he is helping somebody by the misbehavior, and the person who he's helping should be the one who helps him get over it. But anyhow, it sounds to me like he's very involved with his mother and that he helps his mother by giving her something to think about, besides her misery, that you can then work with. A therapist should be able to make her husband help her. I am not saying that this is true. It's a hypothesis, a map that covers the territory. There needs to be a map for this situation that is consistent in planning the therapy. The hypothesis is not necessarily true, but it gives you a map to have a helpful way to think.

The therapist is unfamiliar with the hypothesis that people can develop problems to protect one another.

HALEY: The twin behaves himself, right?

THERAPIST: The twin holds it together at school. They are in different schools. When they were in the same school, they fought with other kids—they would gang up on other kids. And she moved them out of there into another home of her sister's, which they hate. It's an all-white neighborhood. She was worried that he was going to get killed by somebody's older brother. You know, from beating up on these little kids at school all the time. And that is a real danger.

This is a unique way that older brothers protect the younger ones, by making peace with the victim's family. At this point one trainee brought up that there is a strong hierarchy in the African-American families that she has known. "Boy you better listen to Mommy or you are going to get it." You know?

HALEY: There has to be a hierarchy.

In relation to parenting, the correct hierarchy should obviously be stepfather, mother, 13-year-old, and twins. Symptoms in a family express problems of hierarchy, and twins complicate the problem. Twins are a standard problem.

THERAPIST: (*She continues presenting interventions already tried.*) And so we resurrected this dead uncle and made him kind of a guardian angel along with Dad. You know, we had all these dead relatives helping, and then he found out that this uncle had been gay. He just lost it, and then he was really upset. But the other twin is larger, he is healthier looking, he was born second, and they were both premature. So he just doesn't have the impulse-control problem that his brother has.

HALEY: I would also think that if he fights like that, he should be in a karate class: he should be in a disciplined place where he can fight. If the mother would go along with that.

It often happens that you propose an intervention only to find out that it had been tried and failed.

THERAPIST: We tried that. He didn't like the structure. Mom said that he just wasn't able to keep up with the different moves, so he dropped out.

HALEY: Everybody behaves like he's serving a function of some kind.

THERAPIST: Right, and that is serving a function. It's keeping them from having to deal with their stuff. It is a protection function.

The therapist begins to change her hypothesis, accepting a protective function. The boy can express a range from temper tantrums to weeping. This range is admired by the therapist. Part of the problem is the improvement doesn't stabilize.

Integrating the Stepfather by Giving Him Authority

In this case the stepfather had never been integrated, and the therapist had neglected the integration up to this point.

HALEY: Usually, what it sounds like, is a stepfather that never got integrated into the family.

THERAPIST: OK.

HALEY: He is on the perimeter of the family, and one of the ways we usually integrate him is by putting him in charge of something and having Mother support him instead of negating him. I think your task is to introduce him as a biological father, really—get him to act that way. But whether you could with this man, I don't know. I wouldn't hesitate about it, if Mother was not just about to kick him out. It doesn't sound like you can integrate him in. But he should be either in or out.

THERAPIST: I know. Yeah, and I was going to take her aside before the session and find out the status on that, because I did try to do that at the beginning. The first time I finally got him in, I got him in for one session, and he never came back. I tried to get him to take Marcus fishing since the stepfather loved to fish.

TRAINEE TWO: What does the stepfather do with the other kids that he is not doing with this boy? I mean, do they get along?

THERAPIST: Well, Mother says that they do get along and that the other boys have accepted him and look to him as Dad.

HALEY: Apparently, the mother hasn't quite accepted him in some area.

THERAPIST: Well, I think that is true.

HALEY: And therefore the boy represents that relationship of the parents because they are neither together nor not together?

Assigning the Stepfather a Task to Take the Boys to a Wrestling Match Functions to Empower Him

Haley asks if there is a wrestling bout held in this area.

TRAINEE: You mean like the wrestling that he watches? They just had a big convention.

THERAPIST: It feels like an addiction—I work with drug and alcohol—and he cries and has remorse and he cannot control his thoughts and he thinks about it all the time. I look at him and say, "You need rehab, wrestling rehab." So many of the kids I work with who have violent problems are wrestling fanatics. It's a very bad thing for these boys.

HALEY: It's a very exciting thing if they go see it. But you need something for the stepfather to do that gives him some interest and authority in the home.

THERAPIST: That's if he stays.

In the search for something positive in a problem person, some ability or talent or helpful behavior is useful. In this case what the boy loves is wrestling. The adults don't approve.

Planning the Order the Family Members Are Seen

HALEY: So when the family arrives what are you going to do?

THERAPIST: I don't know. What should I do?

HALEY: I would start with the mother first.

THERAPIST: OK. I will start with Mom first and ask her the status of Dad.

HALEY: Then one of the problems is if she is accepting him or not.

THERAPIST: She probably has some reason why she couldn't make the decision right then.

HALEY: And you go to get the others, "Come out here for a few minutes and we can discuss what you learned."

THERAPIST: OK, what was I going to do? I was to push on the boys to find out what they think about what's going on with the problem boy, and what have they done about it.

HALEY: I would start with what changes do they want as a family.

A summary of the interventions already tried:

1. Move to another neighborhood.
2. Suspend the fighter from school and place him in a special school.
3. Provide individual therapy, with the mother in the interview at times.
4. Get them to imagine resurrecting dead relatives.
5. Place the boy in a karate class.
6. Object to boys' watching wrestling.
7. Give the boy various medications.

A Most Ingenious Paradox Is Proposed

HALEY: One possibility would be to get the twin who is behaving himself to stop behaving himself and take the place of his brother to see if he can get in a fight and be hostile. You can get them talking about what he does and would this other twin do. I mean, Twin A shouldn't carry the load. The other guy should carry some of it. So could he begin to misbehave the way his brother does. They are passing it back and forth. Or you may, if you decide to—I don't know the kids involved—one of the others might replace the fighting boy.

THERAPIST: The well-functioning 13-year-old, I would like to see him do something here.

HALEY: Well, then, you can get him to take over. Keep in mind, there is more here than just fighting and getting Mother upset; he's bringing her into therapy.

THERAPIST: He threatens her job, her livelihood.

The family arrives for the first live supervised session but without the stepfather. The lights behind the mirror are turned out and the trainees scurry around to find a seat to see the family through the one-way mirror. Will their fellow student be able to carry out the therapy plan? They all feel the tension of the live supervision. Haley delivers his suggestions to the therapist in the room with the family by computer to a monitor that the therapist can see but clients cannot. The agreement is that the therapist will follow the suggestions of the supervisor. If they have a conflict, the therapist comes out and discusses it. The therapist begins by seeing the mother alone to find out if she wishes to continue the marriage. The mother says she feels sorry for the stepfather as her reason for staying with him. The supervisor recognizes that as a complex situation because the marriage is still undecided, but the mother is not about to separate at this time.

OBSERVING THE FIRST INTERVIEW

THERAPIST: So I guess I wanted to ask, if you wanted me to pull Father into things? I think he's kind of pivotal in what's going on. If you are going to have him around, are you interested in couple's counseling?

HALEY: (*to group behind mirror*) I would like him to get more involved in what's going on, but I don't want to pull something in that unstabilizes the situation.

Computer Suggestion: How will the kids react if he leaves?

THERAPIST: Do you know how you are feeling about it? Do you think you are having a hard time because you feel bad for him?
　　　You know we have been doing this stuff for a long time. We need to do something different.

The twins and older brother are brought in. The stepfather did not come. The plan was to assist Mother so that if her life improves, the boys will behave better.

Computer Suggestion: Ask what you would like the husband to do with the boys?

THERAPIST: (*to boys*) Here we are. Why are we here today?
The boys are quiet.
THERAPIST: This is a pretty strong family.

Computer Suggestion: Who is in charge of the chores?
The boys don't answer

Presentation of the Paradox to the Family

Computer Suggestion: Some twins can take turns in being bad. Maybe the other brother can have a bad week next week.

MARCUS: He doesn't know how. He's a sissy most of the time.
THERAPIST: You have to be the fighter. I think it's time for you to give it up. What would happen if you traded places with him [twin] and he can have a bad week next week? Would that help you?
MARCUS: No.
THERAPIST: No?

MARCUS: You don't know how to be bad.

The bad twin says that he is embarrassed because older brother takes a beaten boy to the boy's home and apologizes to the family for the twin's hitting the victim. This is what a father might do. An older brother here replaces stepfather in the hierarchy.

THERAPIST: (*to older brother*) Can he show you how to be bad? Can you practice at being bad this week?

Computer Suggestion: Ask mother what one of them can do bad.

The climate in the room changes from silence to playful laughter with everyone talking together.

THERAPIST: I think it's time for you to give it up. I think your brother can be bad. What does your brother think about you?

Computer Suggestion: Can his brother do this bad act with the microphone?

In response to the suggestion that someone do a bad act, the good twin was mad and turned off the microphone. The fighter would not let the good boy turn off the microphone. He stood up to take over and be bad at the microphone.

THERAPIST: (*to older brother*) Can he show you how to be bad?
ELDER BROTHER: No.
THERAPIST: He'll have to show you because you don't know. What would you have to do to get him to be bad?
    You wouldn't know how? Which one was the most bad with the microphone? (*The boys argue about fooling with the mike.*)
MARCUS: Because I touched the mike.

Computer Suggestion: Can you practice at being bad this week?

THERAPIST (*to Marcus*): Do you usually have to teach him [older brother] how? Could you [older brother] practice being bad? What would you have to do to get him to be bad?

Computer Suggestion: It's not fair for one person to be bad. They need to take turns.

Computer Suggstion: Your older brother needs the practice.

Computer Suggestion: Ask mother what the agreement is.

For hierarchical reasons, Mother should be in charge of the children in general and of this paradox.

THERAPIST: But in this family somebody has to be bad, so you know what? He [twin] is going to be bad for the next week and you are giving that up for one week. And then guess what? He's [eldest] going to be it.

Computer Suggestion: Make sure mother is in charge.

THERAPIST: Mom, who is in charge?

MOM: Marcus is in charge. (*They all laugh.*) I'm in charge. Wouldn't it be better if all of you guys were good. (*Older brother covers his face with a handkerchief.*)

MARCUS: I don't know.

THERAPIST: The other twin has to be bad for a week. Then the oldest is to be bad for one week. You'll have to teach him. (*The eldest boy stands up and pretends to pull down his pants.*) So you'll report to me next week how things went, Mom. You're in charge. You guys really care about each other. You are a very close family. Thank you guys for coming.

Computer Suggestion: If the bad boy is good, he gets punished this week.

If he is a bad boy being good, he will be punished for not doing what he should, which means he will be punished for being good.

DISCUSSING THE FIRST INTERVIEW

When the therapist came back behind the mirror for a debriefing, she remarked that she was a little overwhelmed and had never worked like this before. She said, "I didn't know where I was or what I was doing." However, she began to think in terms of systems in which "someone in this family has to be bad." After the supervisor expressed regret that the stepfather was not mentioned sooner, the supervisor began pointing out reactions to the paradox.

Paradox and Play

HALEY: Did you think it was the boy saying that he would have to be bad and then he went over to the microphone—do you think that was related—that that was a bad act he was demonstrating?

Haley began alluding to the cultural response to this paradox that the family accepted it as a game.

HALEY: You know, usually when you do this, you have a mother who gets indignant saying, "You mean you want my child to be bad." Usually, you get indignant parents. You mean you are telling my kid to fight again when he can't stop fighting? I thought she would get indignant and say, He's getting in enough trouble and you don't want to make more. She got right in the spirit of it. I think it's partly your manner. You were cheerful about it and she picked that up.

THERAPIST: She even volunteered to be bad. Well, then she confessed. Did you hear the confession? She said, "I didn't tell you what I did to a coworker today." And I went, "What!" I said, "So we are all bad in this family." I said, "Raise your hand anybody who is bad in this family" and they all did.

HALEY: They are willing to play—playing in the sense of a metaphor. One of the studies of Gregory Bateson showed that animals have to differentiate between the bite of combat and a bite of play, and every once in a while they don't differentiate, and they bite each other and get into a battle. But Bateson was interested in the fact that you have to be able to communicate at two levels in order to play—communicate about communication.

And I think kids just have to learn that. They learn how to establish a relationship and then begin to play within the relationship. In this case, apparently Marcus had not learned that. But often you can have kids pass the symptom, and what that does is thin it out. This implies if you can encourage the symptom in a different context, you can do away with it. It becomes a minor symptom when they have to do it and they must do it at a certain time. It works out a hierarchy among the family members, too. Twins are special because they are supposedly equal and have more difficulty establishing a hierarchy. The paradox forced an inequality. One had to instruct the other in how to be bad.

Summary of Interventions

1. Interview the whole family, not just the individuals.
2. Integrate stepfather into the family by giving him some authority.

3. Get stepfather to take the boys to a wrestling match, a live one, which is their favorite show on TV. Previous therapists opposed such wrestling.
4. Rather than resurrect father and uncles, Marcus should visit the grave and acknowledge them gone.
5. Propose a paradox to let the boys take turns being bad. This paradox requires a bad boy, a good boy, and a peacemaker with authority.

The good boy is asked by the therapist to do something bad because the bad boy is overloaded with being bad. The good boy goes and fools with the microphone being bad, and so he is being good as he should. When the bad boy sees the good boy being bad, he also goes and fools with the microphone to be bad, not wanting the good boy to be bad alone, since he, the bad boy, is accustomed to being bad. So the bad boy is not obeying. The good boy is obeying by being bad. If the good boy is being good, he will be punished for not doing what he should, which means he will be punished for being good. This is a type A paradox. A type B paradox is when the therapist tells the client, "Disobey me." He disobeys whether he obeys or not. Type C paradox is when the therapist asks the client to resist when the client is already doing so. In strategic therapy, you have to plan the interview but anticipate cancellations for unclear reasons.

The family did not arrive for the second family interview; however, the supervisor and the group made a plan. There were two main issues. The first was to integrate the stepfather and the second was to find out whether the paradox was carried out. Haley suggested that the therapist see the stepfather alone. Haley said to the trainees, "If you give him special attention, he has some chance of getting authority in the family. You should treat him as a biological father rather than a stepfather and inform him of what was discussed in the previous week." A strategic therapist would be expected to deal with his having only one arm as well. Haley said, "You are trying to empower the parents to stop the way they are handling the boys when they are divided almost to the point of separation."

Another implied paradox is that the mother wants the husband to take charge, but if he does, she is in charge of him taking charge. Haley instructed the therapist to be firm with the father.

HALEY: You know, if you think about how to handle him, if he complains to you, you could say that it is really important now not that you complain, but that you do something, because the boy is really getting hurt out there and is getting bigger.

HALEY: And get the boy to be bad and the other boy to be good. You might tell the father that that's been part of what was planned so he isn't just bewildered by it.

The other issue brought out in this plan is *how to follow up a paradoxical directive.*

HALEY: When you bring him in, you've got to say to the boy, "Did you do what you were supposed to do?"

TRAINEE: What happens when he says no?

HALEY: Then you say how can this be possible? I am very disappointed in you. And then you say to the brother who was supposed to be bad—if you would have been bad enough, he would have been able to be good enough, and blame him for not being bad enough. You ought to play with this. Ultimately, you might blame the mother and say perhaps she could have done something about this.

HALEY: And you can have them all explain whether they should be taking turns on being bad.

TRAINEE: And so what if somebody has to be bad. . . .

HALEY: Somebody has to suffer by being bad. But I am trying to figure how to phrase it for them. It started last week. One of the ways, after you see the whole group, is to ask what happened this week or did it work this week and see if they even remember.

The supervision parallels the playfulness of the paradox.

HALEY: Anybody want to bet whether the boy was good this week?

There was a difference of opinion in the group. Whether or not they followed the paradox, they followed the paradox. If they did not follow it, they were bad anyway. Figure this one out.

Case Follow-up

The family did not appear for their appointment. The therapist saw the fighting boy and his mother in one final session. After that, they were not in therapy. The brothers did not successfully trade places, but they talked and giggled about it for some time that week, as if they had discovered play and not combat. They began to recognize that they encouraged one another to escalate the violence. The fistfighting was reduced and became more verbal than physical. Mom said that things were better. Stepfather was more integrated into the family and, as was suggested, took the boys to a wrestling match. The boys' relationship with Dad improved, and they treated him with more respect. The mother focused on her career, where she was promoted.

African-American Language, Play, and Paradox

This case illustrates the cultural compatibility of African-American language patterns and the paradoxical directive employed. Jiving is a form of slang that has various meanings, some of which are to tease, to jest, to deceive but not seriously, and to mislead playfully (*Dictionary of American Slang*). It often involves verbal skill and semantic inversion. For example, the word *up* would be replaced with *down*, similar to the changing of good for bad in the paradox. Jiving is very comfortable with paradox, as in the family illustrated. The interview showed that the family was silent and hardly spoke until the paradox was introduced. To everyone's surprise, instead of being indignant, the family found the paradox comical and played with it, including the mother. It was compatible with playful jiving, an oral ritual so commonly used in the rap generation. The paradox changed the symptom from "threat combat" to "play combat." It is an example of the strategic approach manipulating the abnormal to the normal. Another function of this paradox was to make the therapist more of an insider. Usually these verbal games are done among black males who are intimates. Introducing this paradox made the therapist less of an outsider in their system and increased her rapport. The paradox worked like semantic inversion, which may be seen in hip-hop and jiving. For example, to be down is to be "up for something." In a popular hip-hop song, "People make the world go round. / They ask me What's up? I tell 'em what's going down." Both slang and paradox relieve tension by humor and playfulness. This recalls Gregory Bateson's evolutionary perspective on the nature of play. Haley (Haley & Richeport-Haley, 1997) remarked, "Bateson was interested in animal communication hoping that there would be fundamental ideas in animal behavior that would be simpler than the complex ideas of humans. His primary interest was animals communicating about communication simulating communication. He discovered with animal play that they have to know that a message was a message in order to play, that a bite of play and not a bite of combat was a major idea." This paradox was an ordeal (see Haley, 1984). The emphasis on the fighter having to teach his good brother to fight, thus passing around the symptom, made fighting an unacceptable alternative.

REFERENCES

Dictionary of American Slang. (1995). New York: Harper Collins.

Haley, J. (1984). *Ordeal therapy: Unusual ways to change behavior.* San Francisco: Jossey Bass.

Haley, J. & Richeport-Haley, M. (1997). *Whither family therapy? A Jay Haley version* [50-minute video documentary]. Triangle Press: La Jolla, CA.

8

Mother–Daughter Incest

A Historical Note on Sex Abuse

Sigmund Freud (1959/1896) reached the conclusion that his young women patients had been sexually abused. As Freud put it, talking about the psychoanalytic method:

> Hysterical symptoms are traced to their origin, which invariably proves to be an experience in the person's sexual life well adapted to produce a painful emotional reaction. Going back into the patient's life step by step, guided always by the structural connections between symptoms, memories, and associations . . . had to realize that the same factor was at the bottom of all the cases subjected to analysis, namely, the effect of an agent that must be accepted as the specific cause of hysteria. It is indeed a memory connected with the person's sexual life, but one that presents two extremely important features. The event, the unconscious image of which the patient has retained, is a premature sexual experience with actual stimulation of the genitalia, the result of sexual abuse practiced by another person, and the period of life in which the fateful event occurs is early childhood, up to the age of eight to ten, before the child has attained sexual maturity. . . . I have been able to analyze thirteen cases of hysteria completely. . . . The experience mentioned above was not lacking in a single case; it was present either as a brutal attempt committed by an adult, or a less sudden and less repugnant seduction, having however the same result. In seven cases out of the thirteen we were dealing with a liaison between children, sexual relations between a little girl and a boy slightly older, generally her brother, who had himself been the victim of an earlier seduction.
>
> These liaisons were sometimes continued for years up to puberty, the boy repeating on the girl without alteration those practices that he himself had experienced at the hand of a servant, or governess; because of this origin they were often of a disgusting kind. In some cases there had been both assaults and an infantile liaison or repeated brutal abuse. (pp. 148–149)

125

What Freud was offering in 1896 was a family theory of neurosis. He found that in 13 cases there had been sexual abuse in childhood. Had Freud continued with this view, he would have established family therapy. He would have had to adopt the position of family therapists today, who must take into account abusers as well as mothers and fathers who have failed to protect their children. His thinking would have become triadic and would have involved not an oedipal fantasy but a real-life family behavior. With this discovery what action did Freud take? He did not have to report this activity as we do today. He did not try to stop it by calling the police. He maintained confidentiality and wrote this paper.

A short time later, however, Freud changed his mind. Apparently he decided that sexual abuse of these patients did not actually occur but was possibly a false memory, a fantasy they constructed of the world. By taking that position, Freud brought the therapy field back inside the mind of the client and away from what actually happens in the social context of the family. One of the most interesting mysteries in the history of psychotherapy is why Freud reversed himself. The issue of whether sexual abuse actually happened or was a false memory had major effects on the lives of many people. It led analysts to force clients to deny what they knew to be true. Moreover, at one time it was routine to hospitalize a daughter if she accused a parent of incest, the reasoning being that such an accusation had to be a delusion.

Abuse Issues

There is no relationship that does not have the potential for abuse. Today therapists with abuse cases carry more responsibility than traditional therapists. They have to decide who to bring into interviews and when. For example, should siblings be brought to a family session when they have not conceded they know about the abuse? Deciding when or whether to put somebody out of the home is a major intervention. Should there be confrontation about guilt? Should there be forgiveness or not? Should one bring out the details of abuse in the past if it is not happening now, or let it go? With serious abuse can therapists restrain themselves from initiating revenge rather than change? Therapists tend to think the safest action is to remove the villain from the family or take the child out to save him or her. The strategic family therapy alternative is to try, when possible, to change the family while keeping it together or, if not, to have as a goal bringing the family back together someday.

Therapy has certain requirements when dealing with abuse cases. The response must be active and not passive. The therapist is an agent of the state and not a neutral observer. The therapist must plan what is to happen and not depend on spontaneity. A unique approach is needed for each case. The change must be sudden to separate the abuser and victim quickly.

There are at least two ways the court is involved. One is court-ordered therapy. There is also court-encouraged therapy in which the abuser goes to therapy in order to influence the judge's decision.

An Unusual Case

Let us look at some of these issues in a controversial case of mother–daughter incest, which is not commonly seen. The mother's lawyer referred Sandy, a 35-year-old woman on public assistance, for family therapy after she voluntarily turned herself in to the police after molesting her stepniece for 6 months. The interview presented here took place eight weeks after she turned herself in. She came in with three children, a 3-year-old daughter and 2 sons, ages 7 and 8. The 13-year-old stepniece she molested was taken out of the home and placed in foster care and was not present. The therapist was a minister.

The session begins with the therapist explaining the one-way mirror supervision. In this case Haley called in suggestions to the therapist on a telephone during the interview. They decided in advance that the goal of therapy would be to have them be a normal family.

SANDY: The reason I'm here is because I called child protective services (CPS) and asked them for help because I sex-abused my oldest daughter, Joy. They asked me to go to the juvenile police station and asked me and my daughter for a statement and took her away from me, of course. (*Sighing deeply.*) I haven't gone to court or anything yet. So I want help to get myself straightened out and my family and my children.

THERAPIST: It has been several weeks.

SANDY: It has been 8 weeks. I can't have any contact at all. My lawyer is trying to change that, but it will probably be a long time.

THERAPIST: And what about Joy's father?

Mother describes her separation from her husband when she discovered that he was sexually abusing the adopted daughter.

SANDY: We separated 3 and a half years ago because he had sexually abused Joy. He's seen a therapist. Up until I called the social worker he was having regular visits with her. They okayed unsupervised visits but now he is not able to see her. We have a court hearing to see what the judge will allow. (*After the father's abuse became known, the family went to the police and psychiatric counseling.*)

THERAPIST: What is your own experience with Joy?

SANDY: I didn't think of it as abuse.

THERAPIST: Having the first one come into the teenage years is never easy for any of us. What kind of relationship did you have with her?

SANDY: She is an adopted daughter. She is my husband's niece. She came to live with us when she was 5. Before that we had a very rough marriage. The first year she was with us, he had an affair that turned things upside down. I had one son who was 2. She had been with my husband's mother. Her grandmother wanted to move, and they would not let her adopt, so they looked for another relative. I took her in cause I felt sorry for her. My mother was raised in a foster home and she never had anything good to say about it. We never hit it off. I was always involved in my own problems and was working a lot. She was fighting me tooth and nail. I didn't understand it at the time, and I always took it that she was rejecting me. I was hurt. I know now that is not true. Because she was my husband's relative, when I had problems with him, I suppose I took that out on her sometimes.

THERAPIST: I imagine it was very awkward when your husband separated and you had your husband's niece living with you in your home.

SANDY: When I shoved him out the door, I told him to take her with him. If you go, she goes. We were disagreeing and arguing all the time. I knew I loved her, but I never expressed it. There was never any affection between the two of us. All this mess with my husband, I cooperated in every way. I didn't want to see a therapist but they insisted. Neither of the boys had any idea what was going on. The social worker advised me to get this book on different kinds of touching, that it was the kind taking place between their father and sister.

The social workers encouraged the mother to be more affectionate with the daughter and that she was too distant. This inadvertently got them involved.

THERAPIST: What response did they make?

SANDY: They didn't understand.

THERAPIST: How much do they know about Joy's moving out?

SANDY: When I called the social worker, they asked me to bring her in. We always reviewed that kind of touching because I feel it's important. You always hear so much in the news and everything. I sat down and told them that I had been involved in that with their sister. I told them I called the social worker and they thought it was better that Joy be taken away from us for a while and I would be doing whatever was necessary to get myself straightened out and that I was sorry to mess everything up.

THERAPIST: It sounds like what you want is to be back as a family.

SANDY: She never wanted to leave in the first place. I knew that's what they were going to do.

THERAPIST: Would you include your husband in being reunited with the family?

SANDY: No. When all this happened with my husband, I was 7 months pregnant. I don't love him, and Joy didn't want him to come back in the house. She was afraid of him. When she goes with her father, her two brothers go with her, so they are not actually ever alone.

I guess after a good year and a half, the social worker was trying to make me see that Joy loved me. You had two people who loved each other, and neither one made it known to the other one. We talked more. I tried to get her to be more open with me. We were getting close in an emotional way, I was incorporating some affection, a hug, a kiss, which there never was before. It just happened one day when were hugging I was sexually aroused. I was attracted to the closeness. I liked the idea of being close and having someone caring for me.

THERAPIST: That is something you hadn't had in some time?

SANDY: I hadn't had any other relationship—man or woman. I don't consider myself gay. That's why I don't understand why I did the things I did with Joy. I wasn't thinking of it as a relationship. To me I wasn't abusing her. I didn't force her. I got sexually aroused by the affection. I spend many a night pacing, wandering around, crying. I didn't know how to stop. One time Joy wanted to stop because she didn't feel right, so I said all right. I wasn't happy because I couldn't separate the sexual part from being close. I couldn't be close to her without the sexual feeling. I think that's why she came back to me in a sexual way, as she said later she wanted the affection, and if she didn't, she wouldn't get it. I told her I couldn't be close to her and not get confused. One day her father took all the kids, and I decided this is it. It's not going to happen again. I told Joy when she got home. I think in a way she was probably relieved. About 3 and a half weeks passed before I actually called the social worker.

Haley calls the therapist on the phone to get the exact sexual details.

THERAPIST: I know it might be difficult to talk about, but do you think you could express to me what kind of sexual abuse took place between you and Joy?

SANDY: It was the kissing and hugging first and then it went to fondling on both parts and then it went to everything, digital penetration. It was like a homosexual relationship. I never thought of myself as a homosexual. I still don't want to be. It was like a man and a woman would have. I guess I was the teacher so I aroused feelings in her being a young girl. I'm not saying she's gay, but she doesn't know how to deal with sexual feelings. Once she said, "Even if we don't have the sexual relationship, can we still have hugging and kissing on the mouth." I said, "Mother and daughter don't do that." And she said, "How do you know?"

THERAPIST: How about her father and the abuse that was taking place? Do you think penetration also occurred there?

SANDY: No, he was forcing himself on her. They could never prove penetration took place. She was about 10. It went on for 8 or 9 months. None of the social workers or the therapist could figure out what happened because the doctor who examined her said they couldn't tell if he penetrated. She said she never wanted it. She ran away twice. She didn't tell me or anyone else. He blamed it all on me, and I guess I really believed it. She said it happened at least a dozen times when I was working.

THERAPIST: Now, was there any sequence of events that took place?

SANDY: Just the affection. It just happened.

THERAPIST: In terms of time of day.

SANDY: At first at night after ten.

THERAPIST: Who would initiate?

SANDY: I always did. In the last few months, sometimes she did. She would get very affectionate. Sometimes once or several times a week.

THERAPIST: She never exhibited the initiating behavior when her father was doing it.

SANDY: Like I said, I didn't force her. I always told her if you don't want to I won't. She never said no. One of the questions she asked the therapist was why her father had done that.

THERAPIST: Would it be possible to have Joy come in? I would agree. I don't know if Protective Services will agree.

SANDY: Just the affection, it just happened.

The goal is to get them back as a family and even if you cannot, you can give them that hope that they will be back together someday. Haley's phone call to the therapist emphasizes the goal of this therapy.

THERAPIST: How can I help you? Can you explain how I can be of help?

SANDY: I want to have normal relationship with my daughter—a mother–daughter relationship and not be confused. How to control it. I don't want a homosexual relationship with anyone. I want to show love and affection and not be confused.

THERAPIST: What about the court?

SANDY: I want to be able to have supervised visitation rights. I want my daughter to have therapy. I want to stop it. I want us to be back as a family. This is affecting the other children.

THERAPIST: I would like to bring in the other kids. Is there anything you would not want me to discuss?

SANDY: I don't want them to know the details between Joy and me. The social worker and police questioned my children and they had a bad experience. They accused me of abusing the other kids. Finally they got my 3-year-old to say that I kissed the boy's peepee. That is not true.

THERAPIST: Do you have fears this might occur with other children?

SANDY: I can safely say up to today these thoughts had not crossed my mind. The social workers don't believe me. They want to take my other 3 children away from me. I was very open and waived my rights to a lawyer. They are using everything against me rather then helping me. It could have been a secret between my daughter and me, so if I had done anything with the three other children I would have stated that then.

THERAPIST: It is important for you to know how much I appreciate how open you have been. What you are doing will help reunite your family. I appreciate your honesty for sharing a very painful experience.

SANDY: Because the kids won't talk they [the social workers and the police] felt they were lying. They wanted to give my son a lie-detector test.

THERAPIST: I would like to meet the kids and have them meet me. And find out what it is like for them to be in a family that is disintegrating.

Haley calls the therapist to have him reassure mother.

THERAPIST: I assure you I will not discuss any of the details.

The three kids walk in smiling. Mother puts the 3-year-old on her lap. The therapist compliments the kids on putting away all the toys. He asks them what toys they like to play with. They are reluctant to talk. The therapist introduces the room and the cameras and one-way mirror.

THERAPIST: Do you know who I am and what I do? One thing I try to do is to try to help families get back together again. That's my job. Can you tell me what its like to be part of your family right now? Why are you here today?

SON: So you can help us.

THERAPIST: What can I help you to do?

SON: Get back into a family.

THERAPIST: Who is not with you?

SON: My big sister.

They discuss why they miss her and what they did together. Then the kids begin to relax and jump around.

THERAPIST: It's been a lot of fun for me today to talk to your Mom. She is a neat lady. She loves you a lot. She needs to know that from you, too. I can't promise to get your sister back but I will do everything possible to get the family back together again.

Haley asks the therapist to get the phone numbers from the mother of the colleagues involved in the case.

Follow-up

The mother was arrested and put in a prerelease center for 1 year. Haley and the therapist visited her. The daughter was put in a foster home. She ran away several times, once staying out all night, and she would telephone the mother. Her mother would say she could not speak to her. We assigned a therapist for the mother, who was overwhelmed by guilt. We wanted to bring mother and daughter together so they could discuss what had happened and plan where the girl would live in the future. CPS (Child Protective Services) refused to allow the mother and daughter to be in the same room even in a therapy interview. When the foster mother heard about the abuse, she was so angry at the mother she would not come to any sessions. Joy had essentially been a parental child with her siblings, but they were not permitted to see her. The grandmother was called to take care of the other children, who were taken away from the mother. The mother blossomed in the rehabilitation center. She lost weight and got a job. She was permitted to come to therapy sessions and visit her children. We asked the foster mother to come to a session with the mother. She refused, saying she would never be in the same room with that woman. She continued to explain to the daughter what an awful mother she had had, and that added to the difficulties of mother and daughter working out a relationship. The mother returned home, had a job, and was taking care of her younger children. The daughter remained in a foster home. The social workers were upset to think that they had encouraged the mother–daughter incest. In one later session the family was brought together again. Finally CPS agreed that the mother and daughter could talk together if the daughter had an individual therapist to help her if she got upset in the family session. We provided an individual therapist to protect her, and mother and daughter met together. The daughter said she wasn't sure whether she wanted to go back and live with the mother or go live with grandmother in another state.

Conflicts among Colleagues

In this case most of the therapist's time was spent dealing with colleagues. Only a small portion was spent in therapy sessions. For Child Protective Services, the responsible position is to assume that change is not possible. The victim must continue to be protected by the community. The abuser must be put out of the family and cut off from contact with the victim. The courts think therapists are soft on villains. Therapists think courts are not fully appreciative of the social context. This contrasts with strategic family therapy, which assumes that change is possible. The family can change so abuse does not occur again, the abuser can change and not wish to abuse anymore, and the victim can leave the experience behind and have a normal life. This can happen while the victim is simultaneously protected from abuse. In this case different viewpoints were apparent as well as conflicts. Yet, both therapists and court representatives have legitimate positions.

REFERENCES

Freud, S. (1959/1896). Heredity and aetiology. In *Collected papers*. vol. 1. New York: Basic Books.

9

Cultural Confusions

How Many Clients Are in One Body?

SPIRIT POSSESSION VERSUS MULTIPLE PERSONALITY[1]

*I*n strategic therapy it is important to deal with cultural issues without getting lost in them. Cultural problems of immigrants entering the United States may involve some type of belief in spirit possession, which is one issue that illustrates dealing with different ethnic groups. Spirit possession is the most common explanation of problems worldwide. Healing through spirit possession is practiced around the world. Specialists or mediums act as intermediaries between the living and the dead. Often they divine and heal through possession trances. Anthropologists differentiate ritual possession from sick possession (Richeport, 1984, 1985a, 1985b, 1988).

Therapists may choose among four alternatives when dealing with cases involving an alternate belief system like spirit possession. These may not be mutually exclusive. First, the therapist can use aspects of the alternate belief system to further therapeutic goals. Second, the therapist can minimize the alternate belief system and treat the case structurally. Third, the therapist can refer the client to a healer in the local healing system. Fourth, the therapist can collaborate with the healer (Richeport-Haley, 1998a, 1998b).

There are people who present themselves as more than one person. This was called multiple personality disorder (MPD) and is today referred to in the *DSM-IV* (1994) as Dissociative Identity Disorder (DID). Therapists find this difficult to respond to. A case was brought for consultation because the Middle Eastern trainee therapist was having difficulty with it. The trainee was a beginner, and Sara, a Brazilian woman in her 40s, was an experienced patient. She was diagnosed as a borderline personality and a multiple personality. She was living in a shelter on disability and was medicated with lithium and Prozac.

Sara showed all the symptoms of multiple personality. She was abused as a child, she reported eight persons inside her, including a violent man, a playful child, and a person who liked to write named Mary. She claimed to be "sensitive," hearing and seeing things before they happen. These same characteristics describe mediums in African-Brazilian spirit religions, which illustrate the problem of differentiating a cultural belief system from a diagnostic category. It was unclear if she lost time displaying amnesia. The supervisory decisions, from a strategic perspective, involved deciding whether she was a multiple personality or a medium in the African Spiritist religions so popular in Brazil. Followers may have identical behaviors. These include being possessed by other selves and writing under a different name. A supervisory question is whether to focus on spirit possession, on multiple personality, or on neither, dealing with a case in terms of family structure and practical matters. If Haley determined this case was a multiple personality, he would deal with her in much the same way he did in other cases following Erickson's approach with 23 cases of MPD (Erickson, 1939/1980, circa 1940s/1980; Erickson & Kubie, 1939/1967; Erickson & Rapaport, circa 1940s; Haley & Richeport-Haley, 1991; Richeport-Haley, 1992, 1994).

Therapists are required to make a diagnosis based on the *DSM-IV*. Although multiple personality was in vogue several years ago, it is rarely used today due to the discredit involving the "false memory syndrome," which revealed that false memories were often produced by therapists to fit their expectations (Yapko, 1994). However, Haley has supervised multiple personality cases (Grove & Haley, 1993; Richeport-Haley, 1994) and the authors are familiar with the 23 cases treated by Milton Erickson, M.D.

Therapies with multiples include two major orientations (Putnam, 1989). One orientation is to attempt to fuse and integrate the personalities, thus eliminating them. This could be considered similar to exorcism, since the alters no longer have a separate identity. The second orientation, recommended by Erickson, is collaboration. One slowly and carefully confronts the primary personality with the realization that there are other personalities in the same body. They are taught to communicate and collaborate. Such an approach is similar to encouraging collaboration among alters in mediumnistic work. In all approaches hypnosis is the choice technique.

One case supervised by Haley was treated by Randy Fiery. The case involved family therapy with a multiple personality, which is unusual. This was a very complicated case and is only touched upon here to underline the factors involved in making a differential diagnosis and in treating a client with multiple personalities using the family in a strategic approach. The client was a woman in her 30s who had serious problems with amnesia, waking up in places and not knowing how she got there. She had been severely abused, was hospitalized repeatedly, and was suicidal at times. Haley supervised the therapist in the use of hypnosis to bring out the different personalities in the sessions to identify themselves and enable them to become aware of one another. The process of learning to control the amnesia and the rapid switching of personalities was a difficult and necessary process. Haley had the therapist develop a plan so that the internal collaborators (other selves) and the external collaborators (family members) did tasks such as driving in one direction without losing time or making a personality stay in the room for a longer period. The husband was passive but attended the therapy sessions with his wife. He interpreted his wife's problems as moodiness, a positive belief in that it showed he was not focused on pathology. For example, when she found herself 50 miles out of her way and not knowing how she got there, the husband called it a "longcut" instead of a shortcut, which is an example of taking it lightly.

The therapy introduced the husband to his wife's alternate personalities and taught him how to struggle with them so that amnesia would not limit her functioning.

THERAPIST TO WIFE: It doesn't mean you have to give the others up if they come here in the room.

THERAPIST TO HUSBAND: Sam, you tell Maureen [an alter] to come out and stay a few minutes.

SAM: I won't hurt you. I just want to talk and you can have them back. I won't force anyone to do anything they don't want to do.

WIFE: (*Cries and brings various persons out while in the arms of her husband.*)

As part of the therapy Haley encouraged the abreaction in hypnosis of the original abuse and suggested amnesia for it. This was done with the client viewing the abuse on an imaginary screen sitting between husband and therapist and then seeing herself getting bigger and older and thus more detached emotionally from the scene. This is similar to Erickson's "February Man," in which the past may be changed under hypnosis with amnesia.

Later the couple's foster children were brought into the sessions. The family watched the personality switching in the sessions. Social Services objected to a foster mother with a problem of suicide attempts and threatened to take the foster children out of her home. The threat of losing the children was an incentive for the mother to change her loss of control of time. The outcome was that one of the foster children had a baby, and the client, now a foster grandmother, successfully helped in rearing the child. Based on Erickson's approach, Haley was very positive about the nature of "other selves" and did not view them as necessarily pathological but a curious fact of human existence. Similarly, spirit mediums in many cultures are awarded a prestigious role and are considered talented individuals. There are complicated issues that can only be touched upon here.

The Brazilian case presented here shows the obvious confusion between multiple personality and spirit possession (this client had been previously diagnosed as multiple personality). At first the spirit beliefs were utilized and a therapy technique was tried to elicit the strongest spirit or spirit guide to help the client help the therapist live a normal life. This is a technique often used by local healers. Abandoning this approach after several attempts, Haley supervised the case practically. The training group considered these problems bizarre, even though spirit possession is the most popular belief system worldwide. In Brazil it is called macumba.

PLANNING THE FIRST INTERVIEW

The group gathered behind the one-way mirror and began to discuss the case of the Brazilian woman who was scheduled.

HALEY: Is this your first interview with her?

THERAPIST: No, it would be my third.

HALEY: OK, what is the problem?

THERAPIST: She is a 41-year-old woman from Brazil. She has been living in the States for quite a while. She has been diagnosed as having bipolar disorder and multiple personality. I cannot say she had an abusive childhood. I would have to say she was tortured as a child.

HALEY: Tortured?

THERAPIST: Practically, yes, and she was often in danger for her own life. Her father would drag them behind the truck "in the fields."

HALEY: So, it was the father abusing her then? What happened to her father?

THERAPIST: He had left the family a long time ago. Nothing ever happened to the father. (*The woman came from northeast Brazil during a time when men were not punished for harming women.*)

HALEY: Does she have any connection with him now?

THERAPIST: No, but she does with her mother—she's quite isolated. She has had two husbands. The last one was wanted by the police, and they lived in hiding for about 4 years in the States and she really liked this life—it was exciting. But now he is in Central America and she is here.

They have been separated for a few months. Sara talks about different persons that she has in her. She has a child [alter] that she really cares for. She was abused and she's abusive. She can be very violent according to her husband and she gets scared at how violent she can become.

HALEY: Against whom?

THERAPIST: Against her husband, against people—I mean, she is afraid of her own strength and her own violence. It seems like when she gets really upset and violent, she seems to block it out, as if she doesn't really realize what is going on. It is not her anymore, yet she knows what's happening. . . .

HALEY: Does she have any children?

THERAPIST: No. She does not.

HALEY: So, just the two husbands? Where's her mother?

THERAPIST: She is in Brazil.

HALEY: Does she have any connection with her?

THERAPIST: I don't think she does. Sometimes she likes writing. She writes a lot and she always gives me what she writes. She writes beautifully. But she just goes on tangents. But she would like to learn how to live with herself. This is what she really wants to do.

HALEY: She doesn't have a choice, does she?

THERAPIST: She wants to be at peace with herself. I mean, she has a lot of resentments toward her father, of course, and she knew that it wasn't her fault what happened to her. She says, "Maybe I should have done something differently. Maybe I provoked him somehow"—even though the whole family was in the same situation.

She Wants a Friend

HALEY: Well, who is involved personally in her life?

THERAPIST: Now, her husband. They talk on the phone.

HALEY: And why are they separated?

THERAPIST: Because she says that she was kind of tired of being in hiding in this very dangerous life.

HALEY: But take me back— What is the dangerous life?

THERAPIST: The dangerous life is that he is wanted by the police.

HALEY: Well, you have had three sessions now. What have you started with her?

THERAPIST: What she comes with, it seems.

HALEY: She comes in with what?

THERAPIST: She comes in with a problem and we talk about that. Last time she was being harassed by somebody and the time before she was talking about her husband and her life with her husband. I still want to know where to go—I mean, how to follow her, because sometimes I am not sure—or do I have to lead and she follows? I am not sure.

HALEY: *You have to have a goal.*

The therapy approach is new to this trainee. She is accustomed to listening passively to the client and saying "Tell me more." Strategic therapy on the other hand is an approach that requires giving directives to bring about change.

THERAPIST: I guess what I would like to get is for her to understand she is a strong person who has been through a lot and she has a lot of strength.

Making a Diagnosis of Multiple Personality

HALEY: Tell us a little more about who is inside of her. (*This will help formulate a problem.*)

THERAPIST: She talked about the child, she talked about a man— Oh, I forgot to mention it that she is sure that there is a man inside her and that she changes features and that other people saw her as a man lying in the bed.

HALEY: Lying in the bed?

THERAPIST: Yes, instead of her. She was lying in her bed and somebody walked in and saw a man there.

HALEY: Who was the somebody?

THERAPIST: Her husband—a friend of hers who saw him, and her husband told her often that she looks a lot like a man. So she is convinced that there is that man that gets out from her and she takes the features of the man.

HALEY: But there is a baby, a man, and who else?

THERAPIST: And there is a girl who writes named Mary. My client writes a lot. She expresses herself much more by writing than by talking. One of the pages was very loving and caring. And she says that there are other people there—about eight people—I mean, they don't all have different names.

TRAINEE ONE: But she is aware of each one. She's not, like, blanking out?

THERAPIST: Yes. We all have different parts of us that talk to us, or do we?

HALEY: Well, not quite like that. The issue is whether she just has a hobby of other people or whether she has other personalities. But it would be very interesting if you had a multiple personality case. Any comment, anybody? What would you do with this to start with?

TRAINEE TWO: What distinguishes a multiple personality from a coping mechanism?

HALEY: A coping mechanism is just a different idea. There is a debate whether or not a multiple personality is pathological or whether there are people with several personalities. Milton Erickson didn't believe it was necessarily pathological. He just felt these personalities got into the same body and he worked on bringing them together.

THERAPIST: Do you find out which one they like to be first?

HALEY: Or at least getting them all communicating with you, so they don't have periods of amnesia, which is their main problem. But she does not seem to have that.

THERAPIST: She doesn't seem to.

HALEY: Does she do anything wrong that would put her in danger? I mean drugs or anything?

THERAPIST: She was abusing alcohol, but she has stopped.

Dealing With Colleagues

HALEY: If she comes off the medication, what is she like? Do you know? Because you could ask her.

THERAPIST: I asked her about the medication and how it was for her to take the medication. She said that she wanted to change it because it makes her dizzy—meaning that she is taking it.

HALEY: Who is her doctor? Do you know? Do you have his records? If you wanted to talk to him— I mean that is a pretty powerful influence he's got in the middle of your case. Well, anything else anybody would do with the gentleman, or this lady, and maybe a gentleman, too?

Utilizing the Client's Writing

THERAPIST: She writes beautifully.

HALEY: How could you use that therapeutically?

Sara's writing as another personality is also part of the African Spiritist beliefs. It is considered automatic handwriting of a spiritual entity. An attempt is made to utilize it a positive way.

THERAPIST: I don't know what to do with the writings right now, but I am reading what she is describing, and because she is more expressive in her writing, I try and talk about things that we would not have talked about in the session and take it to the next session and discuss it. And I feel that this is a powerful tool that she has.

HALEY: I think there are two ways you can use the writing. One is to have her write all her misery that she went through as a child—an autobiography—and hope that relieves it by writing about it. She will get more objective and distanced from it. The other way is to have her go very positive with the writing so that she describes the way she would like to be, and what kind of a family she would like to have, and what kind of a society she would like to be in. So you would make her come out with her goals in the writing rather than in the talking. You would have to decide two extremes you could go with. Is she writing novels about people who are wicked?

THERAPIST: Her feelings, her thoughts.

HALEY: And they are not positive thoughts?

THERAPIST: No, they are not.

HALEY: Well, with the diagnosis she shouldn't be very cheerful.

TRAINEE TWO: You know, what I was thinking is that maybe she is trying to cross over. I wonder if that was possible from the African-Brazilian way of life into our culture and that is why she has is getting upset.

HALEY: Spirit possession is the most common religion in the world, you know. One of the things that is positive in this lady is that she writes.

Richeport-Haley, who is very familiar with the Brazilian religions, explained macumba to the group. "It would be interesting to know whether this client is a practitioner or follower of any of the African-Brazilian religions, which may be confused with her diagnosis of multiple personality or borderline personality. In many countries where spirit possession is common, it is often difficult to differentiate between acceptable cultural hallucinations and pathology. Spirit religions in Brazil are very popular. People consult these healers for all kinds of problems, including physical complaints, marital difficulties, and serious mental illness. The mediums receive four major spirits similar to the client's expression of other selves: the strong and aggressive Indian, the patient and wise old slave, playful and innocent children, and a trickster spirit. While possessed by an old slave, a father can, for example, give advice to his daughter and grandson, who are much more likely to follow his wishes. They also receive ambiguous spirits representing good and evil. Some people say if you put all the spirits together, they make a well-rounded personality."

The group believed that the trainee was inexperienced and too tolerant and accepting of the client's words. She had no plan after three interviews but to listen and admire the client's often fragmented writing. More positively, the trainee was very open to practicing the strategic approach, which included utilizing the client's belief system in this interview.

GROUP OBSERVES THE FIRST LIVE INTERVIEW

The lights were turned off behind the mirror, and the trainees observed this tall heavyset woman with her head down enter the therapy room. The supervision uses the African-Brazilian belief system to make a differential diagnosis between DID and cultural beliefs and to use what is positive in the client. Haley transmits his suggestions to the therapist on a computer monitor in the therapy room that the therapist can read but the client cannot.

THERAPIST: I was thinking about you because I was reading a book about Brazil and the spirituality of Brazil.

Sara describes macumba to the therapist when she inquired about the client's religion.

SARA: I am very psychic. My grandmother had it, too. Mother Nature guides me. If you are receptive, it comes out. I try to bring good out. I feel there is a power to do things without knowing. I know things ahead of time.

THERAPIST: It must be good to predict things. What do you predict?

SARA: My husband John was lifted in the air.

The directives that follow utilize the client's African-Brazilian belief system as an entrance into possible DID. This system shares many commonalities, including amnesia and possession by alternate selves.

Computer Suggestion: Do you have a spirit guide?

THERAPIST: Do you have a spirit guide?

SARA: It is not a person. It is supernatural. John can get a person out of me that is very strong. I can kick things when I feel threatened.

THERAPIST: Can't your guide help you with that?

SARA: What is the question? What was I talking about?

Computer Suggestion: Your spirit can protect you.

THERAPIST: Do you have a guide, you know, a spiritual guide or something?

SARA: It seems that way.

Computer Suggestion: Do the spirits around you get along with each other?

Computer Suggestion: Can you bring the male personality in here?

THERAPIST: Can you bring them here or do they come by themselves?

SARA: There are too many lights here so they can't come out.

THERAPIST: Can you call them?

SARA: No. They just come.

Computer Suggestion: Your spirit guide can help you when you are mad.

THERAPIST: When you get mad, can your spirit help calm you down?

SARA: It doesn't come with me. It doesn't come here. It wants to be protected. Talk to John. He knows a lot of things I don't see.

THERAPIST: Do you forget when parts come out? Do you forget?

SARA: Is it called switches? Mary [alter] writes because if she doesn't write she will forget.

THERAPIST: Who writes?

SARA: The writer is a person between 10 and 14 years old, someone who reads a lot.

Computer Suggestion: Can you do something for your spirit guide?

THERAPIST: What can you do for your spirit guide? Can you do something for him?

SARA: What was the question? I have to understand it first. I have a place where I go which is secretive.

Computer Suggestion: What is your worst problem?

The supervisor felt it was important to get back to the real world since it was difficult to utilize Sara's belief systems in a positive way.

THERAPIST: What is your worst problem?

SARA: I love something and then it dies. People disappoint me who have no heart. Sometimes I don't like men. Other times I protect a man. I do this with John.

Sara could not utilize the strong spirit guide to help the therapist help the client, nor ask for the guide's protection only. We could not elicit a spirit guide, as Sara said the spirit guide was a secret. She said her biggest problem was fear. To end the session it was suggested that she use her talent in writing in a positive way.

Computer Suggestion: Could you write something for me? Write how you would like things to be.

THERAPIST: Would it be okay if you write something for me—something of how you would like things to be?

SARA: What I write happens.

THERAPIST: Write about a good life and bring it next time.

SARA: The cops wanted to talk to me. That face [the violent self] came out.

THERAPIST: The spirit guide can really help you yet.

DISCUSSING THE FIRST LIVE INTERVIEW

The therapist comes back behind the one-way mirror to discuss the interview.

THERAPIST: I thought that was wonderful that the spirit guide could help her and was so much more powerful so all the others are going to be small and there is only one person in charge. That is great.

HALEY: Did she seem to have amnesia in the room while she would say, "What was that question?"

THERAPIST: I think that she was being very overwhelmed. She had a lot of feelings coming out today, and usually I let her talk more and let her lead. Today, I was asking her the questions. So, in a sense, maybe it is because I didn't let her get everything out of the way. I don't know.

This trainee has been taught more to listen than to act.

HALEY: You have to find some protection for her. I mean, exploring the fear doesn't necessarily help. But finding something in the structure that protects her is helpful. And that spirit guide comes along, as Madeleine said, is a helpful creature.

THERAPIST: Thank you so much. (*Laughing*) I haven't seen them [spirits]. Give me a bit of time and I'll find one.

HALEY: But she says, Nobody is interested in the war now, and I think she is saying, Nobody is interested in my husband and me. That kind of metaphor she used a few times. It is also a characteristic of writers. That is how they make their living, through metaphors.

The supervisor is normalizing the client's behavior wherever possible. Here he puts her in the category of other people who write.

PLANNING THE SECOND LIVE INTERVIEW

The group was not sure whether or not Sara was a multiple personality.

TRAINEE TWO: A couple of years ago we read in the paper about the physician who was treating all of these people who had multiple personalities in his practice.

HALEY: I know of one practice that is made up entirely of them. They have a curious logic, but if abuse causes multiple personalities, then if somebody was abused they were multiple personality. So they assume all of them are multiples if they have been abused.

TRAINEE TWO: This is the first one that I have seen—a couple of people have changed who said they have changed, and I don't believe it. But this one, I don't know. This one raises doubt in my mind.

HALEY: They always have an ambiguity about them. But anyhow, we are going to have this one tonight. What is the latest?

Dealing with the Real World

THERAPIST: She was very depressed and angry.

HALEY: At somebody?

THERAPIST: Yes, but they were after John, and they were trying to set him up to kill him. She was very upset, and she says that there is injustice in this world. I just got a message on the voice mail that on Saturday one of the ladies who lived in the same house as she does has died. She was very upset over the phone.

HALEY: You think this will be the subject tonight?

THERAPIST: I am wondering if you want to begin with that.

HALEY: What would you like to have it on? What would you like to focus it on?

THERAPIST: I want to know which direction to go with her. I want her to have a strong—What you had suggested last time is really building one spirit to help her through whatever so that she feels that strength. When she was in the crisis center, I did try to get her back to nature and the strength that she used to get from nature and she said that it calmed her down.

HALEY: Where is she living now?

THERAPIST: It's a shelter for multiple diagnoses.

HALEY: Multiple diagnoses? They have a shelter for multiple diagnoses?

THERAPIST: It is a house, and they have group meetings, and they are being taken care of, medicated, and sheltered.

HALEY: You have to have several diagnoses to get in there?

THERAPIST: I believe so. Yes. At least two.

HALEY: But she is living there and is she working?

THERAPIST: No.

HALEY: What is her income?

THERAPIST: Her income—I believe she gets social benefits.

HALEY: I would try to find out the real world for her—where she lives or where her husband lives, what friends does she have, what kind of a job she is looking for.

THERAPIST: She wants to write and sell her stories.

HALEY: That's a tough way to live. But that's at least something practical. In a far-off land, if you are good enough, you can publish stories. But you don't know whether when her husband comes she sees him?

THERAPIST: She does, and then he goes back to Central America. There's a lot of things that just don't match up.

Disengagement

HALEY: I would, if I were you, be worried about how she's interesting you with these human dramas that she is involved in. That is, there ought to be a way to test it experimentally, to bring up something and see if she then develops that because she knows you are interested in it. I mean, you're her audience is what it sounds like. There're not many friends or people around her. And you must be very important to her.

THERAPIST: I think I am and it is getting scary. She really wants to see me twice a week, and I am wondering whether it is in her best interest. On the contrary, I'll be pushing the dependency on her.

HALEY: How often do you see her now?

THERAPIST: Now I see her just once a week.

HALEY: But I would think some of what she says is exaggerated as a storyteller and also somebody who is interesting you so you will keep on seeing her. What is your destination with her? How long will you see her?

THERAPIST: As long as she needs to see me.

HALEY: But how long will you be available?

THERAPIST: For about a year.

HALEY: Does she know that?

THERAPIST: Yes, she does. And she is very motivated. She's even willing to see different therapists if I cannot see her. She really wants to get better. Or does she want a bigger social system, now that you raised this question?

HALEY: Can she describe what better is?

THERAPIST: I don't know.

Creating a Goal

HALEY: I would just try to get clear a goal, to say that therapy is to help people who can't solve a problem. What does she need? How will she be when she is over it? Does she need to go to work? Does she need another man? What is her destiny?

THERAPIST: When I asked her, she told me that what she wants from therapy is to be able to live with herself.

HALEY: Well, she has no alternative. She's got to live with herself.

But she must indicate she doesn't care for part of herself then? Well, let's think of doing an interview where she says something like she wants to do something about herself. I would say, How would you know you had that? What is the practical thing you can do to achieve that? But I would try to get some more facts about her life—how she supports herself, and why she is in a shelter instead of getting a job and getting an apartment. She's a bright woman. Has that ever come up?

THERAPIST: She likes the shelter. She feels safe and secure in her shelter, even though security is not something that she thrives on, because she was in hiding for about 5 years with her husband.

HALEY: And they won't hunt for her in the shelter? Whoever might be after her.

TRAINEE TWO: It sounds like it's a delusion.

TRAINEE THREE: That supports this idea that she needs an audience. It's like the movies.

HALEY: It's hard to sell a story, but some people sell movie scripts if they are imaginative enough. How would you like this interview to end today?

THERAPIST: I would like to be on the right track—to know how to continue with her.

HALEY: It would be nice if you ended the interview feeling something satisfying. I would be satisfied if we knew more about her in the real world, because she lives in a metaphoric world—if you read her writings. You gentlemen have a suggestion?

TRAINEE TWO: I like the idea that you were having that we need more clarification on what type of a lifestyle she is living right now. She's very comfortable living the way she is living right now. I think it sounds like the more she sensationalizes a lot of the events in her life, it keeps her in a very secure and nice arena.

HALEY: A shelter. If you get her first to say that she enjoys it there and likes it there and get her to say that she has to leave sometime, because you can't stay forever in a shelter. And then have her set a date and begin to organize therapy toward that date, because then she has to get a job and she has to find a place to live. She has to cultivate some friends. I mean, the various things she would have to do if she left the shelter. Can she stay there as long as she wants?

Well, I think one of the things about it is you are a very nice person and she likes you. And it is easy to be kind to her, when you need to be more firm with her, I think, really, about making some plans for her future.

THERAPIST: Yeah. (*The therapist looks pensive.*)

HALEY: And after all, living with people with multiple diagnoses is not the most pleasant time in the world. They must be pretty difficult people. But two diagnoses. I mean, one, maybe so.

THERAPIST: Two is one too many.

Predicting a Relapse

TRAINEE TWO: Would you predict some acting out if you were to set a date for her to leave? Would you predict for her to somehow sabotage that and somehow create that crisis?

THERAPIST: She would get, probably, deep depression crisis, crying, and go straight to the hospital.

HALEY: I would predict that with her, if you think that would happen, and say you are going to begin to resist this and you will begin to develop symptoms so you can't leave. What kind of symptoms would you prefer? Because, if you anticipate it, it is harder for her to do it.

THERAPIST: I need to let her talk about the death of her friend.

HALEY: You have to deal with that, sure.

THERAPIST: And then I'll try to see—from there I'll try and go to the goal of leaving and when does she think she might be able to do that and how would she do it and what are the problems she might be facing.

HALEY: Sure. I would ask her if she knows whether she'll have to leave—if there is a limit.

OBSERVING THE SECOND INTERVIEW

Sara describes the death of her housemate in detail. She talks about her fears, particularly in relation to her husband. All of the directives focused on practical matters to get the therapist to expect action in the real world and not just listen. They emphasized the normal things of everyday life. The client brought in pictures of her family.

Computer Suggestion: Why not get practical?

THERAPIST: What do you want to get out of our meetings? How will you know when you get it?

SARA: I want to get help out of our meetings?

THERAPIST: How do you know that you are getting the help? How do I know that I am giving you the help that you need?

SARA: (*Smiling, as if expecting the therapist to know and showing surprise at the direct question*) That don't sound very good.

THERAPIST: It's just because I want to know what direction to go.

The therapist gave the client all of the following supervisory suggestions.

Computer Suggestion: Would you like a man in your life?
Computer Suggestion: Are you supporting your husband and will you always support your husband?
Computer Suggestion: Would you be safer in your own apartment?
Computer Suggestion: Do you have anyone to protect you?
Computer suggestion: Isn't it normal to be afraid?
Computer Suggestion: In what other ways are you normal?
Computer Suggestion: I'd like you to do something normal next week.
Computer Suggestion: I want to stay with you until you are normal.

THERAPIST: I want to make sure we are getting somewhere.

SARA: All right.

DISCUSSING THE SECOND INTERVIEW

HALEY: The therapy is talking about the interesting problems and bizarre experiences and fears and so on. Talking to her earlier about being normal might have upset her—in getting a job. If I understand it right, she is supporting her husband? We [U.S. taxpayers] are supporting her husband.

THERAPIST: Yes. This is so nice of all of you.

HALEY: But she changed when you gave her a directive—even a simple one like that. She got very serious, and then she got very funny.

THERAPIST: She was so weird today. I could not feel her from the beginning of the whole session.

HALEY: In the beginning she was far out. I think that's right.

TRAINEE FOUR: When she changed her position, she became a different person to me. When she was bent over—I don't know if it was because you were changing your way of dealing with her or it was a way she just changed, as if switching selves?

THERAPIST: And that was the picture of her younger brother and a picture of her when she was 10.

HALEY: Where's her brother?

THERAPIST: He still lives in Brazil with their mother. And he is the only one who has not been abused by the father.

HALEY: And the mother— Do you know anything about the mother?

THERAPIST: The mother lives in Brazil and she has her little house.

HALEY: Does she work?

THERAPIST: No.

HALEY: Do they support her?

THERAPIST: Her children do.

HALEY: I was wondering back here about her mother. She had not been mentioned, and it seemed like, obviously, she should be mentioned. I think she would be very important in this case.

Family Therapy at a Distance through Letters

HALEY: Once you have the mother in the picture, you can take a simple directive like that and turn it into a letter to her mother or a telephone call. She could write her mother a letter saying that I have been having hard times but now I am getting back to normal. Then she is obligated to do that—to support the letter. But you can do things like that.

Learning to Disengage

THERAPIST: How do I deal with her fear that I am abandoning her?

HALEY: Well, there are different things to do.

THERAPIST: My own reaction to that is we're just going to abandon her. She feels that I want out.

HALEY: What you can do, if you really are worried about it, is call her. Say, when we left, we were talking about you becoming normal and getting a job—I mean you seem to think that would mean you would have to leave therapy, but maybe you don't. I want you to continue.

TRAINEE TWO: Is there some truth that when she does become normal, she will not want her therapy?

HALEY: That's right. That's the discovery a lot of patients make. That has been the case of those in analysis for 18 years and this woman has had a lot of therapy.

THERAPIST: So if she gets normal, she is going to lose a lot. She is going to lose therapy, she is going to lose the place where she lives, she is going to lose the support—

HALEY: Her disability. Her husband, probably, if she is not supporting him. She is an adventuress.

TRAINEE THREE: Yeah. It is very exciting and scary, but it's not going to a job everyday and trying to cope in the real world. It would be very boring.

TRAINEE TWO: "Are you afraid to have a child?" What was the plot behind that? That question threw me.

HALEY: You are talking about getting a job and doing all the normal things. Having a husband is normal, having a child is normal. So, I just suggested that. But also, apparently, that convinces many women their life is a little more serious than they thought. They begin to think whether they can have a child or is it too late. I think she has been thinking about it every time she saw a kid. Are you going to visit your husband, which is a rather normal thing to do if he is so far away. So it is all about creating normalcy.

It is partly what I was thinking and reacting to last week—the last interview with her, where she was bizarre and weird and we followed up the various ideas that might lead to this or that. And the idea that she is in here in order to get over these problems and be a normal person and you tend to forget it when it gets fascinating. And the patient often forgets it—thinking therapy is where you talk about abnormal things and it is not a place where you get practical and get a job.

Follow-up

Sara expressed her interest in being normal by calling the therapist at 5:00 A.M. to say she had two job interviews. The therapist finished her training program and that was the end of that therapy. Some months later, Sara called the therapist to say she was being expelled from the abuse shelter for smoking marijuana. She was on the street for 2 days and went to a homeless shelter. She said the rules were too strict, and she left. She said she was too tired to work. We did not know whether she wrote to her mother in Brazil, following our suggestion for family therapy at a distance. The trainee was no longer permitted to communicate with the client, who was not living in a shelter anymore.

This was a difficult case to work with in such a short period of time. This case shows the approach used rather than a finished case. There are many reasons for switching course from the first interview, utilizing the African-Brazilian religions, to the second interview, where they are minimized. Sara's belief system was not fully developed, and she did not receive these prescribed alternate selves in special places like a ceremony. If she had manifested the spirit guide, Haley would have suggested that this spirit guide offer her protection and help her get back to work. Because this was the therapist's first case, and she was enthralled with its eccentricities, it was not practical to supervise her by delving into complicated cultural systems or teach her hypnosis, which might have revealed some well-developed personalities. The question of whether or not Sara was a multiple personality was never fully resolved. The supervisor believed that the client needed to redefine therapy as a place not to be interesting and create mysterious scenarios but to do something to get over the problem.

The directives were:

1. To utililize what is positive in the client, which was her writing, to have her write all the bad things or have her write how she would like things to be, leading to her goals.
2. Have her contact her family and do family therapy at a distance through letters.
3. Have her act normally, which she defined as getting a job.

Then there was the problem of whether Sara was a multiple personality or expressing different personalities in cultural terms. Because she did not show amnesia, Haley did not work with her as a multiple personality and decided to deal with her structurally and guide her into a normal life. On a more general level this case illustrates the problem of dealing with ethnicity issues in the supervision of a case. Cultural sensitivity is politically correct these days, and often cultural exploration may prolong the therapy rather than make it be better. When to utilize belief systems and when to minimize them is a decision that the therapist must confront in almost every case where therapists and clients come from a variety of backgrounds. In general, regardless of the ethnic group or the diagnosis, we must express courtesy and respect for cultural differences and flexibility while assuming that, regardless of diagnosis, complicated problems can be dealt with practically.

NOTE

1. According to Ellenberger (1970), the question posed in the last century was how one might explain involuntary behavior. A person would do something and say he could not help himself. There were three hypotheses that became popular: the person had several personalities functioning independently of each other; the person was possessed by spirits who took over at times; or the person had behavior outside awareness and so was doing something unconsciously. The theory used has implications for therapy.

REFERENCES

American Psychiatric Association (1994). *Diagnostic and statistical manual of mental disorders* (4th ed.). Washington, DC: Author.

Ellenberger, H. (1970). *The discovery of the unconscious.* New York: Basic Books.

Erickson, M. H. (1939/1980). Experimental demonstration of the psychopathology of everyday life. In E. Rossi (Ed.), *The collected papers of Milton H. Erickson on hypnosis, Vol. III.* New York: Irvington.

Erickson, M. H. (circa 1940/1980). The clinical discovery of a dual personality. In

E. Rossi (Ed.), *The collected papers of Milton H. Erickson on hypnosis, Vol. III.* New York: Irvington Publishers.

Erickson, M. H., & Kubie, L. (1939/1967). Permanent relief of an obsessional phobia by means of communication with an unsuspected dual personality. In J. Haley (Ed.), *Advanced techniques of hypnosis and therapy: Selected papers of Milton H. Erickson, M.D.* New York: Grune & Stratton.

Erickson, M. H., & Rapaport, D. (circa 1940). Findings on the nature of the personality structures of two different dual personalities by means of projective and psychometric tests. In E. Rossi (Ed.), *The collected papers of Milton H. Erickson on hypnosis, Vol. III.* New York: Irvington Publishers.

Grove, D., & Haley, J. (1993). *Conversations on therapy.* New York: Norton.

Haley, J., & Richeport-Haley, M. (Eds.). (1991). *Milton H. Erickson, MD In his own voice. Erickson on multiple personality* [50-minute audiotape]. La Jolla: Triangle Press/Norton.

Putman, F. W. (1989). *Diagnosis and treatment of multiple personality disorder.* New York: Guilford Press.

Richeport, M. (1984). Strategies and outcomes of introducing a mental health plan in Brazil. *Social Science and Medicine, 19*(3), 261–271.

Richeport, M. (1985a). The importance of anthropology in psychotherapy: World view of Milton H. Erickson, M.D. In J. Zeig (Ed.), *Ericksonian approaches to hypnosis and psychotherapy* (pp. 371–390). New York: Brunner/Mazel.

Richeport, M. (1985b). *Macumba, trance and spirit healing* [16-mm film]. New York: Filmmakers Library.

Richeport, M. (1988). Transcultural issues in Ericksonian hypnotherappy. In S. Lankton & J. Zeig (Eds.), *Treatment of special populations with Ericksonian approaches (Ericksonian Monographs number 3,* pp. 130–147). New York: Brunner/Mazel.

Richeport-Haley, M. (1992). The interface between multiple personality, spirit mediumship, and hypnosis. *American Journal of Clinical Hypnosis, 34*(3), 168–177.

Richeport-Haley, M. (1994). Erickson's approach to multiple personality: A cross-cultural perspective. In J. Zeig (Ed.), *Ericksonian methods. The essence of the story* (pp. 415–432). New York: Brunner/Mazel.

Richeport-Haley, M. (1998a). Ethnicity in family therapy: A comparison of brief strategic therapy and culture-focused therapy. *American Journal of Family Therapy, 26,* 77–90.

Richeport-Haley, M. (1998b). Approaches to madness shared by cross-cultural healing systems and strategic family therapy. *Journal of Family Psychotherapy, 9*(4), 61–75.

Yapko, M. (1994). *Suggestions of abuse: True and false memories of childhood sexual trauma.* New York: Simon & Schuster.

10

A Positive Approach
With a Psychotic Couple

Outcome Studies of Schizophrenia

*T*here are at least a half dozen outcome studies of the therapy of schizophrenia in recent years. The outcome results have been impressive. One-half to two-thirds will become normal and be back in the community after a period of time. A brief summary can clarify the issue.

Manfred Bleuler (1968) did a 23-year follow-up on 208 patients in a Zurich hospital. He found that 23% had fully recovered after 20 years. An additional 43% had significant improvement.

In the United States there was a 32-year longitudinal study of 269 chronic patients in Vermont State Hospital (Harding & Brooks, 1984). One-half to two-thirds were significantly improved or recovered.

Ciompi and Muller (1987) in Switzerland examined 289 subjects 37 years after admission. They report that 29% had complete recoveries and that between 24% and 33% had only minor residuals; that is, more than half had favorable long-term outcomes.

In 1975, Huber, Gross, and Schutter studied 502 subjects an average of 22 years after admission and found 26% had achieved complete recovery and 31% had sustained significant improvement. Again, over half recovered or were significantly improved.

There were 1,300 subjects studied for longer than 20 years, and one-half to two-thirds achieved recovery or significant improvement. Not many "psychiatric disorders" have so good an outcome. This major finding suggests the need for helping people with a diagnosis of schizophrenia and the need to prepare schizophrenics for normality.

THE CIRCUMSTANCES OF THE CASE

This case presentation offers a way to make a fresh start with a therapy approach to schizophrenia. A therapist who is part of a training group brought in a couple to see whether the supervisor and group could do something with them. Previously, the trainee therapist had seen them individually for a period and had given them up. This interview is the first in which he sees them as a couple. The supervisor tries to persuade the therapist that normality can be expected from the therapy with this couple. To believe they are incurable and then proceed to offer therapy creates a double bind and a difficult therapy.

THE CLIENTS

A 36-year-old man, Joe, is brought in for a consultation. The trainee therapist had seen him elsewhere for a long time and wanted special help for him since the therapy was failing. Joe has a diagnosis of schizophrenia, and it had been decided to bring his 26-year-old wife, Ellen, in with him. Her diagnosis is schizoaffective disorder. She frequently threatens suicide. The couple lived together for a few months and has been married for 4 months. Both the husband and wife have been hospitalized frequently, and when in conflict in their marriage, they call upon a kindly psychiatrist who increases their medication and hospitalizes them if they are out of control. The wife was last hospitalized when she threatened suicide in the presence of her husband. The husband also has tardive dyskinesia, but he continues to be treated with the antipsychotic medication that causes it.

PLANNING THE SESSION

The supervisor asks the therapist-trainees to discuss the case and make a plan for the first interview. The therapist tells the group that the client has had a diagnosis of schizophrenia since his mid-20s. He says, "The wife also has the diagnosis of problems with her voices and the way she interprets things. As a couple they try to understand each other. The problem is, when his symptoms start acting up and her symptoms start acting up, their marital relationship doesn't seem to work."

Haley asks, "What are the *symptoms?*"

The therapist replies, "He has auditory hallucinations. The man is disorganized in his thinking, as is the wife. He is very, very cautious about things. He wants some things really planned. This is one of the reasons for him arriving here at 3:30 or 4:00 P.M. [5 hours before the appointment]. He didn't want to be late. He's really concerned about that."

What does he do for a living? Haley asked. *This question implies that the couple is capable of making a living. The therapist-trainee assumes that they are both mentally disabled and living on SSI and SSA. Their rent is paid and they have a car.* The supervisor could suggest a helpless orientation by exploring their symptoms or choose to focus on wellness by asking them to go to work. He chooses a framework of normality while expecting objections from both therapist and clients. The client says he is on medication and so he cannot work.

Trouble with the Marriage

The therapist says, "I think both of them are on antipsychotic medication and a mood stabilizer, and she also is on an antidepressant. I see him on a regular basis. Regular meaning once or twice a week, and then she comes in to the therapy and counseling alone. Most of his problems have to do with their relationship. He's been hospitalized numerous times. Joe says the reason is because he's having more and more fights and problems with Ellen."

Concerned about conflicts with colleagues, Haley asks, "Does either one of them have an individual therapist? "The therapist says he is the only therapist now. He says, "Joe's also attending a day program in a partial hospital program, where I work."

What Does Everyone Want Out of This Interview?

Since the therapist needs to be focused on a goal, Haley asks him, "What would you like to get out of this interview?" To this question the therapist replies, "I would like to set up specific goals for therapy. I would like to set up a length of time— I want to have some kind of a finish here. I am thinking about five or six interviews just to look at some particular issues and then decide if we need to go on. He's very distant from his parents. He wants nothing to do with his parents. It was like cut off from there. Haley inquires, "Does he associate with his parents at all?

The therapist answers, "Maybe a phone call, and that's it. He doesn't want anything to do with them. As I recall, they were running his life and controlling his life and treated him like a kid. "

Haley asks, "You want to set some goals to establish that? What do you think is preventing them from being normal?" (*continuing to make a normal framework for the interview*)

The therapist says, "I believe that there is a biological component to their schizophrenia. I think they're easily distracted and at times disoriented.

What keeps them from being normal as a couple, you mean? Normal is such a hard word."

Haley pushes for normality, surprising the therapist, "You are going to make them *normal*, presumably, if you can!"

THERAPIST: (*Thinking he could not have heard Haley correctly*) Say that again?

HALEY: That's the problem. You're thinking of them as incurable.

THERAPIST: I'm not saying they're incurable. But, you know, I think there are some limitations to what they can do.

HALEY: That's true of all of us.

THERAPIST: Yeah. And as far as them getting in a relationship, I think that's possible. They can learn how to communicate and how to involve each other and learn how to work with each other well.

HALEY: Why don't they go to work? (*continuing to stress normality*)

THERAPIST: He says that he gets overwhelmed with putting in the day, having to be there, having people telling him what to do.

Haley stresses Joe's problems as similar to those of ordinary people, "An authority problem." The therapist agrees. The discussion then turns to the primary gains of having something wrong with you.

HALEY: He's paid to be abnormal at the moment. I don't know how you feel about that.

THERAPIST: I think that's true. I think that we do compensate for some behaviors in our society. I know that's true. And he's getting paid to act out. That's a viable possibility.

HALEY: Do they have to keep getting benefits?

THERAPIST: They're on permanent disability is my understanding, and it doesn't really end up changing. In other words, people don't get better under that system. Medicare and SSA—it's like being retired. He has become suicidal. He has made a lot of threats but doesn't do anything violent. He doesn't act out or anything like that. He'll call his doctor and say, You know, I just can't handle this. I am having problems. And the doctor will arrange hospitalization.

Haley continues to focus on normality.

HALEY: Suppose you decided that there was nothing wrong with this couple, how would you have a session tonight?

THERAPIST: I think I would do the same things. Try to reestablish the goals and reestablish, perhaps, a little boundaries with each other.

HALEY: And you would assume they're capable of that?

THERAPIST: I believe that they are capable of doing that.

The attitude of the therapist is beginning to change. Now that therapy is possible with the couple, a further focus on normality is suggested.

HALEY: They're not interested in having children?

THERAPIST: He has one son from a previous marriage and has some contact with him. But no, they don't want children. He doesn't want any more children.

HALEY: How seriously do they take their own state of mind as an illness?

THERAPIST: I think they are very invested in their illness.

HALEY: Well, I think you have the proper view of them. It will just be interesting if you can shift your view of them.

THERAPIST: How so?

HALEY: Well, if you started off by saying to the guy, "I would like to set a date for you to go to work. And that should be our goal here and your wife could help you with that. And it could be a month from now; it could be a year from now. Just so we know that you are going to be normal and work."

THERAPIST: (*shocked*) Paid position working?

HALEY: Yes.

THERAPIST: Wow! (*not expecting normality*)

HALEY: Any kind of work. He's qualified to do something. That leads you into what he is qualified for and what is his attitude about a boss. But you are treating this like some deviant thing that he accidentally got into, instead of this is a career, which is a mental illness career. It's a very tough case to have a mental illness career and the assumption of a biological problem. Because what you tend to do is to try to remain stable. Like there is no trouble or he's not going into the hospital this week and she's not upsetting him or he's not upsetting her. It isn't that they are going to recover in 5 years from now. They each have an interesting career or something like that. If they are not having kids, they've got to have something else. They must just spend all their time together?

THERAPIST: Yes. They do. In fact, they are very dependent on one another. And, yes, they are together 24 hours a day just about.

HALEY: They are locked in some mutual protective system.

THERAPIST: I think they are.

HALEY: Or they provoke each other to stabilize each other. But anyhow, it would just be interesting to treat them like they are normal and see how they react.

One of the trainees who knew the wife remarked that in the past the wife had held a good job at a mental health agency. She took classes and drove her own car. Now she calls hotlines saying she is suicidal.

THERAPIST: I don't think each one is capable of holding down a full-time, 4-day-a-week job for days and days and days. I don't think they would be able to do that. But I think they can do like part time or consulting.

TRAINEE ONE: Short term. (*Again the couple is considered incapable.*)

THERAPIST: Short term or a couple hours here and there. Yeah, I think that is possible.

HALEY: I think they will drive each other nuts living together and neither one of them working.

THERAPIST: I think they do drive each other nuts. (*Everybody laughs.*)

TRAINEE TWO: So I wonder what happened that they got together and they got really decompensated or did this relationship drive them into permanent disability?

Improvement Is a Threat

Haley (1989) brings in research of four studies that show that when schizophrenics get older, they become normal in up to half the cases. "And he's getting near 50. So he might recover, and you should be prepared for that. I mean, he should have a job when he's recovered. He should have some training at least to get caught up on the latest. (*This is a classic double bind for him to prepare for normality.*)

Haley asks how Joe behaves in the hospital. The therapist replies that he feels less anxious and more secure, which lasts 3 or 4 days. Haley instructs the therapist: "Say, you know he's been mentally ill, and that's why he is on disability. I would like you to suggest that he pretend he's normal, and if he pretended he's normal, how would he talk to you and how would he talk to his wife? And make a framework of pretending. I mean that is one way to do it. There are other ways, but it is a framework in which he's expected to be normal and see if he can do any part of it. I mean, he's either got to do it or he's got to not do it and be just more and more bizarre to make it clear that he deserves this."

The therapist says, "So, I need this on normality in this session. What do normal couples do?"

Haley continues, "And if he asks you what is normal? You can say, 'Whatever you think is normal'."

The therapist expresses the traditional, proper point of view. The couple has difficulties because of biological causes, which define them as psychotic. The supervisor assumes that many schizophrenics are capable of being normal if a therapist can establish that expectation. It is assumed there is a social and family function to the behaviors (Haley, 1997).

THE SESSION

The therapist went into the room to interview the couple. The trainees and supervisor observed behind the one-way mirror. Suggestions were transferred from the supervisor to the therapist by sending them on the monitor, where the therapist, but not the clients, could see the message.

The suggestions from the supervisor can be grouped. Primarily the suggestion was that the therapist should ask the couple if they would like to be normal.

THERAPIST: Do you see yourself as kind of a normal couple? That these are kind of normal things that happen between people? Let's see if we can pretend that that this is a normal couple with some normal reactions here. Would you have handled yourself any differently?

The second major suggestion was to ask when the man planned to go to work. The man reacted normally by saying it would be scary to go to work after being out of it for 8 years. The wife evidently wanted him to go to work. She suggested he could use his computer knowledge to make web pages at home.

THERAPIST: You worked in computers. Is that right?
JOE: Yeah.
THERAPIST: When do you plan to work again?

The man said that he had always been treated badly at home and at work. He had been used as the world's punching bag. He discussed his upset when the wife threatened suicide in front of him. The therapist went to the issue of work.

Computer Suggestion: Did he say what day he could go to work—the husband can go to work?

THERAPIST: Do you both plan to go back to work and start developing a life for yourselves?

Do you think in therapy here that we might set a goal in regard to work? Again, it doesn't have to be tomorrow, it doesn't have to be in a couple of weeks, but maybe get the idea out there that there is a possibility of returning to a type of work that's been satisfying to you.

Computer Suggestion: Ask her to hold his hand and encourage him.

THERAPIST: Can you hold hands here? Let's see if we can do this. You want to look each other in eye and I want you to encourage him. I want you to give him some encouragement about maybe going back to work and how this might affect you and the relationship and maybe getting that spunk. He needs some of that spunk.

Computer Suggestion: Say, if you are up to it, or if you think it's right, mention that sometime you could bring in Mom and Dad.

THERAPIST: You also may want to consider—and I think this might be kind of interesting, not next session or the session after that, but maybe down the line—I just want you to think about bringing in Mom and Dad.

The therapist shifts to the parents. Could they be brought in? They say both sets of parents might come in, but the husband said his father would not and should not be asked. The three main points covered were:

1. The premise is established that they can be normal. They began to argue like a normal couple.
2. Being normal means going to work and becoming self-supporting.
3. The parents need to come in to therapy.

DISCUSSING THE INTERVIEW AFTERWARD

The group said, "Oh my god, the therapist gave the suggestions to Joe to go to work. Yes, he was brave."

THERAPIST: It was the work option. It was the interesting point. Remember how I told you they were really invested in his *illness*. He's really very negative about that.

HALEY: We'll shake him out of that.

THERAPIST: Yeah. We had a couple of good responses from him or good reactions from him.

HALEY: He smiled a couple times.

THERAPIST: Yes, he did.

HALEY: I thought you handled it very well. It isn't the usual way you've handled it.

THERAPIST: It's pretty close. It's pretty close. I like the suggestions.

TRAINEE THREE: Yeah. You wouldn't have said those things.

THERAPIST: I don't think so. Not this time. I felt like I was pushing work a little. I thought he was going to respond. Because I've seen him get angry and maybe it's because of the camera and this stuff. I don't know. I think he shut down, though, in response to that. I don't have to get better.

HALEY: He has a patient look about him.

TRAINEE: Now he's got tardive dyskinesia

THERAPIST: I saw the tapping of the foot.

TRAINEE: He's been taking the meds for a long time.

THERAPIST: The reason why he has the beard is because he will clench his teeth so bad and tighten up.

TRAINEE: Is that ultimately changeable?

THERAPIST: No. That's damage from the neuroleptics.

HALEY: And they are still giving the medication to him?

THERAPIST: You can give him other medications to offset that. Did you see him jerk a couple times?

HALEY: If they are serving him a medication that is still harming him, he won't have to go to work. He can manage with litigation to do very well. Because they are supposed to stop those drugs when they show some physical harm.

THERAPIST: Some of the symptoms are irreversible even though they stop the medication.

I think he got really overwhelmed when she was trying to commit suicide in front of him. Can you just imagine the chaos—the yelling, the screaming, the fighting, the tears, and all that stuff and the trauma? I think that is what they went through about 2 weeks ago.

HALEY: If she threatens suicide, you have to put them in the hospital.

THERAPIST: She has strange common symptoms. I mean, when she talks about hallucinations and some disorganization.

TRAINEE: No. See that's new. She wasn't hallucinating when I knew her.

HALEY: There wasn't any sign of that tonight. Did you see any?

TRAINEE: No.

THERAPIST: I didn't see any of the psychotic symptoms. Although they are both pretty well medicated.

HALEY: Well that's a "twosome." There used to be and there are enough symptoms to still diagnose them. You know, one alternative to going into the hospital is to ask them to prepare themselves so they don't have to go in by doing what they have done before, and get them to yell and get her to swear at him.

To keep them out of the hospital the therapist asks them to deliberately do the behaviors that usually precipitate hospitalization, and that is a paradox.

HALEY: In the next interview I would really like them to set a date to go to work.

THERAPIST: I think I suggested that two times, three times, and he was resistant about doing that [going to work]. I think we got him thinking about work and what he can do.

HALEY: I would say that anybody would be really worried about that after 8 years whether you could adapt to it now.

This reframes the client's negativism into a normal reaction for anyone out of work for so long and stresses normality that the therapist begins to accept as well.

THERAPIST: Anybody would have those fears.

Being Supported

TRAINEE: Do you know how they live? Who supports them?

THERAPIST: They have lucrative funds. They really do.

HALEY: I would spend some time figuring out how much they make and what about their medical bills and so on.

THERAPIST: He didn't want the dad to know. He and his dad are really apart.

HALEY: He said he [dad] wouldn't come in. Right?

THERAPIST: His dad would not come in.

HALEY: Because I think if you called the father, he would come in. He's not going to come in if his son requests it.

THERAPIST: Right. He'll come in if somebody else wants him to come in. That ought to be interesting.

Protection Theory

HALEY: One of the things, if you have a proper family theory, you assume that guy is failing in relation to his parents. And it's going to be hard for him to get a job, if that activates the change with the parents.

THERAPIST: Say that again.

HALEY: One of the assumptions of most family therapists from different schools is that the kid fails in life as a way of helping the parents, and they have a problem in their marriage for which they blame the son. If he goes normal, if this guy started to go to work tomorrow, his father would be upset. It's the theory, even though the father wants him to go to work and succeed. It doesn't mean the theory is true. Family therapists like this theory because it gives them something to do. Let's just bring the parents in and work with them to resolve issues so the kid is free and at least temporarily no longer has to be psychotic. That's the sequence that's happening. When the kid goes normal, the parents start to split. He gets upset and is hospitalized, confirming the parents' view of the son as a failure. They pull right together to take care of him. He gets normal, and they start to split, and the sequence goes on forever. This is only one aspect of his psychosis and does not mean that his parents are to blame. Some parents are, while others are not. Parents object to blame and form an organization to object. The parents and child are equally caught up in the situation. If he came out of it, the parents would ultimately be pleased with the change and even be willing to take credit. The young man would be an interesting guy.

THERAPIST: Yes, and he has a nice smile. And he's really invested in staying in his rut. You know when we first started seeing him many months ago before we ended the therapy, I kind of had that hunch that it was between him and his dad. He never was good in math problems, so he was beaten as a child, he says; he was the punching bag, and he was the brunt of all the jokes.

HALEY: (*switching to present behavior, not past symptom history*) Did you see any sign of him being schizophrenic?

THERAPIST: I have in the past. I don't think I see it now.

HALEY: I know, but I mean in the interview?

THERAPIST: I did see some of the negative symptoms. I mean the withdrawal. It was more like an affective disorder than a schizophrenic process.

HALEY: There was no sign of him hallucinating again?

THERAPIST: No. No. I didn't see him being preoccupied or responding to internal stimuli. I didn't see any of that—that process. I have seen it in the past with her, but not with him.

Being Practical

HALEY: The problem is when you get people who have had so much experience in therapy, it is very hard to not get involved in the things they are involved in. I mean, like how they treat each other, what they say to each other, and what they think of each other. But neither one is working, going to school, or doing anything useful. You know you tend to forget that as you get involved in how they fight with each other. It is very tempting. The whole language and the style of therapy fool the therapist. All this person has to do is to wonder, Do I really understand? and off they go. One of the problems is deciding what you are a therapist of when you get a multi kind of problem. Or if you find his father is very upset, it is your responsibility to do something about his father. But it is interesting what responsibilities you feel you should take. I mean, a guy who is so compulsive that he leaves home at 1:00 to get here at 5:00 for a 15-minute trip, something should be done about it. I know what we can do with it. It's a classic paradox. Ask him to come at 11 next time so he gets the feeling of what it is like to really wait.

THERAPIST: Yeah. He would do it.

HALEY: He wouldn't do it twice.

THERAPIST: He won't come back.

TRAINEE: (*The trainees are learning to be more positive.*) Most therapists that approach these people with chronic mental illnesses hope for increased functioning. You are looking at trying to get them to relate better.

THERAPIST: To stay out of the hospital.

TRAINEE: Yeah. But when you start saying, Go to work and do these things, they are going to say, oh my god! You know.

HALEY: Ellen gives Joe a double bind by taking leadership by saying he's in charge.

THERAPIST: I like that—a double bind.

HALEY: If you were an expert, you would bring both families together for one big session.

THERAPIST: That's what I thought we were going to do.

HALEY: I was thinking it would be two at a time but you could do all four.

How Many People Should You Include in Therapy?

HALEY: The genius of family therapy was that it shifted from the individual to the social matrix. Bateson said, "The mind is outside the body." He was expressing this idea that it's not an individual problem. The therapist was unfamiliar with the variety of ways to involve the family and assumed that at least four members would be involved. There are also therapists who tell the kid to leave—don't see your family again. Family therapists tend to bring them together because they think they ought to be together. But there are some who just feel this is impossible, and they get family members out of the home to be safe. This is rare. One contribution of family therapy was that it explains that if you have a guy who is acting strangely, you really have a choice whether to explain it because of his ideas and manners and medication or because of his social situation. You have two whole different theories and ideas, depending on which one of those you pick. With Joe you can pick the idea that he's schizophrenic and that that's compulsive and full of medication and that's the problem. Or you can think that his relationship with his wife is the problem. Or you can think of his relationship with his wife and his mother or his father is the problem. These are all hypotheses that you must select from.

THERAPIST: But I think the environment creates the biology.

HALEY: That's a classic question. For you people, what's the best theory for the therapist to have? There's another theory for a researcher to have or another one for some other purpose in examining human beings. But for the therapist the best theory is what gives you an ideology and a way of thinking that helps you as a therapist and gives you a chance to take some action.

A WEEK LATER

A week later the therapist reported that the client protested in group therapy he could not tolerate the idea of working. He also went over the therapist's head and complained to the therapist's colleagues that the therapist was forcing him to go to work. This made the therapist uneasy in relation to his colleagues. It became clear there were a number of people involved in stabilizing the young man as a chronic case.

THERAPIST: He got very angry and got very upset because of the suggestion that we wanted him to go back to work and he says that he is not capable.

HALEY: You know I would have predicted he would either get very normal or he would get angry and upset and a bit bizarre.

THERAPIST: Yeah. He got more and more upset and what he did was he actually went to a couple of other people and was saying, you know, "Oh my therapist is trying to get me back to work." And I even heard it from his physician that I'm trying to get him back to work and he just can't. He said he didn't sleep all night. That he was tossing and turning, that he got very, very upset over the whole situation and his symptoms came back. He told me that he was hearing voices all night long and just was so worried about the whole work detail.

The wife wasn't aware of these symptoms. She wasn't aware of all the problems and only he was a little more irritable. But he let her know that he was having great difficulties and problems with what has been said. How he distorted it was that I was mandating him to go to work next week and that he needed to prepare himself next week to get a job. I was the supreme being telling him that he has to do something and that he got very angry toward me. I could still tell that he was quite angry that I would ever, ever suggest that he was normal; that he can get a job and go back into the work force.

One expectation and hope was that the client would get angry at being forced to go normal. It would be considered a positive move on his part. This is a successful patient. He has survived hospitals and he lives on total disability and married a woman who does the same. So neither one has to work. This is one reason for his anger.

HALEY: Did she have any objection to work?

THERAPIST: You know, she didn't. Actually, she wants him to go to work. He comes in and says, "Oh, not for me I just can't do it. I'm just not going to be able to do that. I can't handle being around people." I mean, I heard everything.

HALEY: What would you assume from that?

THERAPIST: I think that he is really invested in the illness. I think he is really scared about losing some of the benefits that he gets.

HALEY: But your hypothesis is that it's an individual problem in gaining money and so on?

THERAPIST: I asked again about his parents—bringing his folks in and bringing, you know, everybody in together. And he said that they would be willing to but his dad won't come in. And I said, "How about contacting your dad?" No. He doesn't want any contact. He doesn't want me to talk to his dad. That made me think that he may feel that I might talk to his dad about him getting a job and about his normality.

HALEY: That's what will happen. Well, if you push him to go to work, he's going to get angry.

THERAPIST: Get angry. Yeah!

HALEY: Then your question is what hypothesis is best for a therapist to have in relation to that? One is family oriented—that gives you more things do. You've got him, you've got his mother, and you've got his father. And you didn't push it any further about going to work?

THERAPIST: You know, I backed off from that issue. My feeling of backing off a little is because he wouldn't let it go. I mean I didn't want him to say, "Oh, my therapist did this and did that." I guess I was kind of protecting myself a little bit—trying to give him a little understanding that I really wasn't pushing him to go next week. Maybe down the line. I wanted to clarify it a little more. So I admit I was somewhat concerned.

HALEY: You would have been thought wrong for pushing him. Is that right?

THERAPIST: Yeah. I think I still needed to get back and have a little more trust there with him.

HALEY: I think the movement would come more from the wife. If you got together with the wife on how improved he would be if he went to work, and she'll agree. Because I'm sure she wants him to go to work.

THERAPIST: Yes, she does. "I wouldn't be doing my job if you weren't showing some improvement and getting better." It kind of made him think just a little bit and then he says, "Well a job is not the thing to get me better. What I need is more medication and more communication." I mean, again, he's so invested in his illness.

HALEY: Well, it's a career and it's a paid career. You didn't bring that up, though.

THERAPIST: I thought it would be a little callous to do that.

HALEY: You could say to her, how much would you lose if you went to work? You could say there must be different motivations for not going to work and one is money.

THERAPIST: Actually, I asked them about their finances also. So they get $185 a month for rent. He gets $720 and she gets $640. And that is tax-free. That's everything. And then they get all their medical and all the stuff paid for. Their medications are paid for. And their car is paid for.

So I think their total expenditures came out around $250 and that's including gas and they are making $1,000. They have about $1,000 extra cash just to buy and spend and do whatever they want with.

HALEY: He's probably made those calculations.

THERAPIST: Oh yeah.

HALEY: But I think you need to get those parents in somehow.

THERAPIST: I think so, too. It's a challenge.

HALEY: But you could always bring the family together and say this is an important time when your son or daughter (or whoever it is) is reaching a point where they can step forward or they cannot step forward and I would like to help you get off into a new world. You say to the parents, If you thought your son-in-law was successful, what would he be doing? And they'll say go to work. That's what they'll say.

THERAPIST: Go to work. Yeah. They don't really want to. He doesn't work and he's made it quite clear that that's not his focus.

HALEY: He's worked hard to get where he is today.

THERAPIST: He's worked very hard to get where he is today.

HALEY: That's right. You could try bringing in the wife with her parents and the couple, just saying you need to gather information.

THERAPIST: And then look at the areas of success.

HALEY: Focus on success, and it sets an example for his family if these people would come in. Because his father must be in trouble, or his mother or somebody is.

THERAPIST: You'd assume that there are problems in their relationship in the marriage of his parents?

HALEY: I would assume there's a problem in his parent's marriage.

TRAINEE: You didn't even know they were married?

THERAPIST: Yeah. I thought that they were divorced for some reason.

HALEY: Well, OK, we'll look forward to future reports. If you want to bring him in here next week, that would be nice too.

TWO WEEKS AFTER THE LIVE INTERVIEW A SHIFT HAS TAKEN PLACE

THERAPIST: He was in a group therapy session. One of the ladies started talking more about how horrible she feels and of her depression and that she's sick. Joe became upset. He became very angry that she is being sick and he said, "Well it seems to me you are playing the sick role and that you are doing it well." So the process actually turned back on him and he says, "Well, I need to start getting my life back together." And I said, "Such as?" He goes, "Well, maybe work." And it was like from anger right after our session, he was angry for about a week and then all of a sudden in a group he turns around and says this. I mean it was great. He started talking about being normal and didn't want to be looked at as abnormal. I mean, words are good but I hope his behavior follows through. He got some anger out of him. A little animation, which I thought was kind of good.

HALEY: I think you should take credit for that.

THERAPIST: Well, thank you.

Another girl in Joe's therapy group got herself a computer through this free computer service that we got her hooked up with and she got a new computer for free, so long as she joins the Internet. He goes over there and programs the whole thing and gets it all set up for her and feels validated for some of the work he's done. And he liked it. He enjoyed it. That's what I think.

HALEY: That's what I would emphasize. That's aggressive. Because I think that session when you pushed him to be more active and get a job sunk in. He's got to react either by doing that positively, because you timed it with the changes in his life, or he's got to relapse and complain and say it's awful and I've got to work. I don't want to work and so on. What he does is he reacted negatively, and then a week later he shifted.

THERAPIST: Right.

HALEY: So, you had that delay first.

THERAPIST: Actually, within the last couple of weeks there has been no hospitalization treatment nor threats of suicide, whereas it was pretty frequent before.

HALEY: What's interesting is they get shocked with the idea that that they should be normal. It's a very upsetting idea.

THERAPIST: Well, it's scary, I think, for a lot of them too.

The following week the therapist reports on a group session Joe attended in the day hospital. The first week in the group the young man complained about being forced to work and seemed in a panic. The second week he said to the group that he decided he didn't like being considered abnormal. He decided to go to work. He began by setting up a computer system for a woman friend that was partly a job and showed he was capable. The therapist and the reader have the choice of believing the client is too abnormal to go to work to support himself, or one can believe he is capable of going to work but does not for social reasons. Each point of view has its merits and its consequences to the life of the couple and the staff.

Joe and Ellen had come to one live supervised session as a consultation. Two months later the husband left for another state to live with an aunt. Neither wife nor therapist heard from him.

At a 6-month follow-up, the wife was back in therapy but no longer threatening suicide. The therapist continued training with higher expectations of change in difficult chronic clients.

REFERENCES

Bleuler, M. (1968). A 23-year longitudinal study of 208 schizophrenics and impressions in regard to the nature of schizophrenia. In R. D. Kety (Ed.), *The transmission of schizophrenia*. Oxford: Pergamon Press.

Ciompi, L. (1987, February). Toward a comprehensive biological psychological understanding and treatment of schizophrenia. The Stanley R. Dean Award Lecture, presented at the *Annual Meeting of the American College of Psychiatrists*, Maui, HI.

Haley, J. (1989). The effects of long-term outcome studies on the therapy of schizophrenia. *Journal of Marital and Family Therapy, 15*(2), 127–132.

Haley, J. (1997). *Leaving home: The therapy of disturbed young people* (2nd ed.). New York: Brunner-Routledge.

Harding, C. M., & Brooks, G. W. (1984). Life assessment of a cohort of chronic schizophrenics discharged twenty years ago. In S. Mednick, M. Harway, & K. Finello (Eds.), *The handbook of longitudinal research, II*. New York: Praeger.

Huber, G., Gross, G., & Schuttler, R. (1975). A long-term follow-up study of schizophrenia: Psychiatric course of illness and prognosis. *Acta Psychiatrica Scandinavica, 52,* 49–57.

Epilogue

It is evident that strategic therapy has become successful as indicated by the multiple training programs. The reader can recognize a distinctive therapy. It is different from others, which is what this book is about. Opposition to the approach during its revolutionary period has become acceptance, and many of the ideas of strategic therapy have infiltrated these other approaches. Films have demonstrated the training value more than in other therapies. Students who could not accept that certain clients were curable came away with a positive explanation for abominable behavior so they would have optimism that change is possible. Rather than have a theory of motivation based on inner hostility, they learn a method of protection that emphasizes solutions. They learn that this is not an awareness therapy. Therapists should not focus on changing clients with insight although supervisors make therapists aware. Curiously, the trainees are encouraged to follow their impulses while at the same time making conscious plans for action. Therapy is carefully planned and delivered spontaneously. Therapy is brief and inevitably directive. Trainees who were originally worried about keeping clients waiting and waiting for clients to come up with something in the session would learn to make a plan ahead of time, which is becoming expected in the field.

The idea that the initial interview might be the last, because single-session therapy is a challenge, often contradicted the reality that trainees need thousands of hours for licensure. The length of therapy is still determined by the need to make money in private practice, on insurance companies deciding how long therapy should be, as well as the length of hospitalization and educational requirements. Haley had always encouraged trainees to be as brief as possible. If the trainee was interested, and psychotics were available, they were especially interesting teachers. Like Erickson, Haley's training is based on common sense and using the resources in the community to help clients.

It wasn't an accident that the value of strategic therapy and Zen was recognized in the 1950s, though Zen had a history of 700 years, whereas strategic therapy was relatively new, existing for only a decade. In the Gregory Bateson Research Project we were introduced to Zen by Alan Watts, Director of the American Academy on Asian Studies. Watts (1961) became interested in therapy as it related to Zen. In 1953, the same year we discovered Zen, we discovered the hypnosis of Milton Erickson. Haley (1990, 1993) found the premises of Zen to be the only way of explaining the strategic therapy of Erickson and his therapy supervision. In Zen, the stories reflect an anti-intellectual view, which was different from the therapies at the time, which had a European origin. The goal of Zen is *satori* or enlightenment, which is assumed to come about in relation to a teacher who frees the student form the preoccupation with the past, future, or enlightenment. The same kinds of problems that keep clients in distress are those that Zen finds prevents people from experiencing the present moment.

> Tanzan and Ekido were once traveling together down a muddy road. A heavy rain was still falling. Coming around a bend, they met a lovely girl in a silk kimono and sash, unable to cross the intersection. "Come on, girl," said Tanzan at once. Lifting her in his arms, he carried her over the mud. Ekido did not speak again until that night when they reached a lodging temple. Then he no longer could restrain himself. "We monks don't go near females," he told Tanzan, "especially not young and lovely ones. It is dangerous. Why did you do that?" "I left the girl there," said Tanzan. "Are you still carrying her?" (Reps, undated, p.18)

Changing a person means changing their classification system. The task is given to supervisors, to therapists, and to Zen masters to induce change. Many Zen anecdotes illustrate the problem of changing classification. In the anecdote above, trying not to think about something creates the class whose items one must think about in order not to think of them. Change is usually done relating around an activity, a task, a directive between master and student, and often generates paradoxes. When the therapist asks a client not to change, which is a paradoxical directive, the client must begin changing to respond to that idea. If you ask a fighting boy to be good and to teach his good brother to be bad, and thank him for doing this, then you are thanking him for being bad.

One problem is finding similarities between Zen and most therapies because in Zen there is no psychopathology. Behavior is seen as a step toward enlightenment. Likewise, in this therapy, behavior is normalized and reframed as positive, and is not seen as pathological. A disruptive adolescent is seen as moving from one stage in the family life cycle to that of leaving home. A psychotic person is defined as rude and without a job instead of chronically ill. An uncommunicative husband is seen as an artist or special person who may be forgiven. The boy who can't stop fighting is displaying a protective function for his mother and is therefore a more likeable client. In strategic therapy, maladaptive behaviors are seen as a response to a social situation and not as a character defect or permanent malady. This Zen story illustrates this positive view:

> Ryokan, a Zen master, lived the simplest kind of life in a little hut at the foot of a mountain. One evening a thief visited the hut only to discover there was nothing in it to steal. Ryokan returned and caught him. "You may have come a long way to visit me," he told the prowler, "and you should not return empty-handed. Please take my clothes as a gift." The thief was bewildered. He took the clothes and slunk away. Ryokan sat naked, watching the moon. "Poor fellow," he mused, "I wish I could give him this beautiful moon." (Reps, undated, p. 12)

In summary, the procedures of Zen and the strategic therapy approach are similar. In Zen, enlightenment is sought through a relationship with a master who joins the student in the task that involves directing him or her; who attempts to escape from intellectualizing about life or monitoring personal behavior; who insists on solutions that may happen rapidly; who has a wide range of behavior and many techniques, including a willingness to be absurd; who focuses on the present and not the past; and, who, in a benevolent framework, uses ordeals to force a change.

Let us end with a case that may seem simple but illustrates the most important ideas of strategic therapy.

"When I was in practice, a man came to me who said he had a symptom which was exasperating him. He asked if I could do something about it. I said I did not know, and I asked what is the symptom. The man said he would rather not tell me what it is. He didn't think I needed to know what it was, he just wanted to get rid of it. I said he was asking quite a lot to expect me to cure a symptom without knowing what it is. I advised him to tell me its nature and I would see what I could do. He was adamant and would not tell me what his symptom was. I was concerned about whether I could solve the symptom and I was also concerned about the ethics of changing a person without knowing what I was changing. I could see he would leave, and have the distress of his symptom, if he did not get his terms, so I agreed to take him on. I said that I would have to know two things about the symptom. One, I needed to know if it was there all the time or intermittent. He said it was intermittent. I said I also needed his agreement to do whatever I said. He said as long as it didn't reveal the symptom he would do what I said. I made my intervention, which was a directive, and he was surprised by it, but it did not reveal the symptom. It was a type of intervention which has been published. The man came in the following week looking a bit distraught, and he said he would like to stop doing the task. I said he had made a promise and sent him on his way (I had anticipated an upset). He came in the next week and said he was improving, but he would like to stop the task. I said he could not. The following week he came in discussing issues with his wife and other matters. I had to ask him "What about the symptom?" since he never brought it up. He dismissed the subject saying that the symptom was nearly gone. The next week, and in a followup, he was over the symptom. I never did know what it was.

"I cite this case as a simple one which is related to therapy procedures of other therapies. This case raises various issues. For example, need we educate clients about the purpose of their symptoms? Is awareness needed for change? If there is to be a change, is insight necessary? Is the past relevant to either the cause or cure? Is skill with directives necessary to get them carried out? Is it unethical to force someone to change, even when they have asked for it? Can a therapist enjoy the work even when dealing with distress and misery? I hope so." (Haley, 2000)

REFERENCES

Haley, J. (1990). Strategies of psychoanalysis and other therapies. In *Strategies of psychotherapy*. La Jolla, CA: Triangle Press.

Haley, J. (2000) What therapists have in common. Presented at the *Evolution of Psychotherapy meeting*. Milton H. Erickson Foundation, Phoenix, AZ. May, 2000.

Haley, J. (1993). Zen and the art of therapy. In *Jay Haley on Milton H. Erickson*. New York: Brunner/Mazel.

Reps, P.S. (undated). *Zen flesh and bones*. New York: Doubleday.

Watts, A. W. (1961). *Psychotherapy east and west*. New York: Pantheon.

APPENDIX A

Case Report: How to Unbalance a Couple

Being Unfair

A couple in their late 20s, who had been married about 7 years, came to therapy uncertain whether to stay together or separate. They were both dissatisfied, but neither one was willing to make a move to change their situation, particularly by moving toward the other. They were professional people and sophisticated about therapy.

The therapist was a former minister with experience working with couples. He tended to bring out a couple's feelings about each other and offer straightforward advice. He was in training because he wished to learn the directive, brief approach to therapy. He presented himself in a professional manner with a somewhat folksy style. One of his primary characteristics was that he gave equal time to both spouses, having been taught that a therapist should be careful not to side with one spouse against the other.

In the first interview the problems and situation of the couple were explored. The wife said that her husband was dissatisfied and sulked. The husband said that his wife was ignoring him and that she was unhappy with the marriage. At home they often argued and shouted at each other. Although their families were involved with them, there appeared to be no in-law problems, and a decision about bringing in the parents was postponed. Both spouses were successful and devoted to their careers. The wife had recently taken a new position and was working long hours. When interviewed alone, she said she often stayed at work longer than was necessary because it was so unpleasant when she came home.

Spouses are seen individually as well as together in this approach, either in the first interview or at the beginning of the second. It is useful to have the information that each is unlikely to offer in the presence of the other spouse. For example, at times one spouse enters therapy with the wish to divorce and leave the other, rather than with a willingness to improve the marriage, not knowing this can cause the therapist to waste time. There are issues of confidentiality when seeing spouses alone, but the advantages outweigh the disadvantages. A therapist should not be trapped into not revealing something, but generally there is nothing wrong with a therapist keeping secrets from one or both spouses and taking responsibility for what to do with those secrets.

There is another reason for seeing spouses separately: The therapist needs to be an authority to get things done, and authority requires power. One way to increase power is to control information. If a therapist only sees a couple in joint therapy sessions, both spouses know all that has been told to the therapist, but if the spouses are seen separately, neither knows what the other has said. But the therapist does. Since the therapist has more information than either spouse has, he or she has more power. When a couple is locked in a struggle, to get movement requires the therapist to have authority.

The focus of the presentation here is the second interview with the aforementioned couple. The first interview had ended without a directive, and the couple came back expecting further discussion of their dissatisfactions. The second interview began with such a discussion, with each spouse complaining to the therapist about the other. The discussion was the kind that sophisticated, articulate couples are able to carry on for many sessions if they are encouraged to do so, as often happens in private practice. In this directive, brief approach, however, such articulate sophistication prevents change, since change requires action.

When the husband said that he doubted his wife loved him, the therapist asked him for evidence of that. The husband said, "She absolutely avoids spending time with me, and she shows me very little warmth or affection, physically and emotionally." The wife interrupted and said, "That's not true." The husband insisted that it was, and continued, "I feel completely shut out of her life. I learn more about what's happening in her life by what I hear her telling people on the telephone. I don't feel that she wants to be around me at all. I think she is very close to moving out, wanting to be alone on her own, away from me." He added, "I've been trying real hard, and I don't get any positive feedback at all."

The therapist said, "How about when she reached out and touched you here? You didn't respond at all." The husband said, "I was aware of that. She wouldn't have done that at home." The wife interrupted angrily, "That's not true! It's an absolute lie!"

The therapist continued, "What evidence is there that she *does* love you?"

The husband replied, "Well, we're here, and we still live together."

The therapist asked, "Do you think she's interested in someone else?" (The wife, when seen alone, said that she was not.)

"I don't think that's the problem. No," said the husband.

The therapist said, "You feel you want more contact, and you're not getting it." "That's right," said the husband. "We're going through the motions, such as this therapy. Out of a sense of guilt or because the last step is a hard one to take."

"Letting you down softly?"

"Perhaps letting us both down softly. Feeling some responsibility to the marriage. At any rate, I don't feel very wanted."

Turning to the wife, the therapist said, "How about you? What is your view about whether he loves you or not."

"Oh, I think he loves me," she said. "I know he says he hates me every once in a while, but he tends to fly off the handle. Although it hurts me when he does that, certainly . . . a lot. I wish that he . . . the way I want somebody to show love is different from the ways which he tries to show it. And he's unwilling to show it in the ways I want it shown, because he doesn't feel that my ways are valid ways. I think we both have to come to terms with each other's way of showing it. And being able more readily to interpret how love comes across." She added, "I think he's losing patience with me. And I'm having a real hard time now."

"Do you think you'll have to go after him again? To court him again?"

"I don't know. Part of me doesn't want to. I feel like I shouldn't have to. If he's not willing to make a few changes here and there, I'm not going to be willing to do much either."

All couples have communication rules embedded in their relationship. What was becoming evident here was that the couple followed the rule that the wife is to initiate what happens, and the husband to respond. Sometimes relationship rules appear to be followed as inevitably as a train on a railroad track. For example, a couple can have a rule that the wife is responsible and the husband is irresponsible. Whatever they do, that rule is followed. If the wife wants to save money, the husband will want to spend it. If the wife wants to go to marriage therapy, the husband will avoid it (the sympathy of the therapist is usually with the wife because she says what a good client should say, whereas the husband won't even come in). And so on. Of course, the behavior of such a couple is mutually reinforcing in a systematic way: The more irresponsible the husband is, the more responsible the wife becomes, and the more she is responsible the more irresponsible he becomes.

The rule followed by this couple is that the wife is to initiate contact and the husband is to respond, a rule followed by many couples. Often, a couple is quite satisfied with that rule. However, if they become dissatisfied with it, a change becomes necessary. At a certain point in the marriage of this couple, the wife stopped initiating contact (as she said, "I feel I shouldn't have to") and began to wait for the husband to do so. He did not. The wife was then faced with the dilemma of having to decide whether to go back to initiating contact or to wait for her husband to do so, with the possibility that he might never come forward.

After about 20 minutes into the second interview, it became evident to the supervisor behind the mirror that nothing was happening in the therapy room except conversation. The couple was willing to talk forever about their ideas and feelings, but action needed to be taken for change to occur. The question was: Who should do what? The husband seemed to be waiting for the wife to initiate something; the wife, dissatisfied with being the initiator, was waiting for the husband to do something; both spouses were waiting for the therapist to do something; and the therapist was waiting for the supervisor to do something. Aware of the situation, the supervisor called the therapist out of the room for a consultation.

The supervisor understood that something had to be done to divert this therapeutic conversation into an action that would bring about change. Conversation does not change people unless there is a directive implicit in it. It seemed apparent to the supervisor that the couple wished to stay together, but that neither spouse was willing to take a step toward the other. The supervisor saw that that first step would need to be arranged by the therapist. The therapist, meanwhile, was actually preventing change by behaving in a neutral way, and so confirming the type of relationship the couple was revealing to him.

It is typical of married couples who come to therapy that one spouse has more power than the other. A primary way of determining who has power in a marriage is to note which spouse can threaten to leave the other. In this case, the wife could do so and apparently the husband could not. (Often one spouse will regularly threaten to leave the other over some issue, and the other will capitulate. However, if one day the one who regularly capitulate says, "All right. Let's separate," this upsets them both and they come for therapy.)

In this couple, the wife was in a superior position in relation to the husband. When she was dissatisfied, she went out and did things. The husband sat at home, frustrated, waiting for her. A therapist who is faced with this inequality and who behaves fairly and equally with both spouses is confirming their unequal relationship by being neutral. Neutrality indicates that no change is necessary, even though the therapist wishes this couple could change. Unfortunately, there is a tendency in marital therapy training to emphasize that the therapist should treat both spouses equally. The concern about inadvertently forming a coalition with one spouse against the other prevents the therapist from deliberately forming a coalition as part of the therapy. Yet by joining each spouse equally, when they are unequal with each other, the therapist is confirming their relationship instead of trying to change it.

It seemed obvious to the supervisor that this couple was locked in a systemic struggle in which each spouse's attempts to change the other only served to more tightly lock them in an unequal relationship. It also seemed apparent that the couple was prepared to talk about their relationship forever (or at least for many months). What was needed was some action that would destabilize them. The rigidity of their relationship suggested that the action would probably have to be extreme. To the supervisor the problem was not the couple but the therapist, who was committed to "fairness" and would have difficulty taking action if that action involved siding with one spouse against the other.

The group of trainees behind the one-way mirror seemed to think the interview was going well since the couple was expressing their feelings and articulating their differences. The structure of the situation, the inequality of the pair, their reluctance to take new actions—these were not obvious to them. Most of the trainees felt the therapist should continue the conversation, in which he was mainly encouraging the spouses to express their views. Their focus was on the couple, not on the triangle of couple and therapist. They were also unaware of the triangle involving the supervisor. Therefore, this was a good teaching situation.

A comment on thinking in terms of triangles is in order here. Some trainees have trouble learning to explain behavior in terms of triads, as any good therapist should. When a therapist sits down with a couple, the situation is a triangle. If a male therapist sees a wife in individual therapy, he is triangulating with the husband and wife in their marriage; the husband assumes his wife is talking to another man about him, which is so. When seeing a couple, the therapist has several choices. He or she can side with the wife against the husband, side with the husband against the wife, or try to be neutral. Each comment by a spouse pulls the therapist in that person's direction or drives the therapist away from a coalition with the person. Every comment to the couple by the therapist represents a coalition offered or declined. The birth of family-oriented marriage therapy began with the discovery that marriage therapy involves a triangle and that a couple changes when the therapist changes in relation to them. Before that discovery, marriage therapy focused on the couple as if the therapist were not there, which is a reflection of the belief that a marriage therapist must remain neutral (which is an impossibility in such a situation).

The therapist, like his supervisor, did not think the interview was going well. He was growing frustrated with the couple's repetitive complaints and was beginning to believe that something had to be done. He just didn't know what. His dissatisfaction made it possible for the supervisor to motivate him to change.

THE SUPERVISOR'S INTERVENTION

The supervisor said to the therapist, "Is it possible for you to be unfair?" The therapist wasn't sure what he meant. The supervisor clarified his question by asking him if he could choose one of the spouses and say that one was entirely wrong and the other was entirely right. The therapist replied that he didn't think he could do that, because it wasn't true. He said he believed that one spouse was never all wrong and the other all right, that spouses make misery conjointly. The supervisor agreed that that was probably true about the cause of marital misery, but that it was not necessarily relevant to therapy. Understanding a cause does not necessarily lead to a hypothesis that is a guide to change.

At this point the supervisor told the therapist that he should side with one of the spouses against the other and tell them that one of them is wrong and the other right. However, this simple suggestion involved a series of stages before it was accepted, stages similar to those in which a therapist arranges an action with a client. The discussion between the therapist and supervisor was not recorded, but such an intervention typically involves a series of steps.

1. The supervisor talked with the therapist about how the couple was unhappy and he was obligated to help them change. He emphasized that, of course, the therapist wished to do this.
2. He suggested that if the therapy continues the way it was going, the couple would continue in their misery and not change.
3. He pointed out that the therapist had to do something because the couple was waiting for him to do something and that if he didn't have a plan, he would have to accept the supervisor's plan.
4. The supervisor said the plan to follow was to be unfair and say that one spouse is all wrong and the other all right.
5. He said the therapist had a good enough relationship with the couple that they would accept his intervention and not flee.

Part of the supervisor's agenda was to expand the range of the therapist. He was too predictable, which would be a problem with some clients. It took at least 10 minutes of discussion behind the mirror before the therapist agreed to be unfair. The supervisor gave him the choice of being unfair or failing with the case. A final comment seemed to help: The supervisor said that other therapists were able to be unfair. The therapist said that he could be as unfair as any other therapist, and he went into the interview room.

The question was: Which spouse should the therapist join against the other? Either one could be blamed for their troubled marriage, and ample evidence could be found to support any choice. The supervisor suggested that the husband be blamed. He should insist that the wife was not at fault at all and that the husband was the problem. This choice was made partly because the husband was not initiating in the relationship and could perhaps be persuaded to do so. This would please the wife, and her responses would ultimately please him. Another reason for choosing the husband was because of gender: It's easier for a male therapist to blame the husband and identify him as the problem. It can be done, of course, with a different gender arrangement, but this is the least complicated. When a female therapist blames the husband, this sometimes creates a situation where the husband feels ganged up on by two women. In that case the female therapist needs to partly escape gender by emphasizing her professional background; in that way the husband will not feel that he is being opposed by two women but by his wife and a professional. When properly trained, a therapist of either gender can choose among coalition approaches that deal satisfactorily with male–female issues.

The therapist and his supervisor planned the intervention before the clinical interview was resumed. He was to ask the couple to give therapy a chance for 3 months with no threat of separating during that period. Such a contract allows different changes to take place. Next, the therapist was to say to the husband that he was entirely wrong in the way he was dealing with the wife. He was to point out that she was not doing anything to create the problem and to insist that the husband save the marriage, which meant courting his wife to win her back because he was losing her.

Anticipating responses is part of this strategy. It was expected that the husband might say he didn't feel like courting his wife because things were so bad between them. Anticipating such a statement, the therapist was to tell the husband that he should at first pretend, if necessary, that he was in love with her, that he should go through the motions, if necessary, and that he would later develop the feelings. As the therapist discussed the therapy plan with his supervisor and understood more clearly what he was to do, he began to feel more enthusiasm. (Trainees are often reluctant to take a particular approach because they don't know how.) He returned to the therapy room committed to and capable of being unfair.

THE THERAPY INTERVENTION

When the therapist told the couple that he would like to see them for a minimum of 3 months, the wife replied, half jokingly, "You mean that's all the time we get?"* From this remark the supervisor realized that there was another explanation for the couple's conversational approach to therapy. Often, a couple indicates by the way they introduce their problems that they plan long-term therapy. That is, they talk in general ways about abstract issues. It is as if they are expecting to play a long game and see no reason to hurry and get to the point. By setting a period of time for the therapy, the therapist can force a couple to deal with real issues in their lives.

The therapist replied to the wife that 3 months should be enough, and there was no rush since the problems had been going on for a while. Then the therapist said to the husband, "From what I heard tonight you really are in danger of losing your wife. I think what you are doing is absolutely wrong. I think you're making a mess of things. You are doing things to turn her off—by not talking to her, by not being aggressive, by not seeking her out, by not courting her." The husband sat still, looking solemn. The therapist added, "I think it's time you started courting her. You're driving her away to other systems, and to friends, letting her work those long hours, not spending time with her. You really need to. . . . I would say, if I had to make a choice right now . . . I'd say you are absolutely wrong. It's your fault. If you want this woman as your wife, you have to get off your high horse and go after her and court her. You really have to take responsibility for this. And this is a good time of the year because it's spring and the sap is rising. I think this is the beginning of new life. This is the time to convince yourself, so that by 3 months you have it clear in your mind that you've done everything you can to win this woman as your wife. It's like a second marriage."

An observer would not know from the calm, firm, and kindly way the therapist delivered this intervention that it was difficult for him. Once he had decided the approach was necessary, he did it well and with enthusiasm. Looking at the wife, he added, "And it's no fault of yours." Turning to the husband, he said, "You might have to pretend in the beginning because you're still mad, still feeling cheated and ignored. You're going to have to pretend the first week or so that you are in love with her. Go through the motions. After you get into doing something, then you'll suddenly realize, 'Oh yeah, our marriage is getting better.' So I'm going to put the responsibility on you. You won't like what I'm saying—it's a hard message I'm giving you. And I don't see anything that your wife is doing that is contributing to this at all."

---

*The dialogue presented here is verbatim, having been transcribed from the video recordings.

The wife interrupted, saying, "I must be doing something."

"No," said the therapist.

The husband sat forward and said, "Let's talk about this. I'm telling you, I think you're bullshit."

"No," insisted the therapist, "You really have to go after her and court her."

The husband said, with emotion, "She spends her time telling me that everything I am and everything I do is bad."

"You have to convince her that it's not," said the therapist. "You have to convince her by courting her, by meeting her at work, by calling her during the day."

"I call her during the day. I can't get through. She never returns calls. She's busy."

"Take time off and go meet her for lunch," the therapist suggested. "Spend time with her, don't let her out of your sight. She's a prize possession. If this is the greatest thing in your life—it's better than margarine—then you better go after her because she's going to melt, she's going to disappear."

"That's right," said the husband, "I believe it."

"You really have to go after her . . . take the offensive here and go after her . . . and don't talk about criticism. She's just giving you a hard time."

"Yes, but her criticism is not just 'I don't like it when you do that,' but 'I'm going out'."

"You go with her."

"I'm not invited."

"You don't have to wait for an invitation; you're the man of the house."

"She's not home. She comes home at 8:30 or 9:00 every night. I'm the first one home every night. What can I do? I'm there."

"Go to her office and meet her there."

At this point the supervisor phoned the therapist. While he was on the telephone, the wife reached out and stroked her husband's arm. (When a wife is absolved of all blame in her marriage, she has to come forward because she knows it's not true.) He responded by saying, "It's okay."

On the telephone the supervisor suggested that he not discuss abstractions with this husband but enumerate the specific things the husband could do the next day. As the therapist hung up the phone, the husband said, "That's a fairly bold statement after 2 hours," referring to the fact that this was only their second interview.

"I want you to think about this and pull out all the stops," said the therapist.

"We've thought about it," said the husband, referring to his wife and himself as a dyad.

"What will you do tomorrow to go after her so she doesn't slip through your fingers, so she's not moving away from you?" asked the therapist.

"Give up everything I believe in." said the husband.

"Well, you've got to modify that for the next 2 weeks."

"I probably won't do that."

"Well, what would prevent you . . . ? What could you do during the day tomorrow to convince her that she is the love of your life?"

"I'm not sure anymore."

"I realize it's hard for you at the beginning, because you're unsure."

"It's a certain type of person that she wants that I'm not. And I never will be."

"Can you be that for just tomorrow?"

"Well, what's the point? Because when I revert to myself, she'll go back to not liking me."

"Well, you can convince yourself that you can take on a new behavior. You're not locked in concrete. Because right now you guys are locked."

"That's right."

"One of you has got to change. By not changing, you're preventing her from responding to you. So you really have to take the first step and court her."

"I know what I have to do, and I've been doing it for the past few weeks. I have to show a lot of interest in her job but at the same time be very careful not to ask any questions that may be sensitive or suggest criticism or suggest that maybe she's not perfect. It's not allowed to have any kind of even-sided dialogue, but I'm supposed to be like I think her parents are. Just 'whatever you do is perfect.' And I'm not that kind of person."

"It would be hard for you. Then you'd have to pretend to be a good listener?"

"I'm not allowed to say, 'Well, what happened? What went on?' I'm just supposed to say, 'Oh, don't worry about it, you're wonderful, and what happened at work is bullshit,' and I'm not that kind of person."

"It strikes me that's not the type of person your wife is. It's being rude to her to say you can't get the facts out."

When a therapist unbalances this way, it is necessary to go to extremes. Not only is the wife absolved of blame, but if the husband criticizes her, the therapist should say that he is being rude and that the wife doesn't seem that way to him.

"I know everything about her job," said the husband. "I know the names of the employees, I know what's going on during the day, but I can't ask anything substantive. Something happens and the boss was upset and I'm not allowed. . . . "

The wife interrupted. "Because my boss yelled at me and I'm upset and the last thing I need is for my husband to turn around and examine me about the situation. I want you to say, 'It's okay'."

"Just to be a listener, and not to give you the third degree. That would be hard for you," the therapist said to the husband.

"He could not do it," said the wife.

"It would be hard for me; it's not my personality."

"But you could learn that behavior, couldn't you?" asked the therapist.

The couple's dialogue changed with this intervention. They no longer talked in abstract intellectual terms. They began to straightforwardly negotiate change. The therapist continued to insist that the husband take action of a specific kind to court his wife, and his supervisor continued to phone in suggestions for different ways of telling the couple what should be done and for dealing with anticipated difficulties. For example, the therapist suggested that the husband might try to please his wife and then make a pass at her and she would reject him. But that would change if he continued to pursue her. This was done to avoid the situation where the husband might halfheartedly pursue this wife, then approach her sexually and have her reject him so that he would say the whole thing didn't work.

The husband then revealed that he had bought his wife a present the day before and was shopping that day for another. The therapist, keeping the pressure on the husband, replied, "Can you do more of that?" At one point in the interview the husband became quiet, and it seemed clear he was at the point of deciding whether to break up the marriage or take the actions he knew were necessary. One of the risks of this unbalancing approach is that it forces the issue of deciding the fate of the marriage. The husband was feeling that he and his wife could no longer just drift along, that he had to act, and that he had to decide if he was willing to take the steps necessary to save the marriage. At this point the wife, sensing the gravity of her husband's thoughts, became increasingly nervous. When she insisted that *she* ought to have to do something, the therapist replied that somewhere down the road something might be asked of her. Then he continued his relentless pursuit to change the husband, suggesting that he buy tickets and surprise his wife with a show, that he take her out to dinner, and so forth. When he wondered aloud if the husband might be angry at him, the husband shook his head. He knew the therapist was on his side and was only telling him what needed to be done. At one point the therapist asked the husband if he thought courting his wife would work to make a happier marriage. The husband replied, "I have no doubt about that." This statement obligated him to either make those efforts or leave the marriage. With encouragement, the husband came out of his silence and began to talk, apparently deciding the marriage was worth the effort.

As the interview ended, the therapist, at his supervisor's suggestion, asked the husband what color roses his wife liked. The husband replied that she didn't like roses. The wife coquettishly replied, "When did I ever say that?" The therapist suggested that her husband find out which flowers his wife liked.

At the next interview the couple came in cheerfully. Obviously there had been a change. The husband initiated the discussion of the week's events, and he described a number of his courting activities. (The therapist, at his supervisor's suggestion, had phoned the husband several times since the last interview to encourage him in his efforts to court his wife.) Both husband and wife had decided to take steps to change their marriage instead of being locked in a struggle in which neither was willing to make the first move.

APPENDIX B

Supplemental Video Programs

Jay Haley and Madeleine Richeport-Haley

R eaders who would like to supplement the text with relevant videos of case materials, supervision, and documentaries may order videos. These are organized by chapter.

Chapter 1

Jay Haley on Strategic Therapy (1978)
Interviewed by Richard Rabkin, M.D., in 1978, Jay Haley discusses how to plan a therapy strategy and how to give directives to bring about change. The techniques are those of brief therapy. (50 min., $95)

Jay Haley on Directive Family Therapy (1999)
A lecture to a training group on Jay Haley's approach to therapy. He provides the viewer with an understanding of his practical teaching premises and information on a variety of issues. These include family therapy and hypnosis; evolution of live supervision; and brief, problem-focused case examples taken from his work. ISBN 0-93151-321-9 (40 min., $79.95)

Milton H. Erickson, M.D., Explorer in Hypnosis and Therapy (1993)
This video is a fascinating portrait of the life and work of the world's foremost authority on medical hypnosis and therapy. It contains rare archival footage of Erickson at work, allowing the viewer to see his extraordinary ability to heal both body and mind despite his physical handicaps. As a child, Erickson was stricken with polio. Having endured chronic pain as

well as early dyslexia, he describes how he discovered strength and healing through hypnosis. ISBN 0-87630-726-8 (58 min., $89.95)

"Erickson understood the dignity of the human spirit."—*Science Books and Film*

Jay Haley on Clinical Hypnosis
A seminar for a class in therapy differentiates personal, research, and clinical hypnosis in which one is trying to change someone. The techniques of hypnosis are illustrated with Milton H. Erickson's 1958 and 1964 archival films. (55 min., $95)

Whither Family Therapy? A Jay Haley Version (1997)
A film about the discovery of family therapy from the past to current issues. It includes the ideas and participants in Gregory Bateson's project on the double bind and the development of systems theory, the contribution of Milton H. Erickson, and Zen, all combined into the directive therapy approach. Included is rare material from 40 years of interviews, seminars, and actual cases. Haley's original and enduring contribution is his brief directive therapy to solve problems, which is of interest to mental health students, colleagues, parents, and educators who are grappling with a rapidly changing mental health care milieu. ISBN 0-93151-313-8 (50 min., $79.95)

"Haley's fascinating personal recollections are interspersed with priceless rare film clips. . . . "—Wendel A. Ray, Ph.D.

Chapter 2

Family Therapy in Bali (2003)
This documentary presents a series of cases seen by Balinese healers. It reveals and examines the similarities between Balinese healing methods and the strategic family therapy approach of Jay Haley and the hypnosis of Milton Erickson. ISBN 0-931513-29-4 (35 min., $95)

Macumba Trance and Spirit Healing
Filmed primarily in Rio de Janeiro, the film shows the art of trance healing and expresses an Ericksonian approach. In today's stressful world, millions of people turn to spiritism for help. This film shows the roots and beliefs of Afrospirit religions as practiced by the privileged rich as well as the illiterate poor. It appeared on PBS. (43 min., $95)

"A fascinating account for public and college library viewers."—*Booklist*

A HOW-TO-DO STRATEGIC THERAPY VIDEO SERIES

In the following videos, the viewer for the first time can experience Jay Haley's live training behind a one-way mirror of actual cases as they progress from week to week with a training group. You will see the presentation of the case by the therapist, Haley's planning the interviews with the therapist, his directives in the live supervision, and the debriefing group discussions. The clients are not shown for reasons of confidentiality. The problems are as varied as are the ethnic groups. Suggestions from the supervisor to the therapist are sent on a computer monitor where the therapist can see the messages but the clients cannot. The goal is to change therapists as well as clients, since they must learn how to change people in distress. The films offer valuable material for discussion of different therapy ideas.

"There is much to recommend these tapes: the opportunity to watch Haley's trenchant mastery and his gentle humor; the *cinema verité* quality where everything doesn't work out smoothly after one intervention; the discussion and intervention planning as trainees struggle with difficult theoretical and technical challenges; the patient-therapist/therapist -supervisor parallel processes."—Michael Hoyt, Ph.D., *American Journal of Family Therapy*

Chapter 3

Brief Strategic Therapy with Couples
This training film illustrates therapy techniques to be used with marriages in distress. Marital relations are defined as made up of rules. They are comprehensive in a couple's interactions ranging from small issues to major crises. For example, a husband will behave irresponsibly. The wife will behave responsibly. The more irresponsible the husband, the more responsible the wife, and vice versa. A marriage in trouble can be viewed as made up of rules that distress the couple and rarely change with insight. The therapy described here focuses on the problem sequences and uses directives to change them, particularly with the use of paradox. ISBN 0-93151-326-X (50 min., $79.95)

Unbalancing a Couple
A therapist who has been taught to be neutral with a couple and not to side with either spouse learns how to really take sides. The emphasis is on the rules of communication that couples follow, which are difficult to change unless the therapist gets personally involved. ISBN 0-93151-316-2 (30 min., $95)

Chapter 4

Family Therapy at a Distance—A Case of Depression
This case of a Middle-Eastern medical student shows the therapist learning to deal with a depressed man using a directive approach. The primary directive was to get the man to write a letter to his father who was living in the Middle East. This proved to be a difficult task for the supervisor in relation to the therapist and the therapist in relation to the family. It illustrates the parallel between therapy and supervision. Haley arranges a change for both of them. ISBN 0-93151-323-5 (55 min., $79.95)

"It's a great teaching tape."—Braulio Montalvo, M.A.

Chapter 5

Changing a Violent Family
This family illustrates how to work with problems of violence between parents and children and children against each other. This is a family that is court-ordered and multiple helpers are assigned to it, who must agree about what is to be done with the family. The techniques are strategic with special emphasis on motivating the family to change and using paradox to make it happen. This video illustrates how a single family therapist can provide effective therapy and keep the family together. ISBN 0-93151-325-1 (43 min., $79.95)

Chapter 6

Compulsory Therapy—A Case of Violence
This is a minority family in which two brothers, high school teenagers, were accused and sentenced to probation and therapy for beating up a kid for a racial slur. Haley's directives involve bringing the whole family together to assure this will not occur again. The family proves to be responsible with the cultural patterns highlighted in such a way that one sees the damage that could have been done had this case been handled wrongly. ISBN 0-93151-322-7 (35 min., $79.95)

Chapter 7

The Boy Who Can't Stop Fighting
An African-American boy was sent from school to school, therapist to therapist, and group to group. The therapist had seen the problem boy for a year and brought him in for a consultation when he was violent once again. A paradoxical approach improved him. The case also illustrates integrating a stepfather. ISBN 0-93151-327-8 (50 min., $79.95)

Chapter 9

How Many Clients Are There in One Body?
A trainee seeing her first case learns to make a diagnosis with a Brazilian woman whose pathology was expressed in cultural beliefs. Practical considerations are emphasized rather, than cultural exploration of this woman living in an abuse shelter. ISBN 0-93151-328-6 (45 min., $79.95)

Chapter 10

A Positive Approach with a Psychotic Couple
This young couple had been in therapy and in and out of hospitals for years. The husband was diagnosed as schizophrenic and the wife with schizo-affective disorder. Both were considered incurable and were on permanent disability. The therapist brought them in hoping for some ideas of what to do with this difficult case. Haley takes the approach, which grew out of the ideas of H. S. Sullivan and Don Jackson, that the clients should be treated as if nothing was wrong except the social situation. He suggests the therapist treat the couple as normal despite past extreme behavior and suicide threats. The consultation shows a way to make a fresh start with a chronic case. ISBN 0-93151-324-3 (45 min., $79.95)

"Marvelous. A new medium which shows the process of changing minds."
—Salvador Minuchin, M.D.

ORDERING INFORMATION

Any of the videotapes may be ordered on www.jay-haley-on-therapy.com. They can also be ordered by sending an e-mail to prizefilm@aol.com or send check or credit card information to:

> Triangle Press
> P.O. Box 8094
> La Jolla, CA 92038
> USA

Institutional prices may be higher. Inquire for special prices for multiple tape orders. Add to the order $6 shipping and handling price for the first item and $3 for each additional item.

Index

12-step therapy
  effects on therapy, 34–50
  vs. family therapy, 45–46

Absurd directives, 9
Action
  vs. understanding, 2
African Spiritist religions, 136–155
African-Americans
  communication patterns, 111–112, 124
  establishing hierarchies, 3, 115–116
  family therapy, 111–124
Alternate belief systems
  Central American family, 20–24
  collaborating with a healer, 23–24, 138
  defined, 19–20
  intervention alternatives, 24–24
  minimizing, 20–21
  spirit possession vs. DID, 135–155
  using a healer, 22–23
  using to further therapy, 21–22
  videos on, 192, 195
American Academy on Asian Studies, 176
American Psychiatric Association, 135–136
Anthropology
  role in therapy, 17–29
  spirit possession vs. DID, 135–155
  therapists studying, xv–xvi
  videos on, 192, 195
Antidepressants, 112, 136

Authority
  building, 180
  Central American beliefs, 20–21
  creating, 115–116
  graceful, 10
  traditional societies, 24–26
Avoiding credit, 11

Bali
  traditional healing systems, 22–23
  video on, 192
Bateson, G., xv, 3, 121, 124, 169, 176, 192
Being practical, 168–169
Being supported, 166–167
Being unfair, 179–184
Birdwhistell, R., 6
Bleuler, M., 157
Booklist, 192
Borderline personality disorder, 136
Brazil
  alternate belief systems, 135–155
Brooks, G. W., 157
"Bug in the ear" intervention, 4–5

Case examples
  bicultural families, 31–51
  couples therapy, 31–51, 157–174, 179–190
  cultural confusions, 135–155
  family therapy at a distance, 53–78, 152
  family violence, 79–95

Case examples (*continued*)
   mother–daughter incest, 125–133
   psychotic couple, 157–174
   treating depression, 53–78
   unbalancing a couple, 179–190
   violent children, 97–124
Central America
   alternate belief systems, 19–24
Change
   cause of, 1–2
   inducing, 10, 176–177
Children
   abused, 79–95
   playing with, 111–124
   sexually abused, 125–133
   violent, 97–124, 194
Ciompi, L., 157
Coaching, 8
Colleagues
   conflicts among, 133
   dealing with, 2, 141
   too many, 91
   upsetting, 169–170
   who disagree, 60–64
   working with, 79–81
Communication
   African-American patterns, 111–112, 124
   between couples, 181–182
   complexities of, 6–7
   metaphoric, 9
Compulsory therapy. *See* Court-ordered therapy
Computer suggestions, 5, 34, 41, 46–47, 66, 69–70, 73, 82, 100, 103, 118–120, 143–145, 150–151, 164
Couples therapy, 31–51
   being practical, 168–169
   being supported, 166–167
   being unfair, 179–184
   bringing in more family members, 169
   discussing, 35–38, 41–44, 47–50, 164–174
   disengaging, 44–49
   ethnicity issues, 42–44
   family vs. 12-step therapy, 45–46

   observing, 34–35, 41, 46–47, 163–164
   paradox use, 34–35, 38–39
   planning, 33, 38–41, 44–46, 158–163
   protection theory, 167–168
   supervisor's intervention, 184–185
   therapist as generalists, 49
   therapy intervention, 186–190
   unbalancing a couple, 179–190
   videos on, 192
   with a psychotic couple, 157–174
Court-ordered therapy, 2, 14, 97–110
   bringing in more family members, 102–103, 105–106
   discussing the interview, 101–110
   observing the interview, 100, 103, 106, 109
   planning the interview, 98–99
   video on, 194

Danna, J., 27
Deconditioning framework, 10
Defining the problem, 10
Delays, 9
Depression, 53–78
   video on, 194
Diagnosis
   defining, 5–6
   Dissociative Identity Disorder, 136–137, 140–141
   multiple, 147
Diagnostic and Statistical Manuel of Mental Disorders (4th ed.), 135–136
Dickens, C., 8
Dictionary of American Slang, 124
Directives, 2
   giving, xv, 7–8
   Haley's approach, xvi
   how to give, 6–8
   indirect, 9
   the ordeal, 8
   penance, 8–9
   straightforward, 8–9
   types of, 8–9
   using hypnosis, xv, 7–8
   videos on, 191

Disengaging, 11, 147–148
  couples therapy, 44–50
  discussing, 90–91
  family therapy, 89–91
  learning to, 152–153
  planning, 89–90
Displaced families
  Central American, 20–24
  cultural confusions, 135–155
  Japanese, 26
  Pacific Islander, 97–110
  South American, 25
  Spanish, 24–25
  working with, 17–29
Dissociation, 60–62
Dissociative Identity Disorder, 135–155
  cultural confusions, 135–155
  diagnosing, 136–137, 140–141
  video on, 195
Doing nothing, 9
Durkheimian theory of deviance, 83

East India
  alternate belief systems, 21–22
Ellenberger, H., 154
Emotional focus, 60–62, 83
  case example, 179–184
Erickson, M. H., ix, xv–xvi, 6–8, 11,
  21–22, 26–27, 136–137, 175–176,
  191–192
Ethical issues, 13
Ethnicity, 13–14
  alternate belief systems, 19–22, 135–
  155, 192, 195
  Central American family, 20–24
  challenging values, 26–27
  cultural confusions, 135–155
  defined, 18
  experiencing different roles, 27
  family violence, 97–110
  in bicultural families, 42–44
  in couples therapy, 42–44
  interventions, 24–25
  issues in therapy, 17–29, 42–44
  Japanese family, 26
  problems of violence, 24–28
  South American family, 25

Spanish family, 24–25
spirit possession vs. DID, 135–155
traditional healing systems, 22–24
treating structurally, 20–21
using culture, 27–28
videos on, 192, 195

"False memory syndrome," 136
Families
  African-American, 111–112
  alternative, 12–13, 32
  bicultural, 33–50
  Central American, 20–24
  Japanese, 26
  Middle Eastern, 53–78
  Pacific Islander, 97–110
  South American, 25
  Spanish, 24–25
  stages of, 11–13
  violence in, 111–124
  violent, 79–95, 97–110
  watching their interactions, 3–5
Family Process, 103
Family Therapy Institute (Washington,
  D.C.), ix
Family therapy
  at a distance, 53–78, 152, 194
  depression, 53–78
  videos on, 192, 194
  violent families, 79–95, 97–124
  vs. 12-step therapy, 45–46
"February Man," 7, 137
Fiery, R., 136
Film ethnographies, xvi, 175
Fisch, R., ix
Freud, S., 125–126
Fulweiler, C., 3–4

Goal setting, 10
  depression, 56–57
  DID, 140, 148–150
  family violence, 80–81
Gregory Bateson Research Project, 176
Gross, G., 157
Grove, D., 136
Guilt, 8–9
Gutierrez, M., 24

Haley, J., ix–xiii, xvi, 3, 5–6, 8, 10–12, 18–19, 22–23, 25–27, 36, 124, 136, 162–163, 175–176, 178, 191–195
Hardin, C. M., 157
Harwood, A., 23
Hierarchies
  adhering to, 102–104
  clarifying, 80–81
  creating, 101–102, 115–116
  ethnicity and, 13–14
  exploring, 3
  identifying, 114–115
  reinforcing, 85–87
Hoffman, L., 3
Hoyt, M., xvi, 193
Huber, G., 157
Hypnosis, 12, 137
  Erickson's use of, 7
  giving directives, xv, 7–8
  videos on, 191–192

Incest, 125–133
  abuse issues, 126–127
Indirect directives, 9
Indonesia
  traditional healing systems, 22–23
  video on, 192
Integration of a stepfather technique, 112–124
Interpretations, 1–2
Interviews
  being practical, 168–169
  being supported, 166–167
  bringing in more family members, 84–85, 91–94, 102–103, 105–106, 169
  couples therapy, 33–50
  cultural confusions, 138–153
  dealing with colleagues, 141
  discussing, 35–38, 41–44, 47–49, 67–71, 73–76, 83, 85–86, 88–91, 93–94, 101–110, 120–123, 145–146, 151–154, 164–174
  disengagement, 11, 44–50, 89–91, 147–148, 152–153

Dissociative Identity Disorder, 138–153
family, 81–95
follow-up, 153–154
goal setting, 140, 148–150
long-distance family therapy, 64–73, 152
mother–daughter incest, 127–132
observing, 34–35, 41, 46–47, 66, 69–73, 81–83, 87–88, 92–93, 100, 103, 106, 109, 118–120, 143–145, 150–151, 163–164
planning, 33, 38–41, 44–46, 64–66, 69, 83–87, 89–90, 98–99, 116–117, 138–143, 146–150, 158–163
protection theory, 167–168
spirit possession, 135–155
using the client's writing, 141–143
with a psychotic couple, 148–174

Jackson, D., 3
Japan
  challenging ethnic values, 26–27
  experiencing different roles, 27
  family violence, 26
  using cultures, 27–28

Kubie, L., 136

Lambo, T. A., 23
Latin America, xv
  communication patterns, 42–44
  family bonds, 25–26
Leaving home, 12
Lithium, 136
Lopez, H., 23–24
Loss of face, 26–27

Machismo, 24–26
  challenging, 26–27
Macumba. *See* Spirit possession
Marriage therapy. *See* Couples therapy
Mead, M., xv, 27
Medication, 136, 158
  negotiating with psychiatrist, 2
  violent children, 112

Mental Research Institute, ix, xvi
Metaphoric communication, 9
Middle East
   long-distance therapy, 53–78
Minuchin, S., x, xv–xvi, 195
Moitoza, E., 25
Montalvo, B., xv–xvi, 24, 77, 194

Neukrug, E. S., 4
Neutrality
   being unfair, 179–190
   sometimes inappropriate, 36
Nicholls, M. P., xiii, xvii
Normalizing the situation, 3, 13, 34,
   80–81, 152–153, 159–164, 169–
   174

One-way mirrors, 2
   using for supervision, 3–5
The ordeal, 8, 124

Pacific Islands
   family violence, 97–110
Palozzoli, M. S., ix
Paniagua, F. A., 21
Paradox, 111–124
   case examples, 34–35, 38–39
   case follow-up, 123–124
   imposing, 9
   as ordeal, 124
   play and, 121
   presenting, 118–119
   proposing, 117–118
   trading roles, 86–87, 95
   types of, 122
Paradoxical therapy
   explained, 9–10
   stages of, 10–11
   with depression, 58–60
Parallel relationships, 62–63, 76
Past
   changing through hypnosis, 7–8
   vs. present focus, 1
Penance, 8–9
Philadelphia Child Guidance Center, xv
Plans, 10

Play, 111–124
Predicting relapse, 150
Present focus, 1
   in couples therapy, 31–32
Problem drinking, 26
Protection theory, 39–40, 167–168
Prozac, 136
Psychodynamic orientation, 60–62
Puerto Rico
   alternate belief systems, 22
   traditional healing systems, 23–24
Putnam, F. W., 136

Rabkin, R., 191
Racial prejudice, 97–110
Rapaport, D., 136
Ray, W. A., 192
Reps, P. S., 176–177
Richeport, M., 18, 20, 22–23, 27, 135
Richeport-Haley, M., xi–xiii, xv, 17, 23,
   36, 124, 135–136, 142
Ritalin, 112
Rituals, 11–12
Rogers, C., 6
Roles
   experiencing different, 27
   theory of deviance, 83
   trading, 86–88, 117–124

Scherl, C. R.,
Schiff, N., xvi, 9
Schizoaffective disorder, 158
Schizophrenia, 157–174
   being practical, 168–169
   being supported, 166–167
   bringing in more family members, 169
   case circumstances, 158
   clients, 158
   goal setting, 159–162
   improvement as a threat, 162–163
   marital problems, 159
   normalizing, 159–164, 169–174
   outcome studies, 157
   planning the session, 158–163
   protection theory, 167–168
   video on, 195

Schutter, R., 157
Science Books and Film, 192
Sexual abuse, 125–133
  abuse issues, 126–127
South America
  alternate belief systems, 22, 135–155
  family violence, 25–26
Spain
  family violence, 24–25
Spirit possession, 135–155
  videos on, 192, 195
Straightforward directives, 8–9
  absurd, 9
  coaching, 8
  giving advice, 8
  the ordeal, 8
  penance, 8–9
Strategic therapy, xvi, 1–15
  alternate belief systems, 19–24, 135–
    155, 192, 195
  at a distance, 53–78, 152
  being practical, 168–169
  being supported, 166–167
  bringing in more family members,
    84–85, 91–94, 102–103, 105–
    106, 169
  cause of change, 1–2
  challenging values, 26–27
  compulsory, 97–110
  couples, 179–190
  criticisms of, xvi
  cultural confusions, 135–155
  dealing with colleagues, 2, 141
  dealing with violence, 24–28
  depression, 53–78
  diagnosis, 5–6
  directives, xv, 2, 6–9, 11, 191
  Dissociative Identity Disorder, 135–
    155
  ethical issues, 13
  ethnicity, 13–14, 17–29, 42–44, 97–
    110, 135–155, 192, 195
  evolution of live supervision, 3–5
  experiencing different roles, 27
  follow-up, 132–133, 153–154
  goal setting, 10, 56–57, 80–81, 140,
    148–150

hierarchies, 3, 13–14, 80–81, 85–87,
    101–104, 115–116
  interventions, 24–25
  mother–daughter incest, 125–133
  normal situation, 3
  paradox, 9–11
  planning the order, 116–117
  protection theory, 167–168
  spirit possession, 135–155
  stages of family life, 11–13
  traditional healing systems, xv–xvi,
    22–24, 138
  unbalancing a couple, 179–190
  unique plans, 2, 32
  using culture, 27–28
  using the client's writing, 141–143
  videos on, 191
  with a psychotic couple, 157–174
  with children, 111–124
  with couples, 31–51
  with violent families, 79–95, 97–110
Supervision
  disagreement in, 60–64
  evolution of, 3–5
  intervention, 184–185
  tailoring therapy, 2
Symptoms, 177–178
  defining, 158–159
  encouraging, 9, 11
  improvement as a threat, 162–163,
    171–172
  paying to lose, 81–83, 95
  resolving with hypnosis, 7
  stage-of-life problems, 11–12
  to protect another, 113–114
  using the ordeal, 8
  utility of, 62–63, 148–150, 152–153,
    161–163, 167–168

Tardive dyskinesia, 158, 165
Therapists as generalists, 49
Traditional healing systems, xv–xvi
  collaborating with, 23–24, 138
  ignoring, 20–21
  using aspects of, 21–22
  using in therapy, 22–23
Triangle Press, 195

Triangulation, 37–38, 85–86, 183–184
Trust, 8
Twins
    problems working with, 80–81, 88–89, 114–115
    reversing roles, 86–87, 117–120
    roles, 114–115
    taking turns being evil, 86–88
    violent behavior, 111–124

Unbalancing a couple, 179–190
    being unfair, 179–184
    supervisor's intervention, 184–185
    therapy intervention, 186–190
    video on, 193
Understanding
    doesn't cause change, 1–2, 32, 53–55, 184–185
    vs. action, 2
Unique plans, 2, 32

Vermont State Hospital, 157
Video programs, 191–195
Violence
    bringing in more family members, 102–103, 105–106
    children, 97–124
    court-ordered therapy, 97–110
    cultural influences, 18–19
    dealing with colleagues, 2
    family, 79–95
    interventions, 24–25
    Japanese family, 26
    Pacific Islander family, 97–110
    problems of, 24–28
    protective function, 177
    South American family, 25–26
    Spanish family, 24–25
    videos on, 194
"Virginity complex," 26–27

Watts, A. W., 176
Watzlawick, P., ix
Weakland, J. H., ix, 3
Weidman, H. H., 18
Wilkinson, D., 18
Woolley, S., xvi

Yapko, M., 136

Zeig, J. K., 27
Zen, 176–177, 192